BEHIND THEIR SCREENS

BEHIND THEIR SCREENS

WHAT TEENS ARE FACING (AND ADULTS ARE MISSING)

EMILY WEINSTEIN AND CARRIE JAMES

THE MIT PRESS
CAMBRIDGE, MASSACHUSETTS
LONDON, ENGLAND

The MIT Press would like to thank the anonymous peer reviewers who provided comments on drafts of this book. The generous work of academic experts is essential for establishing the authority and quality of our publications. We acknowledge with gratitude the contributions of these otherwise uncredited readers.

This book was set in ITC Stone and Avenir by New Best-set Typesetters Ltd. Printed and bound in the United States of America.

Library of Congress Cataloging-in-Publication Data

Names: Weinstein, Emily, author. | James, Carrie, author.
Title: Behind their screens : what teens are facing (and adults are missing) / Emily Weinstein and Carrie James.
Description: Cambridge, Massachusetts : The MIT Press, [2022] | Includes bibliographical references and index. | Summary: "Presents a teen-level view of stresses and joys behind digital screens, including peer relationships, conflict, digital footprints, and civic life"—Provided by publisher.
Identifiers: LCCN 2021059165 | ISBN 9780262047357 (paperback)
Subjects: LCSH: Social media—Psychological aspects. | Internet—Psychological aspects. | Anxiety. | Adolescent psychology.
Classification: LCC HM742 .W4526 2022 | DDC 302.23/1—dc23/eng/20220421
LC record available at https://lccn.loc.gov/2021059165

10 9 8 7 6 5 4 3

For Nina, T, and Ella.

You're growing up in a world that's changing fast. We're here for you every step of the way.

CONTENTS

INTRODUCTION: WHAT ARE WE MISSING? WHY DOES IT MATTER?

Oleg Shupliak, *Double portrait of Van Gogh*, 2011.

At first glance, the image above just looks like a bearded man. You may even recognize the man as the artist Vincent Van Gogh. But if you shift your perspective a bit, you'll see that Vincent's nose is also a person sitting in a field and his ear is the wide-brimmed hat of a girl in a flowing dress. His eyebrows are the rooftops of buildings in the distance.

What does this have to do with teens and social media? In short: there's more than at first meets the eye.

Over the last decade, we—Emily and Carrie—have studied teens' digital lives. Our team at Harvard Project Zero has had incredible access to the ins and outs that are often hidden from adults' view. Time and again, our research has shown there is more than meets the eye about teens and social media. Our latest research reveals surprising, important gaps between adults' common assumptions and teens' realities. Just a few examples:

Digital afterlife.[1] Adults often assume teens are oblivious to the ways their digital lives could come back to haunt them later in life. With the aim of protecting teens, we double down on messages like, "What you post lasts forever" and "Your digital footprint stays with you for life." But teens' digital missteps happen for other reasons. Plus, posts aren't always in teens' control. Digital documentation and sharing are constant and other people perpetually upload and tag content without permission.

Digital habits. Adults assume teens are reluctant to part with their phones or turn off notifications because they are "addicted." Design features compel ongoing use. And teens' developmental vulnerabilities amplify effects well beyond what adults often see. But teens also describe how friendships are on the line. Disconnecting means being out of the loop socially, risking being seen as rude or, worse, being unavailable for a struggling friend. These burdens are in constant tension with parents' messages to "get off your phone."

Digital activism. Some adults worry about teens facing backlash for speaking up online about civic issues yet fail to appreciate pressures teens face that make staying silent feel just as risky. While many adults dismiss digital activism as shallow and easy, teens feel the stakes for the issues they care about and for their social lives and reputations. For example, the Black Lives Matter movement brought to the fore powerful opportunities for civic expression on social media alongside

pressures to post, concerns about performativity, and harsh social consequences for misposts.

Digital upsides. Adults assume that screen time undercuts "meaningful"
opportunities for healthy relationships and other pursuits. In some
cases, it does. But the "screen time is wasted time" mindset is a barrier
to seeing positives. Online gaming—from Minecraft to Fortnite—offers
real opportunities for necessary social connection and play. Apps can
be used to tap interests, as on "BookTok," a subcommunity of TikTok,
where teens source book recommendations and describe their favorite
series. Zoom, Facetime, and even Discord servers are used for mutual
homework and study support. And there are many more examples
that adults miss.

There are good reasons for the misses. Adults (ourselves included) are
often balancing instincts to protect young people's present well-being
and future lives in a world that is starkly different from the one in which
we grew up.[2]

FROM THE MOUTHS OF BABES

As social scientists who study teens and social media, we've spent the
last decade chasing answers to the following questions: What is it like for
today's young people to grow up with social media and smartphones?
How do these technologies affect their social, emotional, moral, and civic
development? What are teens actually *doing* on their smartphones and
how do they make sense of what they see on their screens?

We pose these as true questions and strive to be open to all kinds of
answers—the good, the bad, and the messy and complicated. Sometimes,
what emerges is predictable. Other times, our findings are truly new and
surprising to the world and to us. This book is about the new and the
unexpected. The pages ahead are filled with the data and stories that
stopped us in our tracks and forced us both to rethink our own tacit
assumptions about teens and tech.

Across the chapters, we draw primarily on our recent Digital Dilemmas Project which took several years and as many unplanned turns. By
early 2021, we had a treasure trove of data collected through surveys,

interviews, focus groups, and observations—all of which brought young people's perspectives to the fore.

Some quick context: The project began in 2017, when we had an opportunity to work with our longtime collaborators at Common Sense Media (a nonprofit leader in media advice for families and schools). Our collaborative team was gearing up to update their digital citizenship curriculum with new and refreshed classroom lessons. We wanted to be sure we were tapping into the most pressing and relevant issues for teachers and, crucially, for teens.

A large survey was the kickoff. We surveyed both educators and students about timely digital topics, such as enduring online posts, pressures to stay connected, and civic tensions. We were astonished by the response. Just a few months in, we had data from almost 1,000 educators and more than 3,500 middle and high schoolers. The youth sample was fairly diverse, comprising students from varied racial and ethnic backgrounds and schools across ten U.S. states. Their ages spanned nine to nineteen, though most were between twelve and eighteen years old. (See more details about our survey participants in the appendix.)

Responses to one question stood out: What worries you most about today's digital world? We didn't ask the question because we see digital life as inherently worrisome or problematic. Rather, we wanted to identify youths' authentic worries so that we could design relevant educational resources.

We first asked respondents to this question to choose their answer from a list of ten options that spanned issues from screen time, cyberbullying, and drama to being asked for inappropriate pictures—or to write in their own reply.[3] Then, we asked them to share an open-ended explanation describing their biggest worry. It was these explanations that captured our attention. They were relatively short, typically just one to two sentences each; some were just a few words. But the explanations were compelling and their sheer volume lent a kind of power: thousands of raw, direct worries "from the mouths of babes."

On digital footprints: *"If you are young and make a post that the older you would regret, it's too late. Especially if that post contains sensitive information. Someone or something has already saved it and stored it so that you have no way of deleting it"* (thirteen-year-old)

On privacy risks: *"It's terrible to know that anyone can get your information and every year it gets easier for people to take it"* (fourteen-year-old)

On digital drama and cyberbullying: *"I never know when I might get a comment that's mean"* (eighteen-year-old)

On too much screen time: *"It's just scary to think that I only get one childhood, and I could accidentally slip into a habit where I just waste it away on some pointless game"* (fourteen-year-old)

On pressures to stay connected: *"I want to not be on my phone too much but I don't want it to seem like I'm ignoring people"* (fifteen-year-old)

We studied worries like these—3,529 in total—systematically, one by one. We reviewed the full dataset several times and with multiple analytic strategies as we worked to organize important insights. Our hope was to achieve what we sensed was missing: a more textured, authentic understanding of teens' worries and experiences. This, we believe, lays necessary groundwork for new or reimagined interventions, policies, and supports.

We'd be remiss not to acknowledge the imperfections of this question from a survey design perspective. Giving people set options to choose from can narrow the realm of what they consider. Permitting selection of just one worry ("what worries you *most . . .*") means that these survey responses only capture perspectives from those who are most concerned about a given topic. These are important qualifications. They mean, for example, that it wouldn't be appropriate to make claims like "x% of teens are worried about this topic." Nor would it be right to say that a certain percentage of teens are *not* worried about a topic just because it wasn't their top concern. Because our work was largely situated in the United States, the research and examples in this book also tend to reflect U.S.-centric emphases (e.g., U.S. politics) and we are limited in the claims we can make about global trends.

Yet there is so much that we *can* say. The data offer an incredible window into different pain points and puzzles of teens' experiences behind their screens.

PRIVILEGING YOUTH VOICES

The obvious bears mentioning: we are not teens. This is important because though we write extensively in this book "about the experiences" of youth growing up in today's digital world, we cannot write *"from experience"* coming of age in an era of Instagram and Snapchat.[4] Carrie, now in her fifties, was in her thirties when cell phones—specifically, flip phones—became ubiquitous. She had her first child in 2005 (when Facebook was just a year old) and used a photo blog to share baby pictures with the grandparents. Today, Carrie parents two technology-loving kids, ages sixteen and twelve. Emily, who is in her thirties, had Facebook as a high schooler, joined Instagram shortly after she finished college, and Snapchatted her way through graduate school. Her toddler does not have a TikTok (yet).

We wrestled with how to interpret and share findings from our research in a way that privileged young people's voices. We are skilled at listening closely to adolescents: trained to notice—and to contextualize—both what youths say and what is left unsaid. Still, we are acutely aware that our positions and identities confer blindspots too. Though we bridge different generational perspectives, we are both White women and researchers who have spent most of our professional lives at an elite university on the East Coast of the United States.

Key to our approach was first collecting and centering data *from* diverse youth, and then co-interpreting the data *with* young people. Working with teens throughout our research process provided additional checks and balances as we continued to consider: What might we be misunderstanding or missing all together? We also repeatedly asked teens: What do you most wish adults understood?

Our advisory council comprised twenty-two teens (ages thirteen to eighteen) and three young adults from different life experiences and backgrounds. These co-interpreters brought to our research perspectives shaped by their own intersectional identities, including as teens who are first-generation American, queer, Asian American, Black, Latinx, White, biracial, and living in communities across every time zone in the continental United States. They brought insights based on their experiences in public school, private school, and homeschool. They had different family structures and living arrangements, interests and identities, and views on the positives and perils of tech.

Their voices feature prominently in the pages ahead, as do the voices of teens we captured through our survey data. When we quote these young people, we have preserved their original wording as closely as possible and used italics for their comments as we did earlier. In some cases, we note that we are drawing on voices from other teens in our past studies on digital life. Through projects we carried out together and separately over the past decade, our research teams have interviewed 275-plus teens about different aspects of growing up in a digital era. We also share stories collected through the course of our work, at times in composite form or with details modified to protect youths' identities. In instances where we use a composite or modified story, the details have been (re)vetted by teens to ensure their validity.

For the sake of brevity, we use the terminology of "teens" to refer to all youths in our sample. We use more specific language where relevant to call out distinctions between the experiences of middle versus high schoolers. In all cases, the names we use for youths are pseudonyms. Wherever possible, we asked the teens to choose these pseudonyms for themselves and we use their self-selected names, which in many cases reflect the cultural identities salient to them.

Beyond our research with teens, we've been fortunate in recent years to be invited into communities where we engage with families and educators around opportunities and challenges of teens and tech. These data offer additional insight into what adults are seeing and what they're often missing.

Centering young people's authentic perspectives on digital life is our principal aim in this book. As we'll say more than once, a crucial part of doing this is underscoring that teens are not a monolith. An essential corresponding acknowledgment: adults are not a monolith either.

An important complement to our account is the growing body of research that delves into tensions different adults face as they parent, teach, or otherwise seek to support young people today. A signature example: Sonia Livingstone and Alicia Blum-Ross's book *Parenting for a Digital Future: How Hopes and Fears about Technology Shape Children's Lives*. Livingstone and Blum-Ross deliver a nuanced and sympathetic account of the perspectives of parents, who engage different digital parenting strategies as they try to protect their children.[5] These approaches reflect parents' hopes and struggles as they guide children through a risky present and into an uncertain future. Importantly, the authors also unpack how digital parenting dilemmas are experienced and navigated differently by families based on social inequities. Although we often refer to "adult assumptions" and "adult messages" we do so with the recognition that there are complexities, too, behind adults' frequent cautions to teens.

TEENS ON SCREENS: WHAT WE SEE AND WHAT WE DON'T

When I (Carrie) traveled to Riyadh, Saudi Arabia, to explore a potential collaboration, my colleagues and I found ourselves in a shopping mall during after-school hours. In Riyadh—as in many places around the world—the mall is a prime place for teens to gather. Yet for Saudi teens, prohibitions on unmarried males and females being in close proximity make certain peer interactions impossible, or at least a bit more complicated. Girls and women also often navigate dress codes that require them to wear abayas (neck-to-floor-length robes) and head scarves that hide everything but their faces.

The teens in the mall appeared to be following the rules. A group of girls congregated together in a cluster around the water fountain. A safe distance (about fifteen feet) away was a group of boys. The groups seemed to respect an invisible boundary, keeping physical distance between them.

I couldn't help but notice this familiar sight: teens, hanging out with friends, a smartphone in every hand. They consulted their screens at regular intervals, in between chatter with their same-sex peers and furtive (and sometimes not-so-furtive) glances toward peers across the way.

Imagine you were in my position, looking on at this scene in the mall. Perhaps you'd sigh or lament how teens around the world seem so focused on the devices in their hands that they aren't fully present for the people right in front of them.

A few young Saudi educators shared some insider intel and a different perspective. A recent phenomenon: when teens are hanging out in sex-segregated groups and appear to be eyeing a group of the opposite sex, they're often "talking" with them below adults' radar. They use Bluetooth to establish connections with close-by peers who catch their interest. Then, they can interact via WhatsApp and Snapchat—staying a respectable distance physically while swapping "uncovered" selfies of their faces and hair, and even building relationships with romantic intent.

This anecdote illustrates a principle we've found to be true time and again: there is more to the teens and tech story than most adults are privy to. There's value in tabling our assumptions long enough to ask, listen, and look anew.

BEHIND THEIR SCREENS, BUT NOT BEHIND THEIR BACKS

Several years later and many miles from Riyadh, I (Emily) was sitting at a conference in Austin, Texas, looking on with permission as a peer scrolled through his Instagram account. In our interview studies, we use different versions of this exercise. We ask someone to browse one of their social media accounts while they narrate their reactions. "What are you seeing?" we ask, even though we can also see exactly what they're looking at. "Share whatever reaction pops into your head."

When we've set the right tone—open and nonjudgmental—people get into the rhythm of thinking aloud. In this case, I saw that thirty-year-old "Ben's" feed was filled mostly with poetry (he's also a poet), a few celebrities, and images of people who looked around his age. If someone were browsing Ben's Instagram from a distance, say by using a monitoring app or plugging in his password behind his back, they'd see an unremarkable collection of his hobbies and interests alongside seemingly benign social content.

But because we were browsing together, I got a more accurate sense of what Ben saw in his own feed. The poetry was "too long" to read and disappeared quickly from his screen as he scrolled past it. He double-tapped on photos from a certain celebrity—adding purposeful likes because, he admitted, he and the celebrity had recently met and he hoped she would reciprocate with likes on his posts. Most notably, his feed was filled with pictures from women he'd previously dated and their friends.

When Ben stopped scrolling, he turned to face me. We both had the same realization: his casual browsing was offering up a steady stream of reminders of failed romances.

The title of this book invites a look behind teens' screens. But to be very clear, the book is not an invitation to covertly peer over teens' shoulders. Philosophically, we aren't keen on digital snooping without cause. Older teens especially see this as a major violation of privacy that shatters trust. More practically, the Ben story illustrates another principle: there is often more than meets the onlooker's eye. And this gap is even wider when the observer is an adult, and the account belongs to a teen.

Our aim is not simply to know what they see on their screens, but also to see it *as* they do. This positions us to have their backs, rather than just looking over their shoulders.[6]

RETHINKING FAMILIAR TOPICS

We chose the chapter topics for this book based on concerns that were salient to adolescents but often misunderstood by adults. Some topics likely seem predictable, such as social conflicts or online politics. But teens' experiences with them aren't. We also give chapter-length treatment to topics like sexting (chapter 5), where a constellation of unique pressures and complexities are illustrated by teen practices, such as "watermarking" nudes: adding a barely-visible digital watermark with the name of the intended recipient as a kind of warranty. Then, the sender will know who leaked the picture if it is ever shared.

We start in chapter 1 with a provocation: you've been misled. Alarmist headlines that shape the public narrative about teens and tech often lead us astray. We need an intentional, data-driven pivot. We talk in this book about "teens," but as we've said: teens are far from monolithic, and their identities and contexts shape their digital experiences. The features of today's networked technologies also inform and amplify their digital interactions in important ways. We then turn to teens' worries, beginning with the pull of the screen.

In chapter 2, we reframe the screen time debate and detail teens' worries, struggles, and strategies related to digital habits. Our research challenges the idea of tech use as an adults-versus-teens battle and instead points to areas of real and mutual concern. We unpack teens' worries about dependence (on devices), disruption (of face-to-face connection and other activities), and distraction (especially from focus on schoolwork). Teens also contend with social media highlight reels and a pull toward social comparison—these are among the dark clouds they navigate. But dark clouds coexist with true bright spots. Overall, new insights point to the fatal flaw of a single-minded fixation on screen *time*.

In chapter 3, we examine the culture of constant connection and zoom into the dynamics of teen friendships. Many adults assume teens crave limitless contact with friends and peers. Yet our research reveals how burdened teens can feel behind their screens as they grapple with what it means to be a good friend in a 24/7 digital world. Teens describe new expectations as friendships play out under a social media spotlight, and stresses related to digitally stratified audiences, from group chats to exclusive "Close Friends" lists.

In chapter 4, we delve into the spectrum of drama and social conflict. We begin with a timely incarnation: tea accounts, where anonymous posts "spill the tea" or gossip about peers. While adults typically register concerns about cyberbullying, teens share how they make sense of more subtle forms of digital conflict that fly below adults' radars. Social media is a context for covert "jabs" as well as blatant call outs—all of which can play out in front of watchful audiences.

Chapter 5 covers sexting. We ask: If teens know sending images of nudes is risky, why do they still do it? Our research challenges the idea that teens are simply unaware of the risks, and instead clarifies the motives and pressures that are typically hidden from adults' view. In reality, not all sexting is equally concerning. We differentiate wanted sexting, pressured sexting, and sexts shared without permission. Chapter 5 also spells out nine reasons why teens send nudes and clarifies why sweeping warnings ("Just don't sext!") fall short.

Chapter 6 directs attention to today's political landscape. Adults at once criticize social media use as shallow and meaningless and simultaneously fret about kids getting in over their heads with real issues. Today's teens feel compelled to get into the issues—both because they care *and* because silence has social costs. Where social media posts are received and monitored by peers, the political is interpersonal and friendships are on the line. Concerns related to cancel culture, performative activism, and echo chambers further weigh on teens, even as they acknowledge the upsides of a digital civic sphere.

Chapter 7 zeroes in on privacy issues including the potential permanence of digital artifacts from the adolescent years. High-profile cases of online missteps and dire consequences abound. Adults often assume teens are unaware of these risks or simply don't care. The natural result is to ramp up messages about harsh consequences, like "ruining your life." Yet our data reveal why such messages can fall short or backfire. We detail teens' perspectives on the risks of misposts that may stay with them for years to come. We complicate the idea that teens can really control their footprints by identifying other "coauthors" who sometimes hold all the cards. And we return to the looming notion of social cancellation. A clearer understanding of the dynamics—developmental, social, personal—begs a rethinking of what adults should say and do to help.

Each topical chapter follows a similar sequence. We open with a story that tees up relevant dilemmas. We then dive more deeply into teen experiences, uplifting youth voices from our own research and putting their perspectives in conversation with key ideas from other research. In various places, we connect apparently new phenomena to existing knowledge from the fields of psychology, communication, neuroscience, and even evolutionary biology. We close each chapter with a synopsis of what "Teens Want Adults to Know" about the focal topic, whether it be digital habits or friendship challenges, sexting pressures or civic participation.

By the time you reach the conclusion, we hope you'll share with us a new sense of empathy for today's teens. How can we translate this empathy into actions that truly support them? The conclusion offers a path forward: we outline "the agency argument" as a new way of thinking about our collective quest to support youth in a digital age. We address adults in diverse roles: parents, educators, clinicians, tech designers, and policymakers.

When adults start by *asking over assuming*, we can hear directly from teens about the digital dilemmas that are most relevant to their lives. By channeling *empathy over eye-rolling*, adults can counter the impulse to immediately judge what we think we hear (or see). This allows us to tune into the details about what's hard (or great) and why. We're then better positioned to provide immediate support to teens, create effective policies, and identify valuable interventions. *Complexity over commandments* is an essential reminder to avoid defaulting to overly simplistic "solutions" that are destined to fail.

The research center we call home—Project Zero—has a long history of developing short, accessible "thinking routines" that invite deep thinking and reflection. "I Used to Think. . . . Now I Think . . ." is a perennial favorite, and we often use it to invite reactions after we share our research.[7] We wrap up this book by sharing a collection of responses from teens and adults, and by revealing how our own perspectives changed in writing it. Surely, there is plenty that you now think to be true about teens and screens. Like us, we suspect you'll find that there is a whole lot that you were missing.

1

DIGITAL WORRIES IN CONTEXT

YOU'VE BEEN MISLED

We've had the same conversation now too many times to count: Someone asks what we do; we say we're researchers who study teens and social media. "Ugh, I know, it's *sooo* bad," the person groans before a presumptive pause for our agreement. Often, they press on with a concerned tone: "I've seen the research." Then our new acquaintance likely tacks on what they're sure is a well-justified conclusion—something like, "It's making us all miserable" or "That's why I don't let my kids have Instagram" or "I would never have survived high school if this stuff existed when I was growing up!"

Alarmist headlines always seem to confirm the instinct that there's something deeply concerning about growing up digital. It's easy to feel like we're doing something terribly wrong by "allowing" teens to use cell phones. But news stories tend to oversimplify the available research evidence. As a result, they can contribute to unproductive panic.

Here's an example of how it happens.

A few years ago, Eric Vanman and his colleagues published findings from an interesting experiment.[1] Their team wanted to study the effect of taking a break from Facebook. The researchers randomly assigned young adults in their study to either keep using Facebook as usual or take a hiatus for five days. They wondered: would taking a break from Facebook lower the participants' stress and improve their well-being?

The researchers monitored effects. They collected reports of how the participants felt, as well as measures of their cortisol levels, which provides a physiological indicator of stress.

If you assume that quitting social media simply improves well-being, you'd expect the participants who took a break from Facebook to report greater improvements in feelings of well-being and greater declines in cortisol levels compared to those who kept using Facebook as usual. But this isn't quite what the researchers found. They *did* find differences in cortisol levels, which suggest the Facebook break reduced stress. However, the break-takers *also* reported lower subjective well-being. Perhaps surprisingly (at least if you're in the camp that social media is making us all miserable), people said they felt less happy and less satisfied after the Facebook break.

There are a few possible explanations. Maybe taking a forced break—one when you haven't really bought into the *value* of a social media detox—is different from taking a break you truly want and need. Or maybe people who take a short break from Facebook are indeed less stressed, hence the cortisol decline, but aren't aware of it yet. There are other explanations too. Maybe the findings are true for Facebook, but they wouldn't hold if people had quit Instagram as well. Or, maybe the relationship between social media use and well-being is more complicated: perhaps these apps add stress to our lives in some ways and help in others. The study doesn't (and can't) tell us which of these possibilities is right.

With these details in mind, take a look at a few media headlines about the study—all published shortly after the study was released:[2]

"Quitting Facebook for 5 Days Can Lower Your Stress Levels"
"Deleting Facebook Could Be Bad for You"
"Deleting Facebook May or May Not Be Bad for Your Mental Health"

If you didn't know the details of the study behind these headlines, you might read the first and conclude researchers produced hard evidence that we should deactivate our Facebook accounts, at least temporarily. Or you might see the second headline and think the opposite: quitting Facebook could be a bad idea. The third headline seems like a nonconclusion and, while arguably the most accurate, actually feels the least helpful.

You've likely seen a steady stream of scary news stories about studies allegedly showing that social media use is toxic. It's tempting to conclude that social media is a disaster for today's teens. We need to be careful. Concerning stories are memorable and it's natural to grab on to information aligned with whatever we already believe. In truth, research findings about technology are almost always more nuanced. Admittedly, nuanced findings don't make for the snappiest headlines.

WAIT: ISN'T SOCIAL MEDIA CAUSING TEEN DEPRESSION?

What about those studies you've heard of that show teens today suffer from higher rates of depression and suicide risk because of social media? And what about the teen you know personally, who started using Instagram and suddenly seemed to develop a collection of anxieties?

It's true that public health data point to pronounced increases in mental health issues for adolescents—girls in particular—beginning around 2010.[3] The timing generally coincides with the increasing ubiquity of smartphones and use of social media. These trends aren't really debatable.

What *is* subject to considerable debate is whether the technologies are to blame for the rise in mental health issues. Some widely publicized research shows correlations between heavy social media use among adolescents and less happiness.[4] But—and this is crucial—correlational data can't tell us for sure whether social media is *causing* teens to be less happy or vice versa (i.e., if less happy teens are using social media more). Longitudinal research from a study that followed adolescents across a full decade of their development (2009–2019) suggests a particular risk to girls of high and increasing media use (including social media, but also television).[5] Girls who used two to three hours of social media daily in early adolescence *and* increased their use patterns over time had a heightened risk trajectory. This arguably indicates an important gender-linked developmental sensitivity related to heavy social media use.

Internal research from Facebook obtained by the *Wall Street Journal* and published as we were finishing this book shows that the company's own research substantiates fears that Instagram "is toxic" for some adolescent girls.[6] A key concern that appears corroborated by the leaked findings: social media is worsening body image issues for some adolescent girls. This is important because we know that body image is core to self-esteem during adolescence.[7] Technology aside, "perceived appearance consistently emerges as the strongest single predictor of self-esteem among both male and female adolescents. The link is remarkably strong and robust."[8] Teens whose social media experiences erode their body image are therefore at heightened risk for other issues.[9]

More generally, such data are yet another call to action: if we are to help those teens who are most at risk, we need focused attention on what's hard for teens about social media, for whom, when, and why.

Given the apparent importance of gender, we need to bear in mind that the vast majority of current research speaks to the social media experiences of cisgender teens (meaning, those whose gender identities align with their sex at birth) and doesn't equip us with all the information we need to understand the experiences of transgender and other gender minority teens.[10] So, we have emerging evidence that is painting a clearer picture yet also much more to learn. As writers, our aim throughout this book is to provide a candid take on what is currently known and what is still up for debate.

What *do* we know? Overall, some studies reveal small negative relationships between screen time and indicators of well-being: they show that higher screen time is, on average, associated with a higher likelihood of reporting psychological struggles.[11] Some scholars call these data alarming while others caution that the findings are simply too minute to matter.[12] Research like the longitudinal study mentioned previously suggests that risk varies based on characteristics such as gender and patterns of use over time.

Even if smartphones and social media somehow amplify adolescent distress, the causal mechanisms aren't all entirely clear. Distress could be a function of screen time itself, of the kinds of thinking it generates (e.g., comparison, body insecurity), or what that screen time is displacing (such as face-to-face socializing, hobbies, or sleep). It could also be the result of broader social and cultural changes that have happened alongside radical connectivity.

At the same time, other studies fail to find relationships between screen time and well-being at all.[13] In one fine-grained analysis of teens' individual tech patterns, heavier technology use didn't predict mental health issues and adolescents didn't feel worse on days when they spent more time on their devices.[14] The absence of evidence can itself be important. Lead researcher Michaeline Jensen acknowledged that these findings (or rather the lack thereof) may be counter-intuitive: "Contrary to the common belief that smartphones and social media are damaging adolescents' mental health, we don't see much support for the idea that time spent on phones and online is associated with increased risk for mental health problems."[15]

If it was just one study, it would be tempting to dismiss it or to wonder if there was just something unusual about the teens who participated in the research. But studies in different contexts with different groups of teens similarly challenge a simplistic, causal narrative that teens + screens inevitably = misery.[16] This doesn't mean social media isn't a huge issue for some teens. But as adolescent mental health expert Candice Odgers puts it: "It may be time for adults to stop arguing over whether smartphones and social media are good or bad for teens' mental health and start figuring out ways to best support them in both their offline and online lives."[17]

Teens wish we would heed this advice. As one fourteen-year-old in our own research said: *"Even though social media or any type of technology may cause some teenagers stress/sadness, adults in our lives try to put all of the blame [for] our anxiety and depression on social media alone, and do not try to get us the help we may need."* Another teen said that the hardest part about growing up with today's technologies is actually *"my mom blaming everything on 'always being on my phone.'"* For sure: social media and phones are a crucial part of the story, especially for some teens. A throughline question of this book is: How can adults shift beyond fatalistic tech blaming toward understanding key issues for teens and building teens' agency to navigate them?

IT'S (STILL) COMPLICATED

Tuning into perspectives of the most vulnerable teens is instructive. One key group: those who are actively struggling with suicidal behaviors. I (Emily) and several of my colleagues partnered with a children's hospital to interview thirty teens who were in psychiatric inpatient treatment.[18]

Our aim was to understand the teens' views on social media, including its influences on mental health. The upshot: There was no single, simple narrative.

Some teens named ways social media exacerbated their mental health challenges. They pointed to struggles like cyberbullying, toxic social comparison, or losing sleep because they couldn't pull away from their devices. But these challenges weren't issues at all for others. And contrary to public discourse, social media really didn't seem to be a net-negative for everyone in the hospital study. Some teens described finding online the kinds of positive social connections you'd wish you could give a teen who was struggling to find offline friends. Others talked about learning positive ways of understanding or coping with their diagnoses or tapping into adaptive interests and hobbies. Much as danah boyd wrote in her landmark 2011 book about teens and social media, the data revealed that *it's complicated.*[19]

To be clear: it wasn't too complicated to see how digital life plagued or benefited individuals. There were teens like Brian who saw social media as a genuine problem: "*Social media is—in my opinion—a depressant,*" he explained, "*it's really unhealthy.*" In addition to navigating offline social issues that were mirrored and amplified online, Brian struggled considerably with social comparison. In his words: "*When you look at [someone's] page . . . you compare that idea of them . . . to yourself. Not just to your Instagram page, but to you. As in: your life. So you're like, I'm here, watching* Parks and Rec *[TV program], not doing crap, and they're just like skiing in the Alps and just like climbing Machu Picchu. And it makes you feel like garbage.*"

In the hospital study, my colleagues and I also interviewed teens like Lei, whose portrayal of social media differed from Brian's on nearly all counts: "*I prefer to be on social media as much as I can be without it interrupting my normal life . . . it's just a creative outlet that I really love to use as much as I can, because it makes me feel happy . . . and it's really fun interacting with people around the world.*"

Lei elaborated:

In my opinion social media really does help me. It really does make me feel like there are people that are there for me . . . it just shows that someone could be 5,000 miles away but still care about you and still support you. And I mean, there's always memes and there are always just funny jokes on the Internet that do make me happy.

And usually when I get really anxious, I'll listen to calm music on my phone or you know, I'll watch a nice funny video on YouTube. And when I'm really depressed, I feel like it's really nice when I get to talk to other people. And even if they post something negative . . . then someone [else] would probably show support.

Listening closely to what teens had to say gave us clearer insight. For teens like Brian, we could identify digital struggles that warranted attention. But our data didn't point to a simple screen time ban as a panacea for all these at-risk teens. In some cases, keeping a teen off tech even seemed ill advised.

This accords with the direction in which research on teens and social media is heading more broadly. There is more and more evidence showing that teens have different digital experiences. It may be fair to say that many—even most—are struggling with some aspect of their digital lives. But what's hard varies. What's valuable and important and even awesome varies too.

THE FATAL FLAW OF THE "SCREEN TIME DEBATE"

In the spring of 2020, as the COVID-19 pandemic took hold across the United States, the *New York Times* ran an article with the pointed headline: "Coronavirus ended the screen-time debate. Screens won." It's true that screens ruled our lives during the pandemic. But that's not the only reason it may be time to table the cultural obsession with screen time. The fixation displaces a more important conversation about details. What are individual teens in fact doing during their screen time, and to what end?

For a time, it seemed like breaking down screen time into two main categories might effectively distinguish "good" from "bad" screen time, at least in terms of impacts on well-being. Some studies show that "active" uses—like the creative expression and social interactions that Lei described—indeed tend to be supportive of well-being while "passive" browsing can spark toxic comparison and negatively impact mental health.[20] This is a helpful distinction.

Yet even differentiating active and passive screen time proves insufficient. All passive uses are not equal. Some browsing is decidedly uplifting, entertaining, inspiring, and valuable. Even when it's not, an hour spent browsing through TikTok videos of dances and whipped coffee recipes is fundamentally different from an hour spent doomscrolling through upsetting news coverage or browsing dieting and workout content, or even more alarming pro-anorexia posts.

One hour is different from five hours too. Acknowledging that screen time is the wrong focus doesn't mean we need to dispense with any consideration of it. At the far extreme, the heaviest screen time users do tend to be struggling more than their peers—girls, especially.[21] This doesn't mean that screen time is causing those struggles, or that every heavy screen time user is in crisis. Again, all screen time isn't the same. And teens aren't either.

ORCHIDS, DANDELIONS, AND SCREEN TIME

We're getting a clearer sense of how much individual differences matter, courtesy of more nuanced research methods. In one study,[22] researchers collected data from 387 adolescents whom they surveyed six times a day, every day, for six weeks. With the resulting dataset of 34,930 surveys, the researchers used statistical approaches to analyze how individual adolescents' trajectories of social media use and happiness changed over time in relation to different kinds of screen activities.

Interestingly, when they looked across the whole group, the data didn't show that active uses were beneficial or that passively browsing others' posts was generally detrimental. This differed from many prior studies. The research design allowed for a more granular assessment of individual experiences and instead revealed different "types" of susceptibility. Whether it was active or passive seemed to matter less than *who* was browsing: some teens experienced only negative effects, others only felt upsides and benefits, and still others seemed relatively insusceptible— their well-being didn't appear impacted at all.

"Differential susceptibility" is a key concept across multiple fields of research (psychology, genetics, environmental science) and it's become an anchoring concept in media research too. Even if all teens browsed the exact same content, posted the exact same types of updates, and spent precisely the same amount of time using social apps, they wouldn't all be affected in the same ways. It's helpful to think about a common metaphor used to explain differential susceptibility: orchids and dandelions.[23]

Dandelions are sturdy flowers that can thrive in a range of climates and conditions. Orchids, by comparison, are much more sensitive to their environments. This is the concept of *differential susceptibility* in a nutshell.

Of course, teens don't all browse the same content. This further amplifies differences in their experiences. A teen who is prone to social comparison might seek out envy-inducing influencers, while another teen who is less prone to comparative thinking fills their social media feeds with body positivity accounts. These complexities are propelling a necessary shift: away from a blanket focus on screen time and toward alertness to teens' different experiences, strengths, and vulnerabilities.

THREE LENSES

There's undeniable power in numbers and big data. At the same time, individual perspectives and stories breathe life into the trends adults so desperately want to understand. In the chapters that follow, we spotlight teens' voices as an intentional pivot, fueled by a sense that important conversations *about* teens and tech too often proceed without their voices.

To adults, teens' digital lives often seem distant and unfamiliar, shaped by twisted and even "upside down" dynamics and logic. As we examine teens' digital lives, we look through three lenses to bring these dynamics into view. A *developmental lens* helps us understand how teens' experiences differ from those of adults in meaningful and important ways. This sets us up to recognize powerful drivers of adolescent behavior, and to identify ways that technologies play (and at times *prey*) on developmental sensitivities. An *ecological lens* reminds us that teens' digital experiences are inevitably and powerfully shaped by their offline lives, contexts, and identities. A *digital lens* alerts us to the ways particular features of technologies shape and even transform[24] adolescents' experiences behind their screens.

A DEVELOPMENTAL LENS

Adolescence is a time of tremendous change—socially, cognitively, physically. Chances are good you still have strong memories associated with the songs that were popular during your teen years.[25] Hearing even the first notes can bring you back to a particular time and place so immediately that you can almost *feel* the excitement or angst or joy of your sixteen-year-old self. The minutiae of a moment remain vivid years later: where you were, who you were with, how you felt, maybe even what you were wearing.

It's not just music. There's some evidence that the teen years hold a special, "privileged" position in our memories.[26] The developmental changes of adolescence prime the brain for strong emotional reactions.[27] Strong emotions—and the neurochemicals released along with them—can make for deep memories.[28] In this way, vivid teenage memories are like an artifact of our adolescent brain's hypersensitivity to strong emotions. This is worth repeating: we feel many highs and lows more deeply during adolescence, and our brains seem to encode the events of our adolescent years differently as a result.

By around age sixteen, if not sooner, adolescents have the same cognitive capacities for logical thinking as adults.[29] Yet teens often behave in ways that confound adults and make risky and apparently irrational decisions. Why?

For one, the adolescent brain has a reward bias. At a neural level, adolescents are more sensitive to potential rewards.[30] At the same time, the circuitry that supports self-regulation is still developing through and beyond the teen years.[31] This creates a period of time when the brain is primed for reward seeking and less adept at impulse control.[32] What's more, the presence of peers amplifies these dynamics.[33] Adolescents are more sensitive than adults to peer validation and to the pain of feeling rejected or excluded.[34] There's actually a neurochemical basis for teens' intense focus on status seeking and getting attention from their peers.[35]

The difference between the early tween years and late teen years is, of course, vast and varied. Because development proceeds at different paces, it's often impossible to make definitive statements about differences between the experiences of, say, a thirteen-year-old and those of a fifteen-year-old. What's more, issues that occupy a teen's attention in early adolescence often fade over time as they find stronger footing in their identities and friendships. For example: social media "likes" remain relevant but may feel less critical as needed evidence of peer approval;

showcasing one's closest friendships via social media Stories remains compelling, but perhaps less essential as an identity statement.

"YOU DON'T EVEN KNOW ME"

One of our most intimate, desperate human desires is to be understood and accepted. Think about how good it feels to be seen for who you are and, conversely, how awful it feels to be misjudged or rejected. Yet this is complicated during adolescence because teens are still *figuring out* exactly who they are and who they want to be.

When my (Emily's) youngest sister Lou was about sixteen years old, a lighthearted family dinner conversation where everyone was discussing who was the funniest, most laid back, and most creative led her to tearfully proclaim: *"You don't even know me!"*

Like teens around the world, Lou recognized that she was changing. She felt like she had a whole "new," emerging identity that was recognized and embraced by her friends, but not even noticed by her family members. The pain of feeling misunderstood was real and deep, even though the conversation seemed low-stakes and playful to everyone else.

Identity development is a core task of adolescence. Neural changes that enable more abstract and complex thinking set the stage for adolescents to reflect on their identities and values in new ways.[36] The psychologist Erik Erikson famously described it as a *crisis* that every individual must resolve.[37] Who am I, and who do I want to be? How do I fit into my family, my peer group, my community, and the world? A coherent sense of self is hard won, though. Adolescents engage in ongoing identity work: trying out different dimensions of their identities, expressing them, and taking stock of how others react. Expression and peer feedback therefore hold particular weight and meaning. Digital technologies did not *create* this reality. Yet, as we'll see, they provide new venues that up the ante.

AN ECOLOGICAL LENS

People make sense of themselves and their worlds *in context*. For teens, their families, neighborhoods, schools, peer groups, religious communities, and sports teams are all relevant. More distant institutions and forces matter too. Mass media and popular culture impact peoples' values and attitudes (even if not in a straightforward, causal way). Governmental policies, laws, and the state of the economy are relevant to the sense of security an adolescent experiences. And sociopolitical events are consequential, like whether a teen is coming of age during a world war, a pandemic, or a major civic movement. In the 1970s, psychologist Urie Bronfenbrenner[38] outlined an *ecological model*[39] that named these powerful influences on development.

Our own ecological lens has a wide scope and includes attention to sociological forces that shape life behind the screen, from the micro to the macro. This lens helps us zero in on dynamics at the micro level of close friends and near peers. We can see how subtle but powerful social forces influence teens' digital decisions from sending nudes (chapter 5) to posting their political views (chapter 6).

This lens also helps us zoom out to recognize how cultural ideologies about sexuality, beauty, happiness, and more are reinforced or resisted as teens use social media. For example, on social media highlight reels teens see images that suggest everyone's lives and looks are perfect by comparison (chapter 2). Yet, they may also encounter, seek out, or produce content that resists such narratives, including body positivity accounts and private Snapchat Stories that let it all hang out—bad days too.

An ecological lens also primes us to see how identities that are sources of privilege or oppression offline shape experiences online, too, from civic expression to sexting pressures and digital aggression. Gender, race, ethnicity, sexual identity and more affect the positive opportunities and risks teens navigate in networked life.

Teens' experiences in digital life are also affected by their differential access to resources and capital. Economic resources are just the tip of the iceberg. Social, cultural, and educational capital grant access to crucial knowledge, skills, and literacies that affect how teens engage and to what end. As mobile technologies have become nearly ubiquitous, there is less talk (at least in the United States) of a digital access gap and more attention to gaps in how technologies are used (the "participation gap") and supported (the "digital literacies gap").[40] Inequities persist on a number of levels. At the same time, teens from historically marginalized groups can and do leverage digital tools in inventive ways that build their interests, learning, and civic agency.[41]

An ecological lens takes on board dynamics from everyday peer interactions to broader cultural ideologies and systemic forces. Our data limit the extent to which we can unpack every factor a comprehensive ecological analysis could reveal; we cannot meet its promise for every topic. Yet this lens is essential to our work and for collective efforts to understand what teens are facing.

A DIGITAL LENS

Studying teens' digital experiences is like chasing a moving target: the technologies teens use continue to change and so do the ways they use them.[42] For example, several years ago, teens typically described Instagram as a space for fairly performative expression to relatively large audiences of their peers. Then, Instagram added a Stories function and Close Friends lists that instantly enabled easy, more fleeting posts to much smaller audience groups. As we'll see in chapters 3 ("Friendship Dilemmas"), 4 ("Small Slights, Big Fights"), and 6 ("The Political Is (Inter) Personal"), these added features had ripple effects for teens' experiences behind the screen. Platforms themselves rise and fall in popularity too. TikTok hardly seemed relevant in 2018 but, as you'll see in the chapters across this book, the platform was a fixture in our interviews and discussions with U.S. teens just three years later.

At the time of this writing, the teens involved in our research talk most often about TikTok, Instagram, Snapchat, and Discord. By the time you read this book, these apps will have changed in various ways and they may well have ebbed in significance. New go-to apps may dominate teens' attention.

Is there any dry land? We could throw up our hands in exasperation that everything is new, different, and impossible to keep up with; we could conclude that this book too will be dated before we even finish writing it. Instead, we train our attention to the core qualities of digital technologies that represent a sea change from the nondigital world and are relatively enduring despite new iterations via new apps. Our colleagues in the field of digital media research have been cataloguing these qualities—often referred to as "affordances"[43]—for some time now. The following distillation draws inspiration from key early works by danah boyd and Nicholas Negroponte, and more recent works by Andrew Cho, Jacqueline Nesi, Sophia Choukas-Bradley, and Mitch Prinstein.[44]

Relevant qualities of note:

Persistence. Digital content sticks around. As danah boyd explained, persistence means that online expressions are archived and potentially viewed outside of their initial context.

Searchability. "Googling" is an everyday practice. Search engines and tools enable quick sorting through huge content databases. Anyone can find an array of digital content connected to an individual (e.g., social media profiles, old forum posts, tagged photos).

Scalability. With no cost and little extra effort, the reach of an online post can potentially be shared to vast audiences.

Replicability. Whether through screenshots or "copy and paste," digital content is readily replicable. It can also be modified in ways that aren't self-evident.

Absence of physical cues. Text-based exchanges are stripped of cues such as facial expressions. The absence of physical cues can play a role in miscommunication and enable anonymity.

Constant connection. Mobile devices and apps offer the possibility of 24/7 access and of uninterrupted contact.

Quantifiability. A variety of metrics, including likes and follows, provides accessible and quantified data. These metrics can signal visibility and reach, as well as social response to online posts. Data logs also quantify individual-level app usage data.

Default publicness. A common design feature of many social media sites, default publicness privileges openness and connectedness to offline networks.

Algorithmically reinforced filter bubbles. By determining what appears first on social media feeds, in search results, and as recommended viewing content, algorithms both personalize content and create ideological echo chambers.

These qualities help us begin to sort through questions such as: How is it different for a teen today to find out in real time that they've been excluded because of evidence they see on Instagram or Snapchat, rather than just hearing about it Monday morning? How does the challenge of "binge watching" differ when it's TikTok or Netflix rather than on a TV in the family room? How do the stakes of speaking out on a controversial issue change when it's a post that can be screenshotted and circulated?

A digital lens helps us think critically about what's new and, crucially, how the design of technologies can undercut or support teens' sense of agency. A developmental lens helps us see what endures, particularly in terms of adolescents' motives and behaviors. An ecological lens helps us consider the importance of context, reminding us that teens' digital experiences aren't happening in a vacuum. Looking through these lenses, we are poised to answer the big question of this book: Behind their screens, what are teens facing that adults are missing?

2

THE PULL OF THE SCREEN

Brynn was about to fall asleep, phone in hand, still on TikTok. She couldn't really explain why, but these short videos just keep her scrolling for hours on end. *"The app TikTok runs my life,"* she reflected. *"I can sit there for hours on end just scrolling through this app. . . . I can't even count how many times I have fallen asleep on TikTok. It has taken over my life."* Brynn has tried to cut back, *"but it's hard,"* she explained, because *"once you get a notification, you just want to go on it and look at what someone sent you, or what someone liked, or who followed you."*

Today's technologies are intentionally designed with features that contribute to the pull of the screen. So it's fair to say that it's truly *by design* that Brynn feels like she can't pull away. Graham shares the struggle. When we Zoomed to discuss digital habits, he wanted to emphasize the extent of his use by revealing how much time he spent on TikTok the previous week—but he worried about even saying the number aloud, lest his mom overhear from the other room. He typed into the chatbox—twenty-four hours—and then gestured as if to say: can you even believe it?

We can. Our research confirmed time and again that many teens feel out of control when it comes to some aspect of their tech habits. It's not just TikTok. Behind their screens, beneath the explicit pleas for "five more minutes," many teens worry about what it's costing them. It's easy for adults to assume all teens want unrestricted, around-the-clock tech time.

The reality is more complicated as the tremendous opportunities of digital life for voice, connection, and more collide with persuasive designs and powerful developmental drives.

"I CAN'T SEEM TO GET OFF MY PHONE"

Apps, games, social media, and even devices themselves are cleverly designed to hijack focus.[1] Features like the buzz of a new notification are strategically iterated to capture attention. As former tech insider Tristan Harris and his colleague Max Stossel like to explain to teens, it's no mistake that notification flags are red. It's far more annoying to see little red flags than, for example, little green flags. This subtly motivates the user to attend to them, which means opening the app and, voila!, the screen has won their attention.

Teens fear yet feel increasing dependence on devices. They say things like:

The most tricky part about growing up with social media is how dangerous and addictive it is. People are always glued to their phones, but so am I and I hate that. (fifteen-year-old)

I can't seem to get off my phone and most of my time is on my phone. (thirteen-year-old)

I feel like I'm too interested in my phone instead of what's happening around me. I wish that I didn't use my phone so much. (thirteen-year-old)

These feelings of dependence are no accident. Long before Mark Zuckerberg was at Harvard creating the beta version of what would become Facebook, a psychologist named B. F. Skinner was at work in a lab on the very same campus researching how rewards influence learning. The wooden box he used in his experiments became known as a "Skinner box."[2] The box had a lever his lab animals could press to release food pellets. Skinner experimented with different reward schedules—releasing pellets in different sequences and intervals—to see how they influenced the rats' behavior. Ultimately, his experiments demonstrated the power of *unpredictable* rewards. Boxes that were programmed to release food pellets unpredictably (rather than, say, every time the rats pressed the lever or even every fourth time) led to more frenzied tapping at the lever.

Skinner's experiments demonstrated that rewards shape behavior. This is true not only for lab rats, but also for human beings. Skinner's experiments are also a landmark illustration of the principle that we tend to pursue rewards vigorously and with intense, enduring zeal when we *can't* predict exactly when and how they will materialize.

HARD FOR EVERYONE, EVEN HARDER FOR TEENS

Technology companies routinely leverage variable rewards to create features that keep teens—and all of us—pulled in by our devices.[3] In his book *Irresistible: The Rise of Addictive Technology and the Business of Keeping Us Hooked*, psychologist Adam Alter describes how the simple addition of the "like" button added the lure of unpredictable rewards to social media. A user never knows exactly how many likes they are going to get when they share a picture. They post and then wait to see their likes and comments amass. Eventually, the post becomes old news. Their followers' positive feedback slows and then peters out. But they can share another post, which offers the promise of a new infusion. Will they get more likes than last time? Will the feedback feel as rewarding, or perhaps even more gratifying?

Adults are plenty susceptible to the lure of unpredictable rewards. Just think about all the people who can't resist slot machines despite their accumulating losses. ($30 billion dollars a year is spent in U.S. casinos![4]) Yet to tweens and teens, the kind of "rewards" social media promise are even more meaningful. Teens are primed to crave and value social validation, which is part of how they make sense of where they fit into their social worlds. Their biological sensitivity to social feedback[5] makes them more susceptible to the pull of social media, which is at the ready with a promise of 24/7 access to likes and praising comments. Capacities for self-regulation and impulse control are also a work in progress during the teen years, which adds to the challenge of pulling away.

Variable rewards are at play in other ways too. Teens describe a *"constant bombardment of content."* Apps like TikTok have an endless database of content to offer users. Some videos are pointless or boring or upsetting; others give a fleeting reward in the form of funny, relatable, or compelling content. Powerfully crafted algorithms are also learning with every click, swipe, and pause—taking careful note of what each user likes, what they skip over, and what they watch again. This enables increasingly personalized content.

Features like infinite scroll make for seamless content transitions. Snapchat is *"so addictive because it's so easy to go on to the next thing,"* one sixteen-year-old explained, *"And you never know what amazing thing could be on the next Story, and all you have to do is tap once and you get to the next thing."* Indeed, users never know what the next video will be, or how many they'll need to watch before something somewhat "rewarding" comes up.

Similarly, Netflix and YouTube autostart the next video before viewers even have time to consider whether they want to keep watching. This design makes binge watching not just easy, but effortless. Tech companies know that natural stopping cues (like the end of a TV show) can give people enough time to pause and think: "Okay, that's enough, I have other things to do." Importantly, there is compelling evidence that teaching teens about "addictive designs" boosts awareness and motivates teens to actively control their social media use.[6]

Video games leverage persuasive design too. Well-designed games provide players with problem-solving opportunities that are "pleasantly frustrating."[7] The path through a game varies such that challenges are introduced right at the edge of a player's skill or ability. This set-up is ripe for a *flow* experience. Flow, the psychological state of being in the zone, involves the kind of full-focus and absorption where one loses track of time.[8] Challenge level is a key to finding flow: too easy is boring, while too hard makes further effort feel useless. Video games also typically provide immediate feedback and they're goal-directed, which also enhance flow.

For developmental reasons, teens are especially susceptible to common persuasive design features. For example, social media exploits natural instincts like social reciprocity.[9] In general, when someone does something for us, we're inclined to return the favor. So, if we've gotten a snap or like on our post, it feels natural to want to reciprocate—and we need to keep checking our apps to do so. For adolescents, these digital features again collide with development. Adolescents are inclined to invest in peer relationships *and* they have still-developing self-regulation and impulse control.

"How do you stop?," we ask Graham.

"I don't," he replies. *"Ever."*

PULLED TO—AND AWAY FROM—PEOPLE

Nearly three thousand miles away from Graham, sixteen-year-old Diego is up late, staring at his screen. He's on Discord, which is a chat app that was originally created for gamers like him. Discord supports multiple modalities: text-based, video, voice chatting, and easy screen sharing. As the pandemic persisted in the fall of 2020, Diego started a Discord server and invited his offline friends who were gamers. As he got more into gaming, he started meeting other teens online and adding them to the Discord server too.

Tonight, Diego is talking to Marcus on a Discord channel he created called "Gamer Minds Matter." It's a space for *"getting things off your chest,"* including *"mental health issues, relationships (romantic or with friends/family), [and] sexuality"* as well as any everyday thing *"that is really bothering someone."* Diego knows from experience that Discord channels like these are a meaningful source of connection and support: *"I have seen people who are struggling with something, [and] we'll talk about it, and then they're really happy [because] they realize that like five different people reached out. And they're talking to them about whatever they're going through, helping them through it. It's really good . . . I can see it helping people."*

For teens, a powerful pull of the screen is social. Sometimes, using tech while hanging out is a conduit for connection or for creative expression—whether teens are in person and gaming together or mastering a new dance routine to share on social media. Yet two things are true: today's technologies offer real, unprecedented opportunities for building closeness *and* their very presence can undercut connection. A key distinction is whether tech is pulling teens toward or away from the people they're with.

Teens are all too familiar with feeling less important than others' phones. *"People are always just on their phones,"* one thirteen-year-old explained, *"so it's practically impossible to have a real conversation without them being distracted."* The feeling is echoed by tweens and teens of all ages.

In real life when I sit next to my friends on the bus, they ignore me because they're on their phones. (twelve-year-old)

I feel a little slighted if [my friend is] on their phone the whole time. Because I made time to hang out with them. And so why aren't they making the same time for me? (sixteen-year-old)

There is a person in my life who is really important to me, and we could be out and about doing something and they sit on their phones a lot. It gets really frustrating when I try talking to them and they don't realize it because they are so into their phone. (seventeen-year-old)

It would be a mistake to misinterpret digital distraction as evidence that teens don't care about connection. Teens want and value strong relationships. Yet the pull of the screen and the impulse to keep devices at hand can be hard to fight. In some cases, the desire to appear digitally immersed is even strategic, as teens try to look busy rather than lost, awkward, or friendless in certain social situations. When phones are used in this way—like a *"digital pacifier,"* as some teens put it—they can send a message of unavailability that may backfire by preventing others from approaching.

There's a term for tech-based interruptions: technoference.[10] The cost can be steep. Allowing tech interruptions conveys the message that what's on the screen is more important than whoever is off screen and in the room. Even diverting attention for just a moment can disrupt the quality of communication. Real people don't come with pause buttons, so the ways we manage tech disruptions matter. So does the frequency with which we let them happen.

In romantic relationships, persistent technoference is related to lower relationship satisfaction.[11] In conversations with friends, technoference leads to lower-quality interactions.[12] For parents of young children, technoference is related to increases in kids whining, sulking, and acting out.[13] Teens notice parental distraction, too, saying things like: *"My parents tell me to put my [device] down and they immediately get back on their own phones."* Notably, adolescent kids whose parents' attention is constantly diverted by tech describe their parents as less warm, loving, responsive, and comforting than do kids whose parents are less digitally distracted.[14]

Overall, technoference seems to change the tenor of our communication and, in turn, the quality of our connections.

Notifications are a key culprit in technoference. Constant notifications lead to teens feeling *"bombarded with messages and pings."* They find themselves on both sides of this dynamic: struggling over the temptation to check a phone rather than staying focused on the person in front of them, but also feeling slighted by others who do so to them.

Cell phones are ubiquitous. They're almost always nearby—if not in hand—when we are talking to others. We might think we can simply ignore or quickly dismiss silent notifications. But the beeps, buzzes, and notifications from smartphones are a distraction and a disruption—even if we don't read or respond to the incoming messages and calls.[15]

LIGHTS OUT, SCREENS ON

Adults are generally alert to concerns that screens are disrupting sleep. This concern is also echoed by teens. Attention to sleep quality is warranted given its role in healthy development, learning, and mental health. Insufficient sleep puts teens at risk of struggles with emotion regulation and depression, concentration and learning, angry outbursts, drowsy driving, and physical issues that range from skin breakouts to catching colds.[16]

Smartphones are thought to disrupt the quest for a good night's sleep in at least four ways:[17]

(1) they displace sleep because teens are plugged in and spending time online when they would otherwise be sleeping
(2) incoming notifications disturb sleep because they wake teens
(3) teens' pre-bedtime digital activities increase wakefulness and make it harder to fall asleep
(4) the light emitted by screens disrupts melatonin release and delays the circadian clock[18]

Researchers are still learning about the extent to which smartphones cause sleep disruption in these ways. We do know, though, that more than 70 percent of high schoolers in the United States consistently sleep less on school nights than the recommended eight-hour minimum.[19] And screen time is, unsurprisingly, associated with shorter sleep duration and diminished sleep quality.[20] In our own research, teens indeed describe how smartphones can displace sleep because *"You get attached very easily and sometimes you just forget about everything and use it without any sleep."*

But another sleep-related issue is especially salient to teens: feeling compelled to wake up during the night to respond to inbound messages. *"I have a tendency to wake up in the middle of the night and respond to people,"* one high schooler acknowledged, *"No matter what time it is, I will respond and then go back to sleep."* They're not alone. More than one in three teens wake up during the night to check their phones.[21] Some even take active steps to ensure it: *"I wake up in the middle of the night to check my phone. I even have alarms set to wake up."*

Why go so far as to set alarms during the night? Both design features and social motives are implicated. Some teens set alarms to wake up because they're playing online games that have timed periods for in-game tasks; if it's in the middle of the night, they may set an alarm to ensure they don't miss the window. Others check messages out of habit, or to ensure they're sufficiently responsive to friends. As we'll discuss in chapter 3, some teens feel obligated to be available 24/7. Especially in cases where a close friend is struggling, responding ASAP can feel like an absolute must. And yet, being there for a friend in this way can undercut personal well-being. Teens who sleep with phones in reach—and reach for them in the night—are bound to have low-quality sleep due to the repeated interruptions.

Sleep researcher Lauren Hale sees the importance of talking to teens about screens and sleep in ways that might especially get their attention. For example, adults might point to data showing that late-night tweeting among NBA players is associated with reduced performance (fewer points and fewer rebounds) in basketball games the next day.[22]

PULLED FROM FOCUS

During the day, teens point to a constant influx of notification buzzes and distractions that can disrupt focus on schoolwork and other responsibilities. Just a few examples, in their own words: *"You are constantly being alerted about everything, and it can be hard to focus"*; *"The most challenging part is getting distracted by games or friends when I'm trying to get work done";* "I tend to watch Stories on Snapchat to procrastinate my responsibilities. I do this daily and wish I was doing more productive tasks instead."

During the pandemic, it was even easier to drift off-task from online school. School rules that prohibited phones on desks during class were suddenly irrelevant and unenforceable; phones could be mere inches away. On the computer screen, other windows, games, and text conversations could be layered behind and competing with Zoom lectures. Michelle, a high school senior, started watching TikTok during class and playing a game called Subway Surfers (reverting, as she put it, to her *"fifth-grade self"*). She explained: *"I started watching TikToks also during class and I was like, wait, I'm supposed to be learning now, and I, like, totally forgot that."* Setting parental controls for herself helped. It wasn't a perfect fix since she could find other on-screen distractions on apps she hadn't restricted, or she could ignore and reset the time limits. But it generally helped her keep distractions at bay.

When we asked teens about managing digital distractions during virtual school, some used strategies like Michelle's screen time restrictions. Others described needing to physically distance from their phones if they wanted to really focus. Still others admitted they didn't try too hard to fight digital diversions because they were a welcome source of distraction or because they felt multitasking wasn't interfering with their learning (*"Sometimes, I'll be on the phone with my friends while I'm in class and they are too, which I know is probably not a good thing, but it's not, like, distracting me from working"*).

In general, "successful multitasking" is a myth. Although it may feel effective, research tends to show otherwise. Unless one of the tasks is more or less automatic (like walking, folding laundry, or—in some cases—listening to background music), people are generally fooling themselves into thinking they can do things simultaneously with no costs.[23] Instead, teens are actually "task-switching," repeatedly diverting attention back and forth between (for example) Subway Surfers and their online World History class. In most cases, the price for task-switching is compromised performance on work or learning.[24] Even if the same quality of work ultimately gets done, it takes significantly more time.[25]

"IT'S BIG BRAIN TIME"

Social apps aren't always at odds with focusing on schoolwork, though. In some cases, they are appropriated by teens to directly support studying and learning. Two examples help illustrate this point: When Mary and her friends started playing Among Us, they downloaded Discord—the platform that Diego and his gamer friends use. They were initially using it to chat while they played the game. Soon after their friend group started using the app, "It's Big Brain Time" was born.

"It's Big Brain Time" is the name that Mary and friends gave to the Discord server they set up for study support. They started with a single study chat meant to *"help each other with homework and keep each other motivated"* as they navigated virtual school during the pandemic. Eventually, it evolved into a series of different channels that they used for different topics—even when some of them returned to in-person learning. Big Brain Time had one channel for STEM, another for humanities, and so on. If someone was struggling, she could post a question and get just-in-time support. It felt good to be the helper too. *"I help a lot with AP Gov and English,"* Mary explained, *"and then a lot of my friends help me with math and science."* The Discord server functioned as a space for both informal peer tutoring and motivational support for staying on track. *"Sometimes I go on there and I'm like, Oh my gosh, I don't want to do school, and then my friends are like: 'you're doing school work!'"*

A Discord study server is fairly unique, but the experience of leveraging technologies for peer-based study support is not. Allahna, for example, got distracted by her phone and by social media when she was trying to do schoolwork on her own. But whenever she and her friends organized a Zoom-based study group, she was able to focus. The virtual accountability was enough to keep her off social media and other digital distractions. It was screen time, yes, but not the kind of screen time that disrupted focus and learning. Sure, not all teens have friends who nudge them toward studying. But these details and distinctions are crucial if we want to understand when screen time supports rather than undercuts activities that adults agree are important.

These stories also connect, broadly, with studies of how online communities constructed for one purpose—whether it's gaming, socializing, or pop culture fandom—are appropriated for other purposes that are beneficial to teens. For example: online fan communities for the *Hunger Games* book series have morphed into sites for "real world" activism and civic learning.[26] The virtual study support groups also connect to a finding from developmental science: peer influence during adolescence isn't just about peer pressure and negative effects, as friends can be good influences too.[27]

Tuning into the details of what teens see, read, and do in online spaces gives us a different view that helpfully spotlights the positives. We see inventive ways in which teens can flip tech from simply a source of distraction to a support for concentration and learning. These kinds of examples are helpful to bear in mind as we continue to dig into challenges and sources of distress.

COMPARISON QUICKSAND

As many adults now recognize, social media can serve up a never-ending stream of other people's best moments. Popular apps can be like comparison quicksand, pulling teens into an envy-inducing scroll hole. Everyone else seems to be happy and thriving, not to mention surrounded by tons of friends.

For some teens, constant comparison to others on social media takes a distinct toll. It *"lowers your self-confidence and makes you feel bad about yourself or like you aren't as good as those around you,"* one thirteen-year-old girl explained. Unchecked, these comparisons can even lead to what another teen (a sixteen-year-old boy) described as *"a sense of self-hatred."* Girls exhibit particular vulnerability.[28] Teens girls explain: *"On social media everyone seems like they are far better and far ahead then me, which is stressful and makes me feel behind, unwanted and stupid."* Also: *"One of the most challenging things I personally have had to deal with is comparing myself to girls on social media. I scroll through my Instagram and see models with perfect bodies and I feel horrible about myself."* But it's not just girls who struggle in this way. Boys, too, acknowledge: *"I do it a lot, and it makes you feel sad and bad about yourself"*; *"It gets [to be] too much."*

People vary in the tendency toward social comparison, both in general and in the context of their social media use.[29] Teens marvel in describing friends who seem more or less immune to comparing and despairing. Especially in a world of social media, this individual difference holds a kind of protective power. At the same time, others find social media triggers constant comparisons that feel escapable only by avoiding the apps all together.

Essena O'Neill[30] was an Australian teen with an "instafamous presence." When she shuttered her social media accounts, she had a final message for her five hundred thousand-plus followers: "Social Media Is Not Real Life."[31] Essena began a mass deletion of all of her old Instagram posts—but first, she recaptioned her past photographs to admit that they were contrived.[32] "Not real life," she wrote under a beach photograph from roughly two years earlier. "Only reason we went to the beach this morning was to shoot these bikinis because the company paid me and also I looked good to society's current standards."[33] To a smiling selfie, she added a self-mocking narration: "'Please like this photo, I put on makeup, curled my hair, tight dress, big uncomfortable jewellery. . . . Took over 50 shots until I got one I thought you might like, then I edited this one selfie for ages on several apps—just so I could feel some social approval from you.' THERE IS NOTHING REAL ABOUT THIS." On her personal website, Essena elaborated. She wanted her followers to know that her smiling Instagram photos were false evidence of an enviable life. And she was quitting Instagram because, she said, "I no longer want to spend hours and hours of my time scrolling, viewing and comparing myself to others."

This is one of the clearest findings about social media and mental health: people who routinely compare themselves to others on social media are more susceptible to everything from minor shifts in mood to depressive symptoms.[34] When teens have a habit of comparing their "real" lives to others' online versions of their lives, it can fuel a vicious cycle. One fourteen-year-old described it as a *"dark spiral"*: *"Comparing your social life to others can make you feel excluded and lonely and that can send you down a dark spiral."* Helping teens who struggle in this way is crucial, whether it's through helping them shift their interpretations and self-talk, shift the content they're browsing, or even avoid a certain app altogether. Tech redesigns are warranted, too, since algorithms can propel the spiral.

"THE PERFECT STORM"—AND A CAVEAT

Why is social media so ripe for comparison? Human beings—adults as well as teens—have a psychological tendency to take thin slices of information and craft bigger stories around them. This is part of how people learn and make sense of a complicated world. It happens even when the thin slices are obviously incomplete and skewed.[35] So, a teen can look at a posted picture of someone who is smiling and happy and think "she's a happy person with a great life," rather than reasoning that she had a single fantastic day or moment (or that the photo was completely posed, or that its subject wasn't actually feeling good at all). We tend to lean into the evidence we *can* see and give comparably little consideration to what we're *not* seeing. This isn't specific to social media. Yet the way people share online often provides a skewed, rose-colored view of their lives that's ripe for comparison.

With respect to body image, social media creates a "perfect storm" for cisgender adolescent girls in particular.[36] As Sophia Choukas-Bradley and her colleagues explain, body image concerns are already at a peak during adolescence. In an era of social media, developmental sensitivity collides with societal messages about gender and beauty on platforms that favor idealized self-presentations. Both teen girls and boys in our own research called out *"workout videos"* and *"diet culture"* on social media as key contributors to feeling insecure and like they aren't *"doing enough"* to look their best.

Filters and other editing tools play a role in the perfect storm. In one study that compared the impact of manipulated versus unedited Instagram selfies of everyday teens, girls who viewed the manipulated photos reported lower body image afterward. The girls didn't consistently detect when others' faces and bodies were reshaped, which may have contributed to unrealistic social comparisons. But once again, teens differed in how susceptible they were to such images: the girls with a higher tendency to compare themselves to others were more negatively affected by viewing the doctored selfies.[37]

So: can we conclude that social media is always bad news for body image? Not so fast. Emerging evidence from research with youth who are transgender and gender nonconforming suggests an *opposite pattern* to what is often observed for their cisgender peers: better body image, not worse, for transgender and gender nonconforming youth who are especially tethered to tech.[38] Why might this be? One possibility is that social media provides them with valuable opportunities for exposure to identity-affirming content and, as the authors of the study say, "being able to present (and be *read* by others) as one's identified gender." So body image issues are a relevant risk of social media use, but not for everyone.

IS AUTHENTICITY THE NEW PERFECT?

Interestingly, recent years have seen a shift from predominantly picture-perfect highlight reels toward more authentic posting. Some influencers rise not despite this but because of it.[39] Their appeal is relatability and *"realness."* Influencers are very much the celebrities of teens' lives. They speak directly and frequently to their followers, inviting them into the minutiae of their day-to-day lives. They unpack groceries from Trader Joe's, livestream Fortnite games with funny commentary, show makeup routines (including unabashed, up-close footage of patchy "before" makeup skin), and describe their daily struggles with the kind of openness one might only expect to hear from a close friend.

The sheer quantity of content that influencers generate contributes to a sense of familiarity and closeness. What's more, as researcher Crystal Abidin aptly describes, influencers build an "impression of intimacy" by engaging with their followers via resharing posts, giving shout outs, and liking or replying to comments. While teens can be heavily invested in the lives of those they follow, these influencers may have little or no idea the teen exists. Researchers refer to this one-way sense of intimacy as a *parasocial relationship.* If you've ever had a personal interest in keeping up with a celebrity, the concept of a parasocial relationship should resonate.

What many influencers have in common, teens explain, is that *"they're really funny and relatable. . . . They're like, really real."* One trend while we were writing this book involved reposting perfect-looking photos that revealed moments "when you looked happy but were actually struggling."

If teens are following people who are *"really real,"* is comparison no longer a concern? For some teens, a feed filled with authenticity indeed seems to provide a source of self-acceptance and inspiration. Watching an influencer post both ups and downs confers a sense that "downs" are part of any life. We also heard teens point to body positivity accounts that really do help them feel more body positive. But other teens say it's even *easier* to negatively compare when people seem real. Essentially, if someone is sharing their worst moments and those moments don't seem so bad—or the person still appears happy and confident despite them—it can create a sense that the poster is even *more* envy-worthy.

Here's an example of one teen's thought process: "*Them posting their worst is what I consider my best. . . . Like [an influencer] last night was talking about how bad their skin looks that day. And then I looked in the mirror and I was like, 'well, that's what I consider to be my skin on a good day.' And that didn't make me feel good. And so, even people trying to be like relatable and like show their real self can still make other people feel bad because their real self is some of our best selves.*"

WHAT'S WITH TEENS AND CONSTANT COMPARISON?

Comparison serves an important function in human development, and it's much more than just a process that leads to an individual feeling inadequate and insecure.[40] Some comparisons are mood boosting and ego affirming: they help us recognize in ourselves particular talents, interests or traits we're proud of, and qualities that make us unique. Other comparisons are motivating as they help us identify goals we want to pursue. Comparisons often happen effortlessly and even automatically,[41] which is developmentally useful in the transition from childhood to adulthood.

The childhood years are marked by age-appropriate egocentrism and unrealistically positive self-concepts. This fuels overestimated beliefs about oneself that can be in turn endearing, frustrating, funny, and wonderful, like: "I am the best swimmer in the whole world!" As social and cognitive development proceed, we gain cognitive capacities that enable more advanced perspective taking and empathy, as well as a more accurate self-concept.[42] In the process, though, there's a new kind of awareness that we're not actually the best swimmers in the whole world. We must reconcile these changes in self-understanding as we each develop a holistic sense of our identity.

Comparison isn't confined to adolescence, but social comparisons are particularly stinging during mid-adolescence.[43] Self-esteem tends to decline as people move from childhood into adolescence before it then increases from later adolescence into adulthood.[44] All of this to say:

comparison has a developmental component and there seems to be a predictable spike during the adolescent years.

Periods of uncertainty and transitions can also temporarily elevate negative comparisons, particularly when they're accented by feelings of self-doubt.[45] Being in a bad mood can also prime us for the kind of negative comparisons that leave us feeling worse about ourselves.[46] Feeling low and then going on social media can activate the *"dark spiral."* Teens described this as a familiar experience. In fifteen-year-old Ashlyn's words: *"I know like if I'm having a really tough day or something like that and I just scroll through my Instagram and I see influencers or my friends posting their happy moments, that just sort of makes me sad that I'm—it makes me feel isolated and it makes me feel like, oh, I'm the only person going through this."*

Jack can relate and acknowledged that it's important to recognize how feeling down sets the stage for dispiriting social media experiences: *"Personally when I'm very emotional and kind of feeling insecure and down myself and I go on Instagram and I see popular guys and girls that I'm crushing on— stuff like that—I get, like, super sad. So, I think that it's important to know . . . when you shouldn't [go on Instagram]. You know, you go on Instagram and compare yourself naturally to people you see, and that can be . . . really anxiety provoking if you're already in a bad state."*

MIRROR, MIRROR ON THE . . . SCREEN

Social media can be the worst kind of magical mirror: reflecting back details that prod directly at one's insecurities. We heard from teens how this plays out.

Teen A hates her appearance and wishes she could lose weight. Any post that features another person who looks thinner seems to spark distressing comparison. She's like the teen in our study who explained: *"I don't exactly like the way I look and seeing other people not have the flaws I have is really discouraging."*

Teen B is struggling with their relationship status, wishing they could have their own real romance. For them, the posts that evoke comparison are those that showcase peers in happy couples or honoring relationship milestones.

Teen C hates when people post screenshots of their class schedules at the beginning of the school year. Seeing how many AP classes others are taking brings on waves of self-doubt that she's not doing enough.

Teen D is an artist. When his friends post to showcase all the works they're producing, he questions whether he'll ever be successful.

Teen E looks at showy pictures of others flaunting their wealth and wishes his family's situation was different. He has plenty of company in this particular struggle, including from teens who explain: "*If someone that might not have that much stuff, or they might not have the best relationship with their family or be rich, when they are looking at like Instagram or something and see like your friend went shopping and got so much stuff and then went on like five vacations with their family, they will start to feel down and start to do stuff that they would regret.*"

What do each of these teens—and others like them who feel the tug of comparison quicksand online—*do* about their feelings? It varies. Some teens recognize posts that bring them down and become vigilant about muting, unfollowing, or even avoiding certain apps. Some curate their feeds by following more of the kinds of accounts that affirm their identities, engage their interests, and inspire their goals. Some teens intuit the research finding that self-doubt can prime comparative thinking and realize they need to avoid social media during particularly vulnerable moments.

Other teens continue to follow envy-inducing accounts, and to browse through them during low moments, which only brings on more self-doubt. The reasons can range from a sheer lack of self-awareness to more complex relational concerns (social consequences of missing out on content or repercussions from unfollowing, for example). Thus, another source of variation in teens' behind-the-screen experiences stems from how they navigate their vulnerabilities. What content and online experiences do they seek out, and what do they avoid?

DARK POCKETS, BRIGHT SPOTS

A discussion of worrying content wouldn't be complete without acknowledging the more explicitly harmful side of digital content. Once easily searchable, many platforms have made real efforts to block or flag self-harm, suicide-oriented, and pro-eating disorder content. Still, it's possible to find accounts that strategically evade detection. Teens can use creative spelling (like "thi.nsp0o" rather than "thinspo" (thin-inspiration → thin-spiration → thinspo) in more public online networks to share images that support disordered eating. Abbreviations and insider lingo facilitate a version of what danah boyd described years ago as "hiding in plain sight" on social media.[47] For example, letter combinations like sw, cw, hw gw1, gw2, ugw each followed by a number might appear as gibberish to an uninformed viewer, but meaningful to a group of insiders who recognize markers for smallest weight, current weight, highest weight, goal weight 1 and 2, and ultimate goal weight.

Turning from the psychologically troubling to the ideologically extreme: White supremacist or neo-Nazi groups also hide in public by using certain sequences of numbers in their username or bio, called "dog tags," to signal affiliation. And sometimes they're not hiding at all, but instead choosing usernames and posting imagery that are unambiguously hateful.

Hateful and harmful online subcommunities are concerning, full stop. The content can be traumatic for teens who encounter it. And adults need to be on alert for teens who are vulnerable to being pulled in and radicalized. Yet it would be a mistake to assume all teens are engaging with the worst the Internet has to offer. Likewise, we shouldn't overlook the kinds of screen time that support unequivocal positives ranging from learning new skills to supporting personal health and well-being. These bright spots exist in ways that are both routine and exceptional and emerge both by design and organically.

Health-focused apps fall into the "by design" category. The growing field of mobile health—"mHealth" for short—aims to use digital connectivity to improve treatment approaches and deliver evidence-based interventions to people anywhere and everywhere. User-generated accounts exemplify the latter—sides of social media platforms where wellness-oriented content proliferates (e.g., on Spiritual TikTok, Instagram accounts that promote self-care; recovery-oriented digital communities that support sobriety, eating disorder recovery, and more). Social media sites also become places for celebrating and validating identities, and for sharing resilience, resistance, and joy. Notable research by scholars Jessica Lu and Catherine Knight Steele, for example, examines online depictions of Black joy that counter dehumanizing narratives.[48] And as Kishonna Gray's research shows, for young Black men, online games can be vital spaces for connection and "solace" even as they navigate subtle and explicit forms of racism in larger gaming culture.[49]

Online gaming is interesting in that it's alternately framed as a prime example of a "dark pocket" or a "bright spot," depending on who you ask. Some adults worry that games are timewasters at best and downright destructive or violence inducing at worst. "Internet gaming addiction" is a common topic of adult concern too. Whether its prevalence really merits concern is hotly contested in the research, though. Plus, studies point to positives that range from social connection to improved aspects of cognitive performance.[50]

What do you need to know? The tailored, immersive experience teens find in gaming is indeed a recipe for prolonged focus.[51] Some teens acknowledge this pull and worry about managing it: *"It's just scary to think that I only get one childhood, and I could accidentally slip into a habit where I just waste it away on some pointless game,"* one fourteen-year-old reflected. *"I am afraid people will lose the real world by spending too much time in the virtual world,"* said another. *"That terrifies me because we're destroying our planet, losing our empathy for those around us, and forgetting the beauty of simplicity."*

At the same time, gaming represents a crucial site of social connection and exchanges with friends—a site that teens acknowledged became all the more important in a moment of pandemic-driven social distancing. Dante (sixteen-years-old) explained, *"it helped me stay connected with my friends while we were unable to hang out in person."* He noted without equivocation: *"gaming has benefitted me with my friend relationships."*[52] When it comes to schoolwork, gaming isn't just a distraction from homework, but also a way to unwind and recharge before digging in. It isn't just a pull from family time, but also a source of shared play. *"Gaming has really helped me relax, like a stress reliever,"* sixteen-year-old Pablo explained. *"It's been helping me a lot and sometimes I play with my sister, like you know, connecting more with the family."* Playing together can meaningfully support bonds between parents and kids too.[53]

TEENS WANT ADULTS TO KNOW

Screen time is so often framed as an adults-versus-teens battle that it's striking to confront the reality of teens' own worries about digital habits. Yet this we heard clearly: teens do not want to feel like their tech use is dysregulated or like they're wasting their lives away because of it. Again and again they shared comments like these: *"I don't want to end up being on technology all of my life"*; *"I want to be able to socialize with people without turning to or checking my phone every minute"*; *"I want to enjoy my actual life, not be obsessed with what others think about my social media."* Many of our wishes for them are their wishes for themselves.

Like adults, teens struggle when it comes to managing the pull of the screen. They describe feeling pulled from sleep, from quality time with friends, and from other activities. And they worry about wasted time (*"it wastes too much time from doing other things"*; *"you could be biking or hanging out with your friends instead of wasting time looking at Instagram posts"*). They also describe valuing time outside yet struggling to get there (*"I like to go outside and play sports and sometimes I just can't get off a computer game"*). Adults can help via nudges in the right direction.

And yet, adults need to recognize screen time isn't always wasted time. Social media and multiplayer games are *"important for us."* These technologies help teens deepen relationships, learn, feel connected to the wider world, and relax and unwind. Teens wish adults would acknowledge these benefits, rather than denigrating all screen time: *"Just because we're on a device doesn't mean we're wasting our time. We can be productive in other ways."* (With respect to multiplayer games, teens also asked us to please emphasize that these games *"can't be paused!"*)

Teens want adults to cast a critical eye on our own habits too. Another repeated sentiment adults should take to heart: *"I've seen family members get highly addicted to their phone or any device really and what I just want is for them to put their phone down and to actually talk and have conversations."* Teens crave focused attention from friends and family members, even as they may struggle to give it in return. They also see hypocrisy in tech-obsessed adults telling them to get off their phones—yet barely making it through a meal without pausing to check our own emails or "just quickly reply" to an inbound text, even when behind the wheel.

Today's technologies are vital, valued, and hard for everyone to manage. When adults just roll our eyes at teens tethered to their devices, we miss opportunities to acknowledge what is a shared struggle to disconnect. This doesn't mean we should just leave teens to their own devices, literally or metaphorically. But when we assume that teens want endless screen time and our sole job is to curb it, we miss opportunities to ask about what parts of their digital lives feel rewarding and what habits they wish they could change. We miss the chance to help them develop *digital metacognition*: moving from mindless use to more active awareness.[54] Managing the pull of the screen requires a mind shift—for us all.

3

FRIENDSHIP DILEMMAS

Lila liked to think of herself as a bridge between friend groups. All through her sophomore year of high school, she stayed close with two different groups. This was somewhat unusual: the social circles in her grade were pretty clearly defined, and most girls were in just one primary social circle. In Lila's case, each of the two friend groups had a group chat. She was active in both.

Group chats are multiperson digital conversations. They take place on different social media or messaging platforms, and they're key to many teens' social lives. Group chats provide a context for teens to share ongoing updates and relevant content throughout the day. They also fuel inside jokes and enable coordination for in-person plans. Those who aren't part of the chat miss out on those plans, as well as ongoing banter and inside jokes that solidify closeness among chat group members. From a technical standpoint, starting or ending a group chat is simple. But the social dynamics can be decidedly complex.

As tenth grade wore on, Lila began to feel less like a bridge between the groups and their respective chats and more like a double agent. One group—self-dubbed "the OGs"—didn't know Lila was in "the Hunnies" chat, and she was pretty sure they wouldn't have been okay with it. Lila became increasingly anxious that her cover would be blown, and she'd be pushed out of the group. This proved to be prescient.

Initially, the Hunnies seemed okay knowing Lila was in both chats. Then, messaging in the Hunnies chat slowed, and Lila discovered they had created a spinoff chat without her. She didn't really blame them or think the spinoff group was created maliciously; she had been hanging out more with the OGs and declining social invitations from the Hunnies as a result. But she realized with dismay that not being in the main Hunnies chat would result in being sidelined in person too. This wasn't melodramatic: she was right. Although Lila kept up individual friendships, she was instantly moved to the periphery of the Hunnies friend group and social plans.

"Could I have asked to be added to their new group chat?," she wondered aloud a year later. *"Maybe. But I knew they made the new chat expressly with the purpose of taking me out."* Without membership in that chat, Lila was no longer a full member of their crew.

Group chats can shape or define offline social circles for boys too. When Lila's younger brother tried to add a friend to his core group chat—which also had its own name and norms—he had to lobby his friends to include the new member. And just as Lila's exclusion from the Hunnies chat had ripple effects for offline hangouts, her brother's inclusion of his new friend conferred immediate acceptance and inclusion. Another boy, Bradley, described the importance of group chats across a much wider group at his high school. In this case, a large group chat was the context for planning a senior prank, meaning that anyone who wasn't in the chat was therefore clueless about the caper.

WHAT'S NEW IS OLD—SORT OF

Much of what these teens shared is not new: the profound importance to adolescents of acceptance from friends, the vigilant attention to one's place in the teen social landscape, and even the inclination to name friend groups in a way that clearly signals who's in and, by extension, who's out. Long before there were group chats to name, a self-assigned moniker was a way to seal and confirm a group's closeness. I (Carrie) was a teen in the 1980s, and I remember my friends referring to ourselves at one point as "The Breakfast Club." And I (Emily) cringe at the memory of friend group names that were formed with the first initial of each person's name and then renamed as middle school alliances changed. The adolescent desire to solidify and signal closeness is hardly a product of the digital age. It endures today, as portrayed vividly in the Netflix series *Ginny and Georgia*, when Ginny and her friends Max, Ashley, and Norah name their group—and group chat—"MANG." (Importantly, though intimate adolescent friendships and related concerns are often understood to be a "girl" thing, boys both need and deeply value intimate friendships too.[1])

Despite concerns about superficial social media likes and text communication altering the very fabric of friendship, research shows that the age-old qualities that make or break friendships endure. Psychologists Joanna Yau and Stephanie Reich reviewed evidence from multiple studies and found that technology is essentially just another medium for core adolescent friendship activities like self-disclosure, validation, companionship, instrumental support, conflict, and conflict resolution.[2] And yet, they explain, digital communication *is* different in ways that matter both for better and worse in how friendships play out.

What is different—and how? Adolescent psychologists have leaned into this question too. Jacqueline Nesi, Sophia Choukas-Bradley, and Mitch Prinstein's work unpacks the ways peer relationships are transformed by social media contexts.[3] Their Transformation Framework highlights how specific social media affordances alter peer dynamics. For example, both *publicness* and *quantified metrics* (e.g., likes and followers) transform the longstanding importance of validation by creating new opportunities to showcase closeness and new signals of peer acceptance—or a lack thereof.

Quantifiability is salient when teens like Judah see that a friend's Snapchat Snap score increased while he was waiting for that friend to reply. Because a Snap score publicly reveals the total number of snaps (i.e., Snapchat messages) a person has ever sent and received, Judah knows instantly that his friend was responding to others—while leaving Judah's messages unread or "on read" (i.e., seen but not reciprocated). Publicness can likewise clue teens into social slights: virtual maps on Snapchat, for example, show avatars of where people are in real-time. So when Sophie checks the map one Saturday and sees her friends' avatars all together in one place, it's crystal clear that she's been left out. In these ways, social technologies enable ongoing access to new kinds of social information.

The qualities of social media transform the social landscape in ways that raise new norms and complications too. Fifteen-year-old Winter put it starkly: *"maintaining friendships online is a completely different ball game, and it has its own set of rules and regulations."* There are also ways to deepen existing friendships, and to make new friends as teens connect through online gaming, over shared interests on social media, and via expansive friends-of-friends networks. Social media is both a burden and a boon. And while the opportunities are tremendous and real, this chapter is about often overlooked friendship pressures and dilemmas.

DILEMMAS OF AVAILABILITY

In our surveys of young people, a clear majority (71 percent of youths) agreed that being a good friend means being there whenever a friend needs you. It's no wonder, then, that new kinds of access contribute to dilemmas for young people about reasonable boundaries for digital availability. How much connection is too much? What response time is just right? Answers are hard to come by.

Setting boundaries in close relationships can be difficult at any age. Values are pitted against each other in ways that evade simple rules of thumb: When a friend says he needs to talk and it's already late at night, disconnecting for sleep is pitted against being a supportive friend. When a peer's private texts begin to sound alarming, getting them the help they need can threaten a promise of confidentiality. For teens, these dilemmas are especially hard because negotiating them requires skills like perspective taking and communication savvy that are still developing.

One sentiment is clear and expressed by teens on repeat: *"I feel like if you're not connected then the friendship will fall apart."* An immense pressure can stem from the belief that meaningful quantities of digital communication are necessary for closeness and essential to a friendship's survival. In other words, being constantly connected—or at least consistently available—is a baseline for preserving cherished friendships. In turn, teens worry that not being available will jeopardize closeness: *"If I don't [stay connected] I'm worried I'll miss out on something and won't be as close to them,"* one thirteen-year-old said. *"If you don't text your friends for a while then they just come up with the dumbest excuse to cut you off,"* explained another.

Because friendships are crucially important during adolescence, any threat of friendship loss can feel like a true threat to a teen's sense of who they are. It's therefore understandable that some teens go out of their way to sustain connection, even breaking family rules or forfeiting other interests. All relationships do require a baseline level of care and feeding to thrive. But the now-boundless opportunities for connection mean that teens may have to intentionally create boundaries amid peer pressure to forgo them altogether: *"There are so many people I text on a regular basis,"* one fourteen-year-old explained, *"and I feel pressure to keep communicating."*

BURDENSOME COMMUNICATION

It would be a mistake to assume that all teens simply accommodate constant connectivity—some do, and some do not. Oshun (fifteen years old) described ignoring people when communication is too much: *"As somebody who likes my space, being in contact all the time makes me shy away from you. Like if you want to talk to me every day, I'm not gonna talk to you: I'm going to ignore you. Because I am already stressed about . . . a lot of things."* It takes a kind of confidence in one's relationships and oneself to buck the norms of availability, though, and it's not without downsides. Some teens describe feeling less close to friends who adopt this tack. They admit that a delayed response time feels like a slight, and for some it's reason enough to start drama or conflict.

Response time is material. This knowledge can lead teens who share Oshun's need for personal space to nonetheless acquiesce to burdensome communication. A key driver: being seen as rude or inconsiderate of others' feelings. Tim noted that the volume of snaps he receives *"gets annoying, especially when so many people—like 10, 12 people are snapchatting you at the same time, constantly."* Nonetheless, he stays on top of it because it's *"impolite to have someone send you something and not to respond."* Makenzie sometimes wants *"to have time to myself and not talk to other people."* But this is complicated because *"they always say I never 'Hit them up' or talk to them and it makes me feel bad for not wanting to talk to them."*[4]

Adults assume teens want constant connection and, while on some level they might, they can also feel stuck between craving moments of off-the-grid time and wanting to avoid *"hurting people's feelings"* or *"people feeling ignored."* The golden rule—treat others how you want to be treated—raises digital dilemmas. Some teens reason: *"Well . . . I don't like it when I text someone and they don't reply for a couple days. So normally, when I get a notification of a new post or a text, I reply or check out the post pretty fast."*

Pressures to respond ASAP create another tension too—between the notifications on your phone and the people you're with in person: *"If you feel like every single time you get a text you have to text them back right away then you are putting your phone and the person you are talking to in front of the people that you are with, and it creates a habit of always checking your phone for new things."* Not wanting to appear rude, ironically, leads to being rude in a different way. Yet while adults may see what looks like thoughtlessness or "phone addiction," teens are often navigating a constellation of hidden social motivations, pressures, and expectations. "Streaks" on Snapchat offer an interesting case in point (see the "What's in a Streak?" box).

What's in a Streak?

Snapchat's Snapstreaks track the number of consecutive days of Snapchat communication between two people. Whether the feature is still a fixture or ancient history by the time this book is in your hands, it offers insight into the ways a seemingly benign digital feature can generate friendship pressures.

To maintain a streak, Teen A needs to send Teen B a snap and Teen B needs to open it and send one back to Teen A at least one time during every twenty-four-hour period. A thirty-five-day-streak is, therefore, a numeric tracker that confirms that Teen A and Teen B have reciprocally Snapchatted at least once a day for thirty-five days straight. If either misses a day, their streak is "dropped" and resets to zero. The number is visible only to the people who are part of the streak. It's not public and it doesn't have any obvious value beyond keeping count within the platform.

For several years, streaks were a fixture in our conversations with teens. We learned that they are maintained for different reasons: at times for fun, but often out of a sense of obligation to friends; or because having a certain number of long streaks is a kind of status symbol in conversations with peers; or because a long streak feels like validation of the friendship, however shallow.

Here, the thinking might go: "We must really be good friends if we've Snap-chatted every day for 220 days." There are teens who have dozens of active streaks and sincerely wish they didn't have to maintain them; it feels like "*a job.*" Yet they experience streaks as an expectation if not a social mandate.

Some teens feel the need to enlist friends to manage the streaks for weeks at a time, sharing passwords so a friend can log in daily on their behalf while they are away at a summer camp, on vacation, or even in inpatient mental health treatment.[5] The meaning some teens assign to streaks is also evident in descriptions about how dropping streaks can cause fights—or be used to sig-nal the seriousness of a friend's anger. In social circles where teens go to great lengths to protect their streaks, dropping a streak can either be an accident or harsh slight. Not knowing which it is can be anxiety provoking for a teen who discovers that a streak was dropped by the other party.

To be sure, there are teens who scoff at the practice and are adamant about avoiding streaks altogether. There are also teens who limit streaks to their "true" best friends or commit to maintaining them only so long as they remain fun. We interviewed teens who named streaks as a real way to build closeness, since daily communication provided a valued excuse for sharing silly updates of daily life.[6] But descriptions of annoyance and stress related to streaks—and of the lengths some teens were willing to go to avoid dropping them—clarify how a metric can take on a life and meaning of its own.

To people who work at Snapchat, streaks may seem like an obvious win since they tether teens to the app for daily use. Their widespread adoption could even be (mis)interpreted as evidence of teens' universal love for the fea-ture. But by listening carefully to teens' different perspectives, a more compli-cated picture emerges. And while Streaks are unique to Snapchat, they capture a dynamic relevant across tech forms, including text messaging, social media commenting, and even email.

Tech features and social norms can collide in ways that pressure sus-tained contact, response times, or both. Adults may relate to the bur-den of having a boss or close colleague who responds to emails within minutes, or responds to every email with a Reply All even when a reply doesn't seem warranted. In some cases, this may be the colleague's per-sonal style but *not* their expectation of others. Nonetheless, their rapid response times can generate an implicit sense that quick email replies are valued and preferred. In other cases, the boss or colleague's explicit expectation may be that everyone responds ASAP to digital messages. Set-ting boundaries can be harder in these instances. The challenge of find-ing boundaries in digital communication is layered: it requires discerning other people's expectations *and* maintaining boundaries that protect a positive relationship with each person, all while balancing personal needs. This juggling act is amplified for adolescents because of the centrality of friendships in their lives. Plus, they are still developing perspective taking and communication skills.

SECOND AND THIRD GUESSING

With close friends, rapid responses may feel necessary so friends won't *"think I ignored it"* or *"get mad"* because they feel snubbed. With less close friends and earlier-stage relationships, a too-quick reply can come off as *"eager"* or *"desperate."* Teens are left to walk a fine line: they try to suss out and then calibrate around peers' expectations for response times with their own desires to seem available but not *too* available. That's why some teens set timers after receiving a text message; this ensures an "optimal" response time, neither too fast nor too slow to send a message of its own. It can become a mind game, with teens' constantly adjusting response time based on the other person's behavior: *"You respond five minutes late, Imma respond 10 minutes late. Honestly, just to be petty. I'm not going to respond right away because I look too eager to talk to you and we need to stay cool."*

While managing one's own response time is complicated, so too is interpreting others'. *"I used to think about it constantly,"* fifteen-year-old Maeve explained, remembering back to the early days of her romantic relationship: *"Like when my girlfriend and I were first talking, I would be like, 'it's been 15 minutes, shit, are we not talking anymore?' Which is kind of ridiculous like looking back, 15 minutes is nothing—but [back] then it felt like hours or days. I think with friends, too, if they leave you 'on read'—like read your text and you can tell, but they don't respond—It's kind of like, 'oh, did I do something to offend you? What did I do?' It's hard to know."*

Anxiety around the timing and frequency of communication is not new, particularly in the context of romantic relationships. This modern day experience has familiar roots in age-old scenes of awaiting a long-anticipated love letter or staying within earshot of a corded phone hoping a crush will call. In digital communication, though, it's especially easy to stare back at one's own last message and start *"second guessing . . . and even third guessing yourself."*

Design features further amplify self-doubt. Read receipts, which signal to a sender their message has been Read, can elevate the sense of being left hanging. On some apps, digital features routinely signal a forthcoming response, whether it's the animated ". . ." speech bubble in iMessage or a push notification on Snapchat that indicates someone is typing a message. This primes and amplifies teens' anticipatory reactions, whether curiosity, excitement, anxiety, or dread. It also puts pressure on the responder since it starts a kind of response time clock. *"I don't like that people know when I'm typing,"* Diego explained, *"because then I'm like, 'Oh I gotta think about what I say before I start typing. Because they already know before you can say anything, like, 'oh, he's about to say something.'"* Diego's reaction points to intersecting concerns: response time matters, as does getting the message right.

Listening to teens describe *"the half-swipe"* again crystallizes how digital features shape their social interactions. The half-swipe is (as of this writing) a hacked-by-teens solution to a tech-created issue. To avoid the message sender knowing that their Snapchat message has been received and read, a teen can half-swipe to see a preview of the message without the app registering it as opened. This buys extra time to strategize a response. But the clock is still ticking (albeit a bit more slowly) because the snap has already been sent. And being left "on delivered" too long is seen as an even more dramatic slight.

PERFORMING CLOSENESS

Responses matter not only in private communication but also, and especially, in public. Seventeen-year-old Nanaa laughed as she narrated examples of over-the-top social media comments—including one that quickly became a favorite among our research team: *"step on meee! i am your cockroach."* What the commenter was saying, another teen explained is, *"you're so great, so above me, so above everyone."*

You may have noticed that teens' social media posts are often flooded with extreme flattery and effusive praise. Comments like, "You are the cutest person ever," "MOST BEAUTIFUL HUMAN," "MY BEST FRIEND PERIOD," "amen," "Obsessed wit u!," "favorite person," "QUEEN," and "angel" are interspersed with emojis, hearts, and flame symbols (to connote that the person is *so hot* or *fire*). Teens portray a gendered dynamic to this mode of commenting and the pressures it creates, but expressions of public praise are not "just a girl thing." Among boys, for example, public support can take shape in comments from one guy to another offering a virtual pat on the back for achievements ("ok I see u," "congrats keep doing your thing bro"), supportive validation ("that's fly," "yessirrrr," "handsome," "stud"), or compliments wrapped with humor ("my man's is wrecking homes out here," "please my girl is on this app have some mercy," "fellas watch out").

Tweens and teens are not the only ones whose social media comments feature gushing compliments. Consider the following Facebook comments exchanged by and for some of the fifty- and sixty-year-olds in our lives: "Looking great <3," "No aging for you!," "Wow—just wow," "What a beautiful family!," "love love." Or among the forty-somethings: "Hot stuff!," "Flawless," "Still a hottie!," "Is this your high school graduation picture? Seriously you look the same," "#BestJawlineEver." Or among the twenty- and thirty-somethings: "OMG MODELS," "Best weekend EVER," "Beyond gorg!!!!," "Love every single thing about this so much."

Comments on social media are often thick with expressions of love and support. Yet their expression in a public context raises questions about what's authentic and sincere versus obligatory and performative. For teens, posts that look joyful and flattering on the surface can also mask underlying pressures that adults may not feel. As adults are well aware, performing a carefully curated identity on social media feels essential to many youths. Teens can feel a similar pressure to perform closeness with friends in full view of an attentive audience of peers, both as part of being a good friend and as a way of validating their own social acceptance and connectedness.

Comment sections become a competition: who is *most* effusive in their response? Special occasion posts—shared to honor a friend or partner's birthday, college acceptance, anniversary, and so on—move expressions of love from the comment section to the digital main stage. Posting a series of pictures is another way to put closeness on display. The ability to easily repost content collides with special occasion posts in ways that further up the ante. Reposting means that a teen's followers can easily see and assess how many friends posted for their birthday and how effusive those posts are. It also allows teens to signal strong ties without seeming too effortful or performative, since reposting is quick and easy.

Birthday posts can be affirming but can also become another kind of comparison quicksand (as described in chapter 2). Specifically, teens read and interpret them in comparison with other posts: why were you the only one of my friends who *didn't* post for my birthday? Why did you call another friend your #1 bestie on their birthday, but only said "happy birthday to an amazing friend" on mine? Why didn't you repost the picture I shared of us, even though you often repost others'? And: is it reasonable if this hurts my feelings?

Bashing friends is a contrast case. In gaming, teens describe the dynamic of *"getting so mad at each other, but, like, having so much fun at the same time."* Banter during these moments can start out in jest, but risks crossing a line when name calling gets offensive or taunts tap into true areas of insecurity—whether they be related to the game itself (gaming skills) or irrelevant attributes (like physical appearance, or even sexual inexperience).

FRIENDSHIPS UNDER THE SOCIAL MEDIA SPOTLIGHT

When Asher adds a new post, they use group text conversations to remind or compel friends to flock to the newly shared picture and begin commenting. Or, they share an Instagram Story that simply says, "LMR" (meaning: "Like My Recent") to direct supportive followers to promptly view and respond to the newest post. Sufficient public validation from friends is part of saving face in a digital age and, again, timing matters. A delay can make one feel publicly vulnerable, like a digital version of walking into the cafeteria and being stuck at the front searching the room for friends. The impulse for social reciprocity is relevant once more. Asher needs public validation from their friends, *fast*, and therefore feels obligated to respond in kind.

These norms raise dilemmas for teens—like seventeen-year-old Michelle, who wants to be authentic but also doesn't want to let down her friends. Michelle recently tapped the button to like her friend's picture but couldn't think of anything to comment. Almost immediately, she saw a notification that informed Michelle that her friend was typing: *"She [was] like, 'Oh, you didn't comment on my post.' It was literally like 30 seconds after I liked it. And I was like, 'Okay, um, like, I'm thinking of something.' Like, let me be. And then I have to comment like three times and it's so annoying. And I get really nervous about it too, because I have to think of something quick, and it has to be something really good. . . . There's* definitely *expectations to comment on a post."*

Expressing closeness and appreciation for others is important, even essential, for healthy relationships. Social media offer compelling opportunities to validate relationships and show public support for others. For less close friends who aren't expected commenters, commenting is an easy yet meaningful way to signal a general positive regard for the poster or a desire to be closer. *"When you get a nice comment from somebody that you don't really know or speak [to] . . . Like that's really sweet . . . it's kind of like establishing a connection,"* teens explained. And yet, when so much of posting is an expectation and over-the-top compliments are the norm, *being* authentic can feel nearly impossible and *knowing* what's authentic can be like reading tea leaves.

The "opportunity" to observe friends' interactions also means today's teens have new windows into *others'* relationships. Noah sees a series of Venmo transactions between two of his friends and wonders when they started hanging out so much. Kailah monitors her ex-boyfriend's follower count on Instagram and gets a pit in her stomach when she sees it's jumped up by one—and then painstakingly reviews the entire list and manages to identify a cute girl as his newest follower. Again, in these ways, social media offers TMI (too much information) via a continuously updated wellspring of social information.

HOW MANY FRIENDS CAN YOU REALLY HAVE?

Digital life has obviously evolved in major ways over the last two decades. One significant shift is the rise of social media sites that are firmly tied to our offline identities. Although there are still spaces for low-stakes, anonymous "identity play,"[7] many modern social media sites are places where people from all different parts of one's offline life coexist.

Sociologists have long written about the ways that social context shapes identity expression. We generally want to be seen by others in a favorable light. At the same time, what's authentic in one space is often inappropriate or odd in another (e.g., contrast one's self-presentation hanging out with old friends versus on a job interview). We therefore tailor our self-presentations based on where we are and who we are with, foregrounding or concealing particular aspects of ourselves in different situations. Erving Goffman's seminal work on self-presentation described this process as "impression management."[8]

What happens, then, when people from different parts of one's life all become social media followers? Researchers Alice Marwick and danah boyd were thought leaders in unpacking this challenge. They wrote in 2010 about how "the need for variable self-presentation is complicated by increasingly mainstream social media technologies that collapse multiple contexts and bring together commonly distinct audiences."[9] For teens, this reality is practically ensured by the social norm of accepting follow requests from everyone they know (and often friends of friends too).

Adults spend a good deal of time worrying about teens connecting with strangers, but comparably little time on the complexities of staying connected to anyone and everyone. Social media sites provide easy opportunities to stay connected and they can engender a sense of obligation to do so. Teens describe new dynamics related to keeping in touch for eternity, and even worries about not doing so ("*I don't want to hurt anybody's feelings if I can't stay in touch with them.*").

It's interesting to consider these concerns in light of what we know about human social networks. Even if it's technically possible to stay connected, evidence from research with both humans and primates indicates that we have a natural capacity to limit our social networks. There is a predictable pattern to the number of ties people maintain at different "layers" of closeness, from the most emotionally intimate (around five individuals), to those we would turn to for support when needed (around fifteen individuals) to those whom we can recognize and name (typically maxing out at around 1,500 individuals).[10] "Dunbar's number," is named for the researcher who initially developed the theory and refers to a middle layer: the typical community size of 150 individuals with whom we can maintain stable relationships. Proponents of the social brain hypothesis (including Dunbar) argue these patterns result from cognitive constraints of our social brains, which set a kind of cap on how many relationships we can manage at different levels of time investment and intimacy. The same numerical patterns have typified social networks since the time of hunter-gatherers.[11]

Social networking sites make it easier to maintain more connections at a lower cost in terms of time investment. But if the very architecture of our brains is the reason we have defaulted to the same average network size throughout history, these technologies make technically possible more relationships than people can maintain. Research suggests this may be the case: even in an age of social media, even with more digital connections, the inner circle of close friends remains small. For teens in particular, Dunbar notes, "promiscuous friending" on social media can result in a heavy burden of connections, including to "anonymous 'friends-of-friends.'"[12]

Large networks of weak ties have benefits. For example, if you want to share information widely or tap your network for job opportunities, it's helpful to have thousands of "friends."[13] Yet maintaining so many digital connections can also create an overwhelming water hose of social information. This may be one reason why app features that allow for audience segmentation are so readily taken up by teens.

CURATING THE INNER CIRCLE

Indeed, in a world where social norms generate pressure to accept Follow and Friend requests from all classmates, acquaintances, and friends of friends, digitally stratifying audiences is a practical necessity. Teens who stratify audiences create their own digital versions of network layers; they also push back on context collapse that can otherwise blur boundaries between school, neighborhood, and family life.[14] In so doing, they try to lessen some of the pressure that comes with impression management and create digital spaces where sharing can be more like telling a story to the friends at one's lunch table instead of shouting through a megaphone to the whole school.

This isn't entirely new. Social media users have for years stratified audiences by creating duplicate, more private accounts.[15] By only inviting and accepting followers whom they trust and consider close friends, teens try to create protected bubbles for sharing with more openness, vulnerability, and authenticity. Now, there are digital features that facilitate segmentation. On Instagram and Snapchat, Stories are a prime place for segmenting audiences. Stories are posts that by default remain viewable for twenty-four hours, though on Instagram they can be added as a permanent part of one's profile.[16] While Stories can be shared with all followers, they can also be posted so that they're only seen by a smaller, designated "Close Friends" group.

On Snapchat, teens curate multiple Stories that represent distinct groups. This allows them to share certain content with their besties or with friends who share certain interests, while other posts are shared with their broader networks. For example: Monet presents a polished identity for her full online audience but loves having a way to share embarrassing and silly moments with close friends. She also has separate Stories that correspond to different interests: one with soccer teammates and another where she shares music recommendations. Genevieve has a music recs Story, too, which she created after first posting to her public Story to invite anyone who wanted ongoing music recommendations to be added to a separate private, music-focused Story. It wasn't meant to be exclusive; she just didn't want to "*spam*" those in her larger audience who weren't interested.

Izzy uses the Private Story feature on Snapchat to stratify audiences because she is gay but only out to certain friends; she has a designated Private Story where she is open about her sexual identity. Ari wants to speak out about political issues without his extended family members—who have opposing views—seeing all his posts. Using the Close Friends Story feature on Instagram offers Ari what feels like a safer space for his political expression.

Stories can be intentionally hidden from particular people too. Noa might hide from several friends a birthday post for Mari if Noa worries that the "hidden" friends would judge or disapprove of Noa's friendship with Mari. In a context where certain kinds of expression and performance are desired and even expected, teens navigate ongoing tensions and adjust audiences for specific posts accordingly. They may very much *want* certain people to see a post, hence the reason for sharing it in the first place. Yet they may also have a host of reasons—from petty to perceptive—why they do *not want* others in their audience to see all posts.

Whether it's on Instagram or Snapchat, being added as a viewer on another person's Private Story can signal closeness, since it extends an invitation into parts of their sharing or posting that are, by definition, not meant for all. It also reinforces closeness since it provides access to ongoing updates and people's whereabouts.

Stories stratify audiences in ways that can be practically useful and empowering, yet also raise friendship dilemmas. As teens add and delete friends from Private Stories, who's in and who's out of the inner circle is crystallized, even if it's only temporary. However, the contents of Private Stories are by no means under lock and key. As we'll discuss in chapter 4, screenshotting can bring a "private" update to a broader audience.

WHEN FRIENDS STRUGGLE IN PUBLIC

As we've described in prior chapters, there are clear signs that mental health issues are on the rise among youth. Documented increases in mood disorders, depressive episodes, loneliness, and suicidal thoughts and behaviors mean that even teens who are not themselves struggling are more likely than in the past to have peers who are.[17] Distinct issues arise when those peers struggle in public, online.

In some cases, situations that feel like *"emergencies"* are social events or gossip that will be forgotten within the span of a few weeks. In other cases, they are serious and persistent issues that would be major stressors at any age: posts that signal mental health issues, family conflict, domestic violence, or health problems. Adults can be quick to lament that empathy is on the decline and to pin the blame on technology. Yet we may fail to recognize how teens' empathy for one another is a reason why they're tethered to their devices. It's also a source of true burdens and digital dilemmas—especially when close friends struggle. We offer Aly and Jaylen's story as an example (see the "When Teens Struggle in Public" box).

Aly's unease when she saw Jaylen's posts stemmed from the question of *how* to respond, but teens also struggle to determine *whether* they should respond. This challenge intersects with at least two open questions. First: is what they see serious enough to warrant some kind of intervention?

When Teens Struggle in Public: Aly and Jaylen's Story

On a Friday evening in February, at the start of public-school vacation week, thirteen-year-old Aly was unusually preoccupied with her phone. Her typically happy face shadowed with worry, she tapped her phone's screen repeatedly. After a few minutes, she looked up. She turned to her mom, who was driving her home from gymnastics practice: "*Mom . . . Jaylen's posting stuff . . .*"

Jaylen and Aly had been friends since kindergarten—even self-proclaimed "BFFs" for a period when they were in third and fourth grade. Although they had drifted apart over the years, they remained friendly. Now in eighth grade, social media sites were key venues for keeping up, third spaces for connection beyond their face-to-face interactions at school or around the neighborhood.

While Jaylen was fairly quiet at school, he opened up online. Over the past few months, he had occasionally posted a worrying Instagram or Snapchat Story. One read, "*I can't do this anymore. I CAN'T.*" Another said, "*I wish I was a better person. I get why ppl hate me. I'm toxic, I'm stupid, and I'm a waste of oxygen*" and "*See you on the other side </3.*" It was clear that Jaylen was struggling. Yet what did these posts really mean? Were they a cry for attention? A cry for help? A sign that he was planning to hurt himself? Each time, Aly responded by sending direct messages to Jaylen, asking, "*What do you mean?*" or "*Are you ok?*" Jaylen's replies were brief ("*Fine*") but the posts continued, which only added to the ambiguity and to Aly's growing sense of panic.

On this night, Jaylen's posts were different. Or perhaps just more explicit. The first one read, "*I can't do this anymore. I'm so close on killing myself. This is too much.*" Another said, "*I very badly want to overdose myself. I can't do this anymore. But I also don't want to.*"

Jaylen's situation was a true crisis. It turned out he was posting some of the Stories from a local emergency room where his mom had taken him for immediate attention. His mom was aware of his distress, though she hadn't realized Jaylen was posting about it in a semi-public way.

Technology did not create Jaylen's mental health issues. Yet social media provided a venue for his expressions of suffering, and in turn raised new dilemmas for everyone in his audience. The messages were also ongoing, meaning that Aly was encountering them at different times of day over several weeks. Each time, Jaylen's posts stopped Aly in her tracks and evoked immediate distress.

For example, when Lila saw pictures of a friend who looked *"scary thin"* she wondered if that friend was struggling with an eating disorder—but she wasn't sure if the photos warranted comment. Second: what kind of response is appropriate given a teen's relationship (or lack thereof) with the poster? Puzzles abound when social media cries for help come from more distant acquaintances, friends of friends, or even strangers. A consequence of the shift we described in chapter 2 to more authentic and open posting is that encounters with the details of others' struggles are more common. As another teen recounted: *"I've seen things about people [whom I don't know] being like, 'Can you please give me money? I need to escape this house, like this abusive household.' Stuff like that, and putting their Venmo in the comments* [as a direct way for people to send them money] *or something like that."* It can be impossible to know whether the original posters are truly in crisis or are attempting to con kind strangers.

Unsurprisingly, when peers signal distress online, cry out for help on social apps, or reach out directly for text-based support, teens feel a sense of responsibility to be available and even, as another teen put it, to *"save"* their friends from self-harm. Fourteen-year-old Martina described herself as acutely concerned *"that I don't have enough contact with friends who are struggling. Because I don't want my friends to do something bad just because I didn't respond in time to stop them from harming themselves or worse."*

Adults encourage teens to be good friends, and to embrace values like trust, kindness, empathy, and responsibility. Hidden tensions and dilemmas of a social media age make this easier said than done.

TEENS WANT ADULTS TO KNOW

Teens wish adults would acknowledge the ways that social media and gaming help create, deepen, and sustain valued friendships. Digital life matters, whether it's staying in close contact with *"my best friend who goes to a different school"* or *"reconnecting with old friends."* Talking that happens while playing Fortnite or Call of Duty extends beyond it in ways that help teens *"form a bond."* This can be a real win, especially for teens who are shy or socially anxious but find that digital exchanges help them build close relationships that are otherwise hard for them to establish.

For many teens, technologies are a non-negotiable for friendship preservation. There's no way to opt out without major social repercussions. They wish adults would acknowledge this reality. *"I think it would be nice if adults realized that our entire social life is linked to social media. It isn't like when they were kids, where your social times were mostly during school. Nowadays, if you aren't on social media a lot, you won't have as many friends. It's all linked to it."*

Listening to teens clarifies a core dilemma they face: what does it mean to be a good friend—or even just a compassionate *person*—in an age of radical connectivity? Developmentally, teen friendships are supremely important. Now, those friendships are under a social media spotlight. This raises unique puzzles for teens who feel the pressure to perform closeness or ensure sufficient validation is always freshly on display. Teens also describe how the potential for 24/7 communication raises dilemmas around availability. What happens when the desire to protect valued relationships is pitted against the desire to disconnect? (Or, in their words, when a real concern about *"losing friends"* means feeling *"obligated to stay connected"*?)

Adults tell teens to get off their phones—and often have good reasons for it. Teens want adults to recognize that sometimes they connect willingly, for fun, and out of desire. Other times, they do so out of a sense of obligation or even a sense of stress that disconnecting will mean being left out, disappointing a friend, or being seen as rude.

A final point here: adults also seem to need more nuance in how we approach the topic of online friends. It's tempting to get stuck on the message that online strangers = danger. Teens are rightly nervous of *"creepy adults"* and other Internet strangers with malicious intent. But teens do connect online with "strangers" who are often peers of a similar age. Whether they're brought together by a mutual friend or by fandom around novels, fantasy basketball, or gaming, these connections can evolve into relationships that teens define as valued friendships. As with offline friendships, they can also be sources of struggle, like when an online friend needs more support than a teen can provide. When adults think about new online connections only in terms of potential predators, we miss opportunities to offer support when teens need it.

4

SMALL SLIGHTS, BIG FIGHTS

"*DM drama/secrets/anything, don't be shy* 🤫" read the Instagram account bio for @Mill_HS_drama.[1] It was a tea account: a designated place for anonymously "spilling the tea," aka sharing gossip and confessions. The premise of such accounts is simple. Anyone can DM (direct message) the account owner to share confessions, tips, or information. The account owner then screenshots and posts each message—without the sender's name—on the account's public page. Reading the posts on @Mill_HS_drama feels a bit like reading notes scrawled on the back of a bathroom door:[2]

I have a crush on [Boy A] and [Boy B] they are so hot and cute i don't know how to tell them. Keep this anonymous.

Make this anonymous but I know for a fact [Girl A] and [Boy C] are dating.

The posts are redacted haphazardly and without any clear logic. This results in a mix of posts that openly name their subjects and others that have strategically placed edits. So, while the readers learn that "Rachel" and "Connor" are dating, they are left to speculate who is being talked about in the post that reads: "*NAME uses a deodorant that we found buried under a septic tank.*"

Some @Mill_HS_drama posts seem helpful, even prosocial. They warn girls about a guy who is asking for nudes and then screenshotting those nudes and using them as blackmail. They condemn homophobia and call out a particular grade: *"Kids going into 9th need to stop being homophobic."* There are also posts like this one: *"Got a piece of tea for u. [Boy X] is a rapist."* The post immediately reminds me (Emily) of an interview discussion I had with a specific teen (see the "Social Media Can Make Things 'Ten Times Worse'" box).

In chapter 3, we described the Transformation Framework.[4] It is built on the premise that fifteen-year-old Brian articulated so well: social media is not simply another context that mirrors social dynamics. Rather, its very affordances *transform* the landscape of adolescents' experiences. People who would never be in a bathroom stall at Mill High School can easily access and read the digital posts. These posts are shared anonymously and are viewable by vast unintended audiences, potentially permanent, and easily spread. In other words: this isn't just graffiti to cover with a fresh coat of paint.

A TOXIC COMBINATION: GEOSPECIFICITY, ATTENTIVE AUDIENCES, ANONYMOUS POSTING

Before the rise of tea accounts on Instagram, apps like YikYak and (briefly) Streetchat enabled similar kinds of publicly available commentary. The specific platforms teens use will surely continue to shift. Yet there's a toxic trio of enduring features that seems to fuel this kind of pernicious gossip.

The first feature is geographic specificity, or "geospecificity." Different tech features are used to tether posts from "the cloud" to very specific physical places, whether it's Mill High School, Arizona State University, or Smithtown. YikYak leveraged geospecificity so that posts were searchable and viewable to people in a small radius, and it was especially popular on college campuses. So, at Arizona State for example, any students who opened the app in the vicinity of their campus could see the bulletin board-style collection of anonymous "yaks" shared by their classmates. In the case of the Mill High School tea account, which was housed on Instagram, simply including the school name in the account's @handle facilitated searchability. As more students started following it, the account became known, recognized, and likely even more readily discoverable

Social Media Can Make Things "Ten Times Worse"

Looking through the @Mill_HS_drama posts takes me (Emily) back to the small hospital room where one of my colleagues and I interviewed Brian a few years earlier (you may recall him from chapter 1 as the teen who said "*Social media is—in my opinion—a depressant*"). Fifteen years old at the time, Brian had been admitted following acute suicidal ideation. Our interview setting—in a wing of the hospital's adolescent psychiatric inpatient unit—served as stark evidence of his psychological state.

My understanding was that Brian had faced a series of traumas in his relatively short life. But I was there to investigate the role of social media in the lives of adolescents who struggle with suicidal thoughts and behaviors. Brian was one of thirty teens whom my colleagues and I interviewed in that inpatient unit. As noted in chapter 1, our study showed that teens' experiences were varied.[3] Even though every teen was in a psychiatric crisis, it just wasn't the case that all—or even most—were having horrific social media experiences. Most described digital life as offering a mix of challenges and benefits. Like many teens, they struggled with things like regulating screen time and comparing themselves to others' highlight reels. They named benefits like access to funny, relatable content, and the ability to stay connected to their most supportive friends. Our interviews revealed how social media, for some teens, provided precious hope, connection, and coping in the midst of crippling despair.

Brian was not one of them. He shared the kind of assessment that justifiably feeds adults' fears about digitally driven harms. One story seemed particularly painful to recount. After Brian turned down a romantic advance from a girl at school, she told everyone that he was a rapist. It was a lie.

As Brian recounted the story, the boundaries between what played out online versus offline were wholly unclear. At one point, I wondered why our questions about social media had even surfaced this particular incident. But then Brian stated plainly: "*It would be inaccurate to say [that] without social media it would be just as hurtful, cause it's not. Social media makes it ten times worse. It's a public forum, everybody can see it. . . . I want you to understand the seriousness of this. Because this is something that, like, high schoolers struggle with daily.*"

As Carrie and I looked through the @Mill_HS_drama account, I thought about Brian. We don't know whether or not Boy X is a rapist. If he is, the post might be a brave PSA (public service announcement) and a possible step toward accountability. Either way, we know that the posts on the @Mill_HS_drama account are qualitatively different from notes scrawled on the back of a bathroom door.

on Mill High students' Instagram Searches. The algorithm supports this by tailoring Search and Explore content based on both a user's likes and those of other people they follow.[5]

The second feature is an attentive and interested audience. The public (or potentially public) context of social media amplifies drama as conflicts are "performed" in front of an audience of peers.[6] Posts are shared to be seen. Even if a teen doesn't want to be part of the drama, she can feel compelled to monitor gossip accounts to make sure she isn't named—or at least to know if she is. People use these accounts for different reasons: curiosity, boredom, anxiety, or malicious intent. Whatever the motive, the presence of an attentive audience breathes continued life into these accounts.

The third feature is the ability to post anonymously. Whether posts are (or remain) truly anonymous, teens feel like they can share without identifiability and, therefore, accountability. This is particularly valuable if a teen wants to *say* something mean, but not be *seen* as mean. As one teen explained, *"The thing about tea pages is that they're anonymous. So I think that's given an outlet for people who don't want to be mean outright. They send anonymous messages to tea pages . . . and that doesn't have, like, any connection [to them]. It's anonymous. So it's an easy way to insult people or cyberbully people without being the cyberbully, publicly."*

Tea pages are a prime example of the ways social media affordances transform the landscape of social conflict. In the pages that follow, we dig into other recent incarnations. Digital information can spread rapidly. It's also easily replicated via screenshots and can be made visible—or rendered invisible—to audiences of varying sizes. However, as we describe in the box "Not Just for Gossip and Bullying," these affordances aren't leveraged only for harmful purposes: they can be tapped in the service of civic goals too.

Not Just for Gossip and Bullying

The summer of 2020 was a revealing moment when many current and former students of elite private schools disclosed their experiences of racism on social media. "BlackAt" accounts were tethered by name to particular schools (e.g., @blackattrinity for Trinity School in New York City). These accounts were used to circulate firsthand testimonials of how racism took shape within those communities. But the trend wasn't limited to private schools. Indeed, a separate tea account for "Mill High," which is the fake name we gave to a real public high school in another state, documented injustices and corresponding institutional failures.

Both current students and alums of various schools shared their own BlackAt stories—in some cases with their names but often anonymously—contributing to a collective call for accountability and change. Without the opportunity to share anonymously, some students and alumni might not have come forward with their stories. Without geospecificity, the stories would not have been so clearly linked to particular school communities. Without attentive audiences reading and responding to the posts, schools might not have felt pressure for rapid steps toward action. And hashtags like #blackatschool and #amplifyblackvoices facilitated attention from wider audiences and connection to a broader #BlackLivesMatter conversation.[7]

The @blackattrinity Instagram account shows one way these affordances and dynamics began to play out. The first post on the account, shared on June 13, 2020, read: "This account was created by Trinity alumni to share the experiences of current and former black students at Trinity. #BlackatTrinity." The caption elaborated: "Inspired by our peer nyc institutions @blackatbrearley @blackatchapin." Dozens of posts followed, some with messages that implicated faculty by name and others that named faculty roles more generally ("My English teacher told his entire class that he was scared of black people"; "My art teacher made me, the only black student, clean up after each class"). Other posts cited peers ("Hearing people in the language hallways say they would never marry a black woman") and even parents ("I was once stopped by a white parent in the hallway because they wanted to know if I was a prep [scholarship] kid").

Exactly one week after the posts began, the account owners posted a letter from Trinity's Head of School along with their own message of thanks. In the letter, the Head of School expressed gratitude to those behind @blackattrinity for "bringing to light the deeply painful stories of our community—stories that we should never have allowed to slip into silence." He described the first in a series of planned actions. The @blackattrinity account posted a message thanking the Head of School and administrators for "the response we wanted, the response we needed." To be sure, there were subsequent puzzles and further issues (including pushback) as Trinity and other NYC private schools began to implement new policies and curricula, and in some cases reckon with the fates of individuals who were named for past behaviors.[8] Yet, the collective influence of these shared stories was undeniably apparent.

"HIDING BEHIND A SCREEN"

Anonymity is implicated in tea pages and the like, and its veil empowers posts teens may hesitate to share from their real accounts for a variety of reasons. But even when people aren't anonymous, they at times behave behind the screen in ways that they would not in person. Teens are well aware of this idea, which scholars call "online disinhibition."[9] Digital communication emboldens people to share more freely and say things they might never say in person. Or, as teens in our research put it, *"Words on the internet hurt just as much as in real life, and the bullies feel more empowered and are generally harsher because they are on a screen. [They] feel their words have no meaning, and that it's just fun and games"* (twelve-year-old); *"It's so easy to hide behind a screen. Behind a screen one can be anything they want"* (thirteen-year-old).

Again, anonymity isn't always a bad thing. For example, disinhibition can lead to more open and honest self-disclosure. On the one hand, such *benign disinhibition* can benefit teens' emotional well-being by supporting closeness and intimacy with friends.[10] On the other hand, *toxic disinhibition* enables antisocial and mean behaviors like name calling, threats, and aggressive swearing.[11]

Interestingly, it's the lack of eye contact in text-based digital communication that seems particularly key to understanding toxic disinhibition. Experimental manipulations show that people are more hostile when they chat without eye contact.[12] Eye contact—even occurring through a webcam—leads to fewer heated exchanges, further confirmation that FaceTime is meaningfully different from texting.

The absence of both eye contact and identifiability can contribute to toxicity and bullying. However, it's not the case that digital cruelty is always or even usually anonymous. To the contrary, teens who are cyberbullied typically know who is behind the aggression. In one study with 451 teens, fully 92 percent who had been victims of cyberbullying reported that they knew the perpetrator.[13] This pattern is replicated in other studies, too, which clarifies that even if anonymity fuels disinhibition and meanness, most cyberbullying isn't anonymous.[14]

For years, we observed and heard about instances in which adolescents shared harsh comments with "friends" under the guise of wanting to be honest. To explore a hunch, we asked teens to weigh in on this statement:

"If a friend asks for honest opinions on an anonymous app, you should respond honestly even if it hurts their feelings." Interestingly, a majority (56 percent or 1,611 out of 2,909 respondents to the survey question) agreed with privileging honesty over kindness.

It's likely that developmental forces are at play. Adolescent egocentrism[15] can mean prioritizing personal concerns, in this case a bias toward thinking "I want to be honest and say what's on my mind" over "my friend might be quite hurt by this." Social perspective taking is implicated, too, since it's required to make such judgments. Perspective taking involves making inferences about things—like what others might want or how they might feel. Importantly, we know that social perspective-taking skills develop over time, rather than all once[16]—and that this competence is still developing across the adolescent years.[17] Thus, adolescents can both care deeply about others and still reason that a friend who asks "What do others think of me?" deserves an unfiltered response.

THE SPECTER OF CYBERBULLYING

There are also times when hostile comments are made intentionally to hurt others. Bullying is traditionally defined as unwanted aggression that is intentional, repeated, and carried out by someone who is in a position of power over their victim.[18] When such cruelty is communicated through digital devices, it falls into the category of cyberbullying.[19]

How common is cyberbullying? Overall, about one-third of youth in the United States report that they have experienced cyberbullying at some point in their lives. Researchers Sameer Hinduja and Justin Patchin have spent more than a dozen years tracking the nature and prevalence of cyberbullying in the United States, including with large, nationally representative samples. They ask youth about experiences when someone "repeatedly makes fun of another person online or repeatedly picks on another person through email or text message or when someone posts something online about another person that they don't like." Looking across their various studies, they found that about 28 percent of youths had been cyberbullied at some point during their lifetimes, and roughly 16 percent had at some point cyberbullied another person.[20] The experience of being cyberbullied was somewhat higher in Hinduja and Patchin's

2019 nationally representative survey of middle and high schoolers as compared to their earlier surveys. Of 4,972 students in the study, 36.5 percent said they had been cyberbullied at some point during their lifetimes and more than 1 in 6 (17.4 percent) had been cyberbullied in the past month. Nearly 15 percent (14.8 percent) reported that they had at some point bullied someone else, and 6.3 percent said they had done so in the past month.

A striking finding from our own research: teens perceive a causal, even inevitable path from being cyberbullied to mental health crises. This was a repeated sentiment as teens described worries about cyberbullying and drama: *"Lots of kids have killed themselves because of cyberbullying."* Suicide is a commonly feared and cited outcome. *"Suicide rates are getting higher due to cyberbullying, and I don't want me or my friends and family to fall into the group of people who have committed [suicide]."* Such fears can understandably amp up anxiety.

Most young people who are cyberbullied do not commit suicide.[21] It's also a pervasive misconception that cyberbullying is the worst type of bullying. In her well-researched book, *25 Myths about Bullying and Cyberbullying*, Elizabeth Englander explains: "Cyberbullying doesn't stand out as significantly worse or different than other social challenges. This doesn't mean cyberbullying doesn't hurt; but there's no compelling body of evidence demonstrating that it hurts significantly more than other harmful social interactions. . . . When we look at cases where cyberbullying is implicated in a suicide, we almost always see that the child in question was already struggling with depression and/or other emotional challenges."[22]

That said, cyberbullying is a serious cause for concern especially when it's happening to youth who are already in distress. It's especially devastating when it co-occurs with bullying at school. Compared to students who had not been subject to such aggression, Hinduja and Patchin's research indicates that youth who experienced both bullying and cyberbullying were more than five times as likely to have thought about suicide and more than eleven times as likely to have attempted suicide.[23]

Teens fear cyberbullying in part because they can feel helpless about both its occurrence and its impact. News coverage isn't helping. In the

United States, news stories about cyberbullying are significantly more likely than those about traditional bullying to use fear-based language, including alarmist words like "tragic" and "epidemic," anxiety-related vocabulary like "fearful" and "worried," and terminology directly related to death (for example: an article headlined "The Top Six Unforgettable Cyberbullying Cases Ever" describes teen deaths from suicide).[24]

BLATANT HOSTILITY

Blatant cruelty takes shape in myriad ways through devices. Some actions clearly meet the criteria for cyberbullying. Others—like receiving a single hateful text message or being publicly shamed by a former friend via a Snapchat Story—may be one-off aggressions but are no less relevant.

Because mobile devices offer anywhere and anytime connection, mean messages sent by text or direct message can instantly reach their target. For teens, this transforms experiences of hostility because it creates a sense that there is no respite. In their words:

When you go home you can't get a break from drama or bullying. (twelve-year-old)

Constant direct access to someone to bully them is miserable. They aren't even safe in their own home, when their phone is with them. (fifteen-year-old)

It's [a] big concern for me because I never know when I might get a comment that's mean. (eighteen-year-old)

Mean messages can also be sent in ways that are intentionally ephemeral, such as through Snapchat, which poses a challenge to documenting evidence of harassment. Although technically snaps can be screenshotted, the sender is by default alerted (unless a teen knows workarounds, which do exist).

Most teens can't just turn off their devices to escape hostility. So much of teens' lives happens with and through devices. Disconnecting comes at a high cost: missing messages from friends, details about social plans, and even timely information about school and extracurricular activities. When drama is unfolding, disconnecting can also mean being out of the loop as malicious content may be circulating. Painful as it is to know, not knowing can bring its own form of anxiety.

IN FRONT OF A CROWD

Hostility is also enacted in front of—even *for*—an audience. Indeed, publicness is yet another quality that transforms adolescents' peer experiences.[25] Someone who wants to embarrass or shame a peer can post harsh public or semi-public comments. They can submit a piece of damaging gossip—whether true or false—to a tea account and then watch from a comfortable distance as tensions escalate.

In rarer and more extreme cases, someone might create a fake account that uses another teen's real name and features unflattering content, like photoshopped images of the teen's face on different animal bodies. Or someone might create an impersonation account that is carefully rendered to appear real, with a username that is nearly identical to the person's actual account handle and pictures taken from their past posts. Such accounts can be used to send messages that damage the person's friendships or reputation; to follow problematic groups that link the person to hateful causes; or to post comments meant to spark backlash and get the person in trouble.

"Airing people out" or "exposing" them is another way to exploit the publicness of social media, particularly when a teen feels their wrath is warranted because another teen has crossed a line. "Receipts" refer to screenshots or screen recordings, which are shared to provide proof in the case against someone. Screenshotting is routine. Damning conversations that were meant to be private are made public thanks to easy replicability and shareability. Past transgressions that in a pre-digital era would have been relegated to distant middle school memories can resurface thanks to the persistence of digital content.

It may be tempting to make the case that much of this drama could be avoided if teens would only take more care with their words and actions. But how does one really manage in a context where a friend might later become an enemy who will scroll back through every bit of conversation history to find something indictable?

The reality is that once a teen is called out and "canceled" (i.e., publicly shamed and socially exiled for stepping out of line in some manner), any new post they share is likely to be scrutinized, at least for a while. Tweets, comments, and shared photos may be screenshotted and reposted along with critical analyses that continue the work of publicly blasting the person's character or behavior. Some audience members are "instigators" who pile on, while others assume the role of loyal defender. Some teens expect friends to publicly have each other's backs when fights or "calling out" escalate online, jumping into the comment section to express support, allegiance, and commitments of solidarity. Doing so checks the box of validating the aggrieved friend, but also comes with the risk of alienating others and creating drama for themselves. Perhaps most often, though, support happens "backstage," through direct messages and private texts that offer support and validation. Being a good friend can also mean talking a friend down if they are escalating a social media conflict unnecessarily. As sixteen-year-old Dante told us, he expects friends to tell him when he needs to *"Stop talking, walk away." "I'd expect my friends to do the right thing, not just coming to help me, but like . . . de-escalating the situation. Like 'Yo [Dante], you're being stupid right now. Like get your head in the game. You're not doing the right thing.'"*

For those who aren't close friends but merely onlookers who want to stay out of the drama, watching a peer get dragged down can nonetheless become a dark form of entertainment. As fourteen-year-old Mai put it: it's *"like a football match."*

PLAYING TAG (BUT NOT THE WAY YOU REMEMBER)

There's another kind of digital *"football match,"* that warrants attention too: the back-and-forth that plays out in comment sections. Tales of threads that devolve into shouting matches abound. When "Girl C" posted a picture of herself at a women's march with the caption *"the future is female,"* a male classmate (we'll call him "Boy D") responded: *"this comment isn't correct."* Girl C responded with a defense of the slogan, unpacking the importance of feminism today and the value of broader human rights advocacy. From there the comment thread blew up: more than two hundred comments poured in, with lengthy arguments on both sides.

Tagging was a crucial mechanism that kept people in and coming back to the thread. Generally, tagging allows commenters to directly respond to and call out others, often via sharply worded retorts that make it *"hard to leave it alone."* Some comments on "the future is female" thread were ideological; others were direct and personal: *"@BoyD, for once, stop giving everyone a very good reason to dislike you."* At least one commenter leveraged the opportunity for anonymity and used a fake account to weigh in.

Boy D never backed down. Eventually, Girl C went through and deleted all comments she didn't agree with, leaving a robust one-sided documentation of the argument.

But, again, tech features go both ways and tagging is no exception. Just as it is used to stoke conflict, tagging is also used for supportive, friendly purposes. If a teen tags her friend in a post that is likely to be of interest, her friend gets a notification and immediate access to that post. This makes tagging an easy way to share content. Sharing found content like relatable memes is a common, fun, and often funny way to build a closeness. It's also a practical method for circulating important news or information.

Tagging and a related practice—DMing (direct messaging)—can cross a line into subtler jabs or even blatant hostility. Tagging someone in a post with the caption "this is you" can be a compliment, a joke, or a jab depending on what the post shows. Even then, it can be a guessing game. The person who's tagged won't always know what it means. Genevieve, for example, is a huge Taylor Swift fan. When one of her more peripheral friends tagged Genevieve in a post about people who are obsessed with Taylor, Genevieve was unsure: Was it meant to mock her fandom? Or was it meant to be a friendly gesture, along the lines of, "This made me think of you since I know you love Taylor." This kind of ambiguous digital tagging is common. Teens often wonder: *"Are they laughing at me or with me?"*

SOMETIMES YOU JUST DON'T KNOW

Social media enables a host of ambiguous acts that can leave teens anxiously puzzling about others' intentions. Consider seventh grader Jessa seeing a social media post from the party she was at earlier. Another girl posted a group picture but cropped Jessa out of the shot. Jessa knew the other girl could deny that it was meant as a jab. The photocropper might argue that the full picture didn't look as good or support the *"aesthetic"* she was going for. Or, she could say that it was an unflattering shot of Jessa and she was trying to spare Jessa embarrassment.

Such is a perennial puzzle of navigating social life in a digital world: it can be hard to know when something on social media is done *in order to* hurt someone's feelings versus done without even considering their feelings. Admittedly, considering every possible viewer's feelings before posting is unrealistic. Because so much is documented and shared, a teen occasionally seeing pictures of even close friends socializing without them is simply a given. Still, sometimes posts are shared with decidedly hurtful intentions. This ambiguity can lead even confident teens into a spiral of self-doubt. As one fifteen-year-old explained:

My friends hung out without me. And of course [when I saw it on social media] it was such an, "oh my God" feeling. Like, "oh my God, am I out of the group now? Oh my God." . . . It's not like I really care about what people think, but it's like we've been friends since middle school. So am I out of the group? Like I'm not in the circle anymore? And as much as we try to ignore that feeling deep down in our hearts we still feel like, "oh my God, is something wrong with me, like, are they ignoring me?"

In chapter 3, we described various ways that teens signal and perform closeness for an audience of peers. Here, we see how online posts can also make teens wonder if they're being sidelined or even pushed out of a friend group. In other cases, posts can imply a desire for distance or even a demotion from best friend status. Again, it's not always clear. Consider Ruby seeing that her friend had tagged her in a TikTok video that linked different pairs of best friends and showed their horoscopes. The poster had paired herself with one friend and paired Ruby with another. Ruby wasn't sure what to make of it: was the poster trying to tell Ruby that she didn't consider Ruby to be her best friend? Was she trying to send a message that she wished they were closer? Or was it a fun and friendly act that was meant to be *inclusive* since she was featuring her three best friends in the video in the first place?

In other cases, teens analyze likes and comments for signs of closeness, distance, or conflict. For example, Dee circled back to look at the comments on her friend's recent picture. She had commented that her friend looked *"so gorgeous"* and saw that her friend had liked the comment. But then she noticed that all the comments left by other close friends had received not only a like from the original poster but also a personal reply.

Dee was instantly worried that her friend might be mad at her. In at least some teen circles, social norms dictate levels of comment replies. Liking a nice comment is the bare minimum of civility; commenting back (e.g., responding with a comment like "thanks gurl miss u lysm [love you so much]!!!") is a level up and seen as more endearing. And liking every comment save one can be downright insulting.

Ambiguous interactions like these also unfold in online gaming, although in distinct ways. Gamers describe how the very same taunts and heat-of-the-moment trash talk (*"you're so garbage"*; *"you're so bad"*) can reflect a relaxed, *"playful"* closeness or be experienced as harsh, rude, or full on *"bullying."* Tone is key, but so too is the nature of the relationship. Microaggressions as well as more overtly sexist, anti-gay, and racist comments are also a persistent feature of gaming culture, especially with the expansion of live streaming on visible digital platforms like Twitch.[26]

SUBTLE(R) JABS

Yes, hostility can be blatant and clear. But there are also jabs that are much less apparent to outsiders. Subtle jabs characterize much—perhaps even *most*—of teens' social struggles behind the screen. Pablo described how his guy friends' banter might seem in jest but can snowball: *"for guys on social media, I see a lot of one-upping each other . . . like a 'I'm better than you' competition. And that's how things escalate a lot. Because it's mainly either jealousy or overconfidence about what other dudes can do . . . it usually escalates that way."*

A further example: when two girls *"have beef,"* a comment like, *"oh my God, you're so gorgeous, I wish I could be you"* might be offered *"through gritted teeth,"* and meant as sarcastic and aggressive. These examples echo the concept of "social steganography" that danah boyd first wrote about over a decade ago. The idea here is that multiple meanings for different audiences are layered into online posts. In the case of a digital jab, coded language becomes a way of hiding the slight "in plain sight."[27] Indeed, posts that appear wholly benign are sometimes masked attempts to hurt a particular person. When one teen was angry at his best friend, he went out of his way to post pictures with other friends on his Snapchat Story—hoping, even *knowing*—that his best friend would see.

Teens can weaponize the chance to control what people see in other ways too. Removing someone from a Private Story is yet another digital jab. Because many teens use Private (or semi-private) Stories to share with their closest friends, the act of revoking someone's viewing access can be a power move to convey anger or stir conflict. People aren't notified when they've been removed from seeing someone's Stories. They find out only by either asking someone or realizing that they're out of the loop.

Creating spin-off group chats has a similar effect, digitally evicting someone from the ongoing group conversation; recall Lila's story from chapter 3. And yet, removing someone from a Story or chat isn't always hostile. It can be an acknowledgment that a friendship is no longer close (*"a good amount of the time, it's not malicious. It's just, hey . . . I don't think that this person who I knew well maybe a year ago but I don't know as well now, needs to be on there. Or stuff like that."*) This ambiguity contributes to stress, which isn't so easily brushed off. Peer rejection is even more emotionally distressing for adolescents than it is for adults.[28] While being excluded can be painful at any age, it's especially hard for teens for whom peer validation is an essential developmental need. Being left out can prompt real feelings of self-doubt and inadequacy.

IF YOU KNOW, YOU KNOW

Take the following example, which is a composite version of stories we heard on repeat: Juliana shares on her social media account a picture with her boyfriend, Marco. One of Juliana's (former) friends was hooking up with Marco previously and some of Juliana's friends have turned on her since she and Marco started dating. One of those friends, Ayanna, leverages the easy replicability of digital content and takes a screenshot of Juliana's picture with Marco. Ayanna then adds her own touch—an oversized vomiting emoji right next to Juliana and Marco's faces—and reposts the screenshot on her Close Friends Story. Only about twenty-five of Ayanna's closest friends see her Private Stories. Although Juliana was among that group in the past, Ayanna revoked Juliana's access when she and Marco first started dating. But Juliana and Ayanna still have a number of mutual friends. About ninety seconds after Ayanna reposted the picture of Juliana and Marco, one of those mutual friends took her own screenshot—a screenshot of the screenshot—and promptly texted it to Juliana to clue her in.

When conflicts erupt online, teens describe different paths that unfold. In one similar incident, the boyfriend went on his own TikTok and posted a video about how people need to stay out of other people's business. He didn't tag or call out the girl directly. But two things were true: one, everyone who knew, knew. That is, everyone who knew the context knew exactly what the boyfriend was talking about. And two, almost everyone who didn't know immediately *wanted* to know. This may be what's most powerful about an ambiguous, frustration-fueled airing of grievances: the whole audience is rapt, digitally rubbernecking to see what's happened and what will go down next.

CONTEXT SHAPES CONSEQUENCES

What goes down next depends heavily on teens' offline contexts. Whether the spark is an ambiguous act, a subtle jab, or a blatant call-out, teens describe meaningful differences in the fallout of digital drama and conflict. Their stories show how context profoundly shapes the nature and implications of experiences behind the screen. In some contexts, when issues start online, tensions may simmer, but they won't lead to much beyond either social awkwardness or perhaps a tense verbal exchange. Mica can call out someone in another friend group and she might get a dirty look in the hallway, but she knows the conflict won't escalate much further. The norms in Diego's school are similar: when people have a beef online, they mostly just ignore each other in person. But other teens have a different experience. *"Where I'm from,"* lil Ronny explains, *"words online lead to fights in the street."*

In one community where online fighting at times carried over to in-person physical fights, a teen in our research recounted how stressful it was to watch peers getting dragged on a local tea account. As tensions escalated, people started *"dropping addresses"* in the comments—that is, posting the home addresses of those teens whose behavior was in question, amplifying the threat of a physical confrontation. Others describe fights that begin online and provoke explicit dares to *"keep up the same [hostile] energy"* when in person.

Researchers Caitlin Elsaesser, Desmond Patton, and their colleagues (including me, Emily) studied the experiences of adolescents who live in disinvested neighborhoods in Hartford, Connecticut.[29] The aim was to understand when and how social media fights escalate to offline violence. Social media features, particularly comments, intensify conflict and spill over into physical fighting. Similarly, teens on our advisory council for this book described people dropping addresses in the comments to expose and threaten others' sense of safety at home. The Hartford-based study revealed that teens also drop addresses to specify locations to meet up and fight. Importantly, the publicness and quantifiability of social media comments can contribute to a sense that fights are expected and even inevitable, which echoes findings from research in other cities, including multiple studies led by Desmond Patton[30] and deep ethnographic work conducted by Jeffrey Lane.[31]

A key finding across the research is that the public nature of social media ups the ante.[32] Other features contribute to conflict too: tagging people allows for direct insults, and references to known public places broadcast where fights will happen. As Patton and colleagues explain, the volume and ease of communication can fuel disinhibition with truly toxic consequences that spill over into street violence.

THE THING WE MISSED

On an evening in early December 2020, we were in Zoom meeting with some members of our teen advisory council. The conversation had toured the varied twists and turns of how meanness and drama unfold in teens' online worlds, as we've described in this chapter. As we were wrapping up, we asked a standard closing question: Is there anything that is important to teens' experiences with this topic (digital social conflict) that didn't come up at all? In other words: What did we miss?

After a brief pause, fifteen-year-old Maeve spoke up. We missed *"a big thing,"* she told us: *"outing people."* That is, revealing their sexual orientation without their consent on social media. Another teen jumped in to agree, *"that's a really big thing."* Turns out, everyone knew someone who had been outed online. A third teen shared a story of a teen being outed on Facebook and, later, seeing a video of him being beaten up. Another told of a gay couple in which one partner was *"ready to show the world"* but the other was not; the public revelation caused extreme backlash from his family.

But for Maeve, outing wasn't just something that had happened to a classmate. It was *her* story. In sixth grade, Maeve was dating a boy but questioning her sexuality. She told him as much and he *"wasn't very nice about it."* The next day, she broke up with him over text. Before too long, the boy told another classmate and, in short order, that classmate *"spread it to the entire school."* *"I think it really defines the rest of your life, being outed,"* Maeve reflected, *"It's like, such an invasion of privacy and an invasion of choice, too. This is something that should be yours, and it's been taken away from you."* As in Brian's story about being called a rapist, the role that social media played (if any) wasn't initially apparent. But like Brian, Maeve then stated clearly, *"It was definitely exacerbated by social media. It's just such a way for news to spread—like on Snapchat, like, 'Oh did you hear?' Stuff like that."*

Teens who have secrets of any kind have a heightened vulnerability in a digital context where anything can be made instantly public at any time. The "default publicness" of certain social media sites (especially sites like Facebook that are intentionally designed to be used with people's "real" names) poses distinct dangers for queer youth.[33] This is pronounced on sites with "linkability" to offline social networks. Yet, risks persist regardless of the site. Notably, screenshotting allows digital content to transverse apps and therefore audiences too. Stories like Maeve's and those of other youth with marginalized identities underscore the reality that the risks of "being in public" are inequitably distributed.

Just as relational aggression, social slights, and physical fighting are far from new, outing and being outed aren't new either. But once again, social media appears to transform the experience in ways that make the proverbial "writing on the bathroom wall" seem almost quaint by comparison. Teen social conflicts—from small slights to big fights—are at once nothing new and profoundly transformed.

TEENS WANT ADULTS TO KNOW

Online drama is *"as serious and harmful"* as drama in real life—and at times even worse. If someone wants to be mean, they can be relentless.

"Even if you escape it on one platform, they'll probably find their way to the next—and it's just a whole, like, cat and mouse game." Digital connectivity makes targeted meanness hard to avoid: *"anybody, anywhere, at any time"* can send a rude comment or mean message. Social conflicts can also *"escalate super fast, from like nothing—zero to 100 . . . one day, [a kid] can be fine, the next day they really can't."*

Subtle digital jabs complicate the challenge of interpreting what's meant to provoke a fight or hurt feelings. Not-so-subtle jabs may be crystal clear to the target audience—but conveyed with enough ambiguity to make them hard to prove and even harder to know how to respond.

There can be value in shutting off one's phone temporarily, whether it's to simmer down, get some emotional distance, avoid further escalation of a conflict, or rally in-person support. But teens wish adults understood that *"you can't just always 'shut your phone off' and be done with it."* Digital conflicts spill over *"into the real world."* Responding can feel like a necessity, particularly when conflicts are playing out in a digital public and threaten a teen's reputation or relationships. Even when exchanges aren't happening in front of an audience, part of the stress stems from anticipating a forthcoming in-person confrontation or interaction.

In years past—when social technologies supplemented teens' lives but didn't necessarily dictate their every move—avoidance may have been a viable option. Complete and prolonged disconnection just isn't feasible for today's teens when these technologies are essential to their everyday lives, jobs, and school. This reality can make for an unfortunate comingling of distressing messages (ambiguous jabs in group chat) with important ones (a text from a parent about a ride home from practice). Plus, steering clear of social media or texts often costs teens access to friends and the *"support network of people who care about you."*

Teens urge parents *"not to blame their child for getting into drama online."* Even if a teen wants nothing to do with drama or fights, they can get pulled in against their will and then struggle to effectively navigate a path out. *"Doing the cliched thing of confronting them"* (someone who is being mean) isn't always the best idea. Even when ignoring a jab feels like the best tack, it doesn't mean teens can ignore their emotional reactions. Painful social moments are *"not a thing you can really get over fast."*

What *can* adults do? Recognize that intense emotional reactions to social slights are expected, developmentally. When in doubt, validate teens' feelings ("That seems really hard"). Consider that a break from tech might help, and what the costs might be. And resist the urge to conclude that everything they're facing is too new and different to understand.

5

NUDES (AND WHY TEENS SEXT WHEN THEY KNOW THE RISKS)

Peter was on the bus ride home from an away basketball game when he covertly pulled out his phone and called over a few of his friends. He pulled up an app that looked like a calculator and typed in a sequence of numbers—a password—that revealed a collection of photos he had stored in its "vault." The pictures offered glimpses of different female body parts, and he divulged to his friends that they came from a number of their eighth grade female classmates. His friends were impressed.

The entire photo sharing session lasted only a few minutes, but it left an impression on Peter's friends, including Harrison. Cool boys, it seemed, were both asking for and receiving nudes. And at least some of the girls in their grade were apparently game to send them.

Later that night, Harrison asked his girlfriend to send him some sexy images. After all, if other girls were sharing with boys in their grade, shouldn't his *girlfriend* trust him enough to?

But the photographs on Peter's phone hadn't really come from his female classmates. Peter simply found the pictures online and cropped them in ways that supported his story. It didn't matter: the faked collection suggested to Peter's friends that asking girls for nudes was acceptable.

"IT COULD RUIN YOUR REPUTATION!"

When adults talk about sexting, we tend to gloss over the reasons teens end up entangled in sexting dilemmas in the first place. Sexting behaviors are shaped by teens' natural sexual interests *and* by peer pressures. Apps provide new tools for sexual exchanges, but longstanding features of adolescence underpin how and why youth tap them—even when they are well aware of the risks. When we ignore the reasons teens sext, we misunderstand the calculus of their decision-making as they grapple with whether to request or "snap and send" a racy picture. And when we dole out only panicked admonitions ("never, ever, ever sext, period"), we slip into a digital age version of abstinence-only education, leaving teens without sufficient information to support complex, real-world decision-making. Notably, various studies show that abstinence messages are largely ineffective at stemming sexual activity and risk-taking.[1]

By the time adults are aware of an unfolding sexting scandal, the situation has often escalated to a crisis point. Our responses can default to a specific mode of victim-blaming: she (it's often *she* in the stories we hear) really should have known better than to send that picture or video. We then rush to warn the teens in our lives, "See! This is why you should never send a naked picture to someone else. It could ruin your reputation." "Once you hit send, you can't take it back!" "Sending inappropriate pics is illegal and dangerous." Important messages, but are they enough?

Some adults do go a step further in their discussions with teens. They think to caution boys (and often, it is *boys*) against asking for nudes. Such warnings carry the crucial message that it's not okay to pressure others for sexts. Still, these messages fail to acknowledge the counter-messages those teens are hearing from peers, who often hold more sway than adults. As in the preceding story, a repository of nudes can be an alluring status symbol, like a digital collection of trophies in the adolescent world.

Research also shows that sexting "scripts" or narratives among adolescents portrays sexting as normative and boys as the typical askers.[2] But, to be clear, large-scale analyses show that most teens are neither asking for nor sending sexually explicit pictures, videos, or messages. And yet: around one in seven teens has sent a sext. About one in three has received sexts. A smaller number, in the ballpark of around one in ten, have forwarded on others' sexts.[3]

WANTED, PRESSURED, AND SHARED WITHOUT PERMISSION: WHAT'S THE DIFFERENCE AND WHY DOES IT MATTER?

Adults tend to use just one word—sexting—to describe a broad range of behaviors most adults would prefer teens avoid all together. But data reveal important differences.[4] Sexting can be *consensual and wanted* by both parties. Sexts can be *pressured* or even actively *coerced*: the result of one person feeling uncertain about how else to navigate requests or even trapped by threats or blackmail. Sexts can also be *shared without permission*, as in the case of pictures that are sent to one person and then shared further without consent from the person who is featured.

Sexting also takes different forms. The term "sexting" can refer to erotic text-based communication, nude or semi-nude pictures (think: full-body mirror pics, "dick pics," "ass pics," "bra pics"), or videos that feature sexual imagery or acts like masturbation. In this chapter, we focus on visual content—photos and videos—because of their graphic and often identifiable nature. Visual content poses unique privacy risks and can persist as part of a teen's long-term digital footprint. In our most recent research, teens most often used the term *"nudes"* to talk about this kind of content.

Teens can play multiple roles in sexting situations: they can be the *askers* who request sexts from others, they can be the *asked* person, from whom sexts are requested, and they can also be the *recipients* of others' sexts. When teens are *recipients* of others' sexts, they may be willing or unwilling audiences, and the pictures may have been sent with or without permission of the person they feature. Teens may receive dick pics they neither request nor want; this experience can be deeply unsettling (*"the most disgusting thing"*; *"polluting my phone"*). Some teens may resist telling adults because they fear adults will misinterpret what has unfolded or immediately take away their phones or both.

Teens who are *asked* for nudes describe requests from at least four possible sources: significant others with whom they are in committed relationships, earlier-stage romantic interests (i.e., people they are *"talking to"* or flirting with), people they consider *"just friends,"* and strangers. These different categories of requesters raise distinct puzzles as teens consider whether and how to respond. A request from a stranger is creepy and unsettling, often best handled by blocking or reporting the asker. A request from a "friend" is challenging in a different way and blocking the asker can feel like it will cause different problems. Requests from romantic interests or partners—people with whom teens are quite motivated to convey intimacy and trust—require weighing these desires against potential risks if images are saved or later leaked. Of note, teens who are asked for sexts by their significant others (boyfriends, girlfriends, etc.) do tend to comply.[5]

Teens who identify as LGB appear to engage more frequently in sexting than their non-LGB identifying peers and to engage in more mutual (two-way) sexting.[6] Researchers have noted that sexting may provide LGB teens with a valuable, nonpublic avenue for sexual identity expression and exploration.[7] At the same time, survey data suggest that queer youth are more likely to report being pressured for nudes, suggesting they may also face heightened risk of pressures and sexting victimization.[8] Being outed and/or harassed just for their sexual identities on social media is a corresponding threat that can add another layer of stress.[9]

WHY SO SHORT-SIGHTED?

When teens consider whether to sext, their calculus includes a number of considerations beyond the risk of leaks or potential long-term consequences.

The way adolescents' brain systems mature skews focus toward near and immediate concerns over more distant future possibilities. It works like this: the brain's arousal systems and regulatory systems mature at different speeds. During adolescence, the neural systems that drive emotional reactivity and a focus on immediate rewards outpace development of the frontal lobes, which fuel the kinds of logical thinking that help keep impulses in check. These asynchronous developments shape decision-making in ways that can seem nonsensical to adults. As adolescent development expert Larry Steinberg describes:

Behavioral data have often made it appear that adolescents are poor decision-makers (i.e., their high-rates of participation in dangerous activities, automobile accidents, drug use and unprotected sex). This led initially to hypotheses that adolescents had poor cognitive skills relevant to decision-making or that information about consequences of risky behavior may have been unclear to them . . . however, there is substantial evidence that adolescents *engage in dangerous activities despite knowing and understanding the risks involved.* Thus, in real-life situations, adolescents do not simply rationally weigh the relative risks and consequences of their behavior—their actions are largely influenced by feelings and social influences.[10]

Adults often assume that teens who send nudes simply fail to appreciate potential stakes and consequences. Accordingly, their approach is to talk with teens in ways that emphasize the dangers—especially the risk that images will be shared with other audiences and follow them into their futures. But understanding the trajectory of neural development helps to clarify why a sole conversational focus on the *consequences* of sexting is destined to fall short. If adults want to intervene in ways that will really shift adolescents' behaviors, we need to understand the more immediate feelings and social influences at play.

DECIDING TO SEND

Decontextualized from actual situations where they are being asked to send or weighing sending a nude, many teens are impressively alert to risks of sexting. They are patently aware of the permanence of digitally shared pictures and get that *"once u send it everyone can see it."* They recognize that *"the pictures can go viral and that would be scary and embarrassing."* Even if the asker promises not to save it, they might create and leak a copy (*"if you send any inappropriate pictures to anyone . . . they can take a screenshot and show everyone"*).

They know, too, that *"these pictures that are sent can ruin your future"* and that *"the person who receives this now kind of has control over you because they can post those pictures anywhere without your consent and you are powerless over that."* And yet, as noted, some teens *are* sexting: according to one meta-analysis of studies totaling more 184,000 adolescents, one in seven teens has sent a sext.[3] What's more, sexting is only becoming more frequent.[3] While the behavior was framed as deviant a decade ago, studies that explore the prevalence of sexting over time signal a trend toward normalization among teens and young adults.[11] It's likely the pandemic hastened this shift, too, as suggested both by survey data of adults[12] and our own mid-pandemic focus groups with teens (who noted that sending nudes had become more common in their social circles amid stay-at-home orders and mandated social distancing).

If teens know the risks, why do they send nudes anyway? Taking a closer look at their perspectives is revealing. The following are some of the most salient motives documented in prior research[13] and echoed in our surveys, interviews, and focus groups with teens. Importantly, these "9 Reasons Why Teens Sext" are not mutually exclusive:

1. It feels pleasurable, exciting, and fun.
2. They hope to impress someone they like. They're seeking praise, validation, or attention from a crush.
3. They're "*talking*" to a romantic interest but not yet serious or exclusive; they want to signal a desire to move things forward and/or keep that person interested.
4. They're in an exclusive relationship and want to deepen intimacy or show trust.
5. They can't figure out how to say no. Sending a photo feels easier than dodging the request.
6. The asker is someone they consider a friend, and they worry that saying "no" will jeopardize the friendship.
7. The asker is persistent and wears them down.
8. They fear consequences if they refuse, e.g., from an asker who might be mean, get aggressive, or spread false rumors.
9. They are being actively coerced, threatened, or blackmailed by the asker. For example: perhaps they have already sent some sexy pictures in the past and the asker is threatening to share those pictures if they don't send new images.

Teens are assessing their own desires and concerns, their perceptions of the recipient's trustworthiness, and even their feelings about their own bodies. They're drawing on their impressions of social norms among their peers, including whether they think the popular kids they know are sexting. An interesting finding from a study of over six hundred adolescents: high schoolers who think popular kids are sexting are themselves more likely to sext.[14]

A developmental phenomenon called *the personal fable* is likely relevant too.[15] In short, the personal fable is a sense during adolescence that one is special and unique—so much so that a teen can reason that they are personally less vulnerable to risks ("Even if sexts are often leaked, that wouldn't happen to *me*").[16]

If they're considering turning down a request, teens are weighing their ability to say no to the asker alongside real or imagined fears about what it will mean for them. Often, short-term outcomes are front of mind and seem guaranteed. These include outcomes teens want to ensure (like attracting a crush) or avoid (like being called a prude). Longer-term potential consequences certainly loom but are often ambiguous and uncertain. These variables are often invisible to adults but weighty for teens. Importantly, many of the "9 Reasons Why" suggest that decisions to sext can fall short of consent. Consent turns out to be a valuable frame for thinking about teens' experiences with sexting (see the "Let's Talk about Consent" box).

CONSENSUAL SEXTING—AT LEAST AT FIRST

Consider two stories that concern consensual sexting, both shared with us by teens who are close friends of the people involved. In the first case, Josephine was a high school freshman, dating a guy who was a year older. He never explicitly asked for a nude, but he had implied his interest. She decided to send one. For Josephine, sending the picture was a signal of her trust in him. She also hoped it would deepen their connection and intimacy.

Her boyfriend apparently thought Josephine looked hot, and he sent the picture to a couple of friends. His friends sent the picture on to other classmates. When it wound up in the hands of a few girls who had never liked Josephine, they seized the opportunity and spread it around further. It became a painful case study of *replicability* and *scalability* in action.

Josephine was mortified. She also felt completely betrayed. Josephine knew when she sent the picture that it *could* be leaked. But she had trusted her boyfriend enough to believe he would respect her body and her privacy. His actions had done irreparable damage to that trust. So, on top of managing the social aftermath of her *"exposure,"* Josephine was thrust into a sudden breakup that she painfully initiated.

Josephine's feelings of betrayal didn't end with her boyfriend either. Some of her so-called friends had circulated the picture too—and she decided that marked the end of those friendships. A number of those girls were Josephine's soccer teammates. She decided to quit the team.

Planned Parenthood's definition of "consent" uses the memorable acronym "FRIES."[17]

F—Freely given: Consent is freely given, meaning that the person was not pressured or threatened into agreeing.

R—Reversible: Consent is reversible in the sense that it's not static. The fact that a person said yes in the past does not mean that they consent to the activity now and indefinitely into the future.

I—Informed: Consent is informed, which means that the person knows what they are agreeing to and fully understands the facts and circumstances.

E—Enthusiastic: Consent is enthusiastic, which means that the person is happy and excited to participate in whatever the sexual activity is.

S—Specific: Consent is specific to the activity in question. Consent to going somewhere private to kiss is not consent for anything more than kissing.

To be sure, this is an aspirational definition of consent. It isn't always consistent with legal interpretations, which may have a lower bar. (We'll turn to the general complexity of the legal landscape of sexting later in this chapter.) But consent is often overlooked altogether as a relevant component of teen sexting. If someone is pressured or coerced into sending a picture, this isn't consent. If someone shares a nude under the condition that it will be deleted and then the recipient doesn't do so, this also isn't consent. Same goes if someone sends a snap that is meant to disappear and then the snap is stored, saved, or screenshotted—again, this is a violation of consent. And if someone shares a sext with one person and that picture is shared with others? That, too, violates consent—even if the picture is just quickly shown from the original recipient's phone, even if it wasn't forwarded digitally, and yes—even if there's no way the original sender would ever know. More generally, reversibility is hard if not impossible to achieve in a context where digital content persists. Importantly, as in offline sexual encounters, sexting can appear consensual but in fact be unwanted. Even in the context of a committed relationship, sexting behaviors can be motivated by subtle pressures to fulfill a partner's needs.[18]

Josephine eventually moved forward. She joined a new friend group and leaned into other sports. Her new friends knew about her experience with the circulated nudes, but they hadn't actively seen or sent them.

Second, we have Anya's story. A few years ago, when Anya's boyfriend wanted nudes, she took a few pictures and sent them to her best friend for consultation: did she look hot? Should she retake them at a different angle? Once assured that the pictures were sufficiently flattering, she sent them on. A year or two later, when the COVID-19 pandemic began, Anya and her boyfriend weren't seeing each other in person, and they started getting sexual over FaceTime. Anya made no effort to hide this from her friends; she wasn't embarrassed and didn't seem to think there was any reason she should be.

By the time we heard this story, considerable time had already passed since Anya first sent her boyfriend nudes. There had been no leaks, no scandals, and no betrayals. Maybe it will take a negative turn, but maybe not. For younger teens, the likelihood of unwanted circulation and the nature of others' reactions to a leaked nude elevate the risk and social consequences of sexting. By contrast, for older teens, consensual sexting may be fairly low-risk: research with eighteen-year-olds who sent nude pictures suggests that in most cases—for as many as 92 percent of "non-pressured sexters" in one study—sending a picture didn't cause any problems at all.[19] In another study, researchers specifically asked college students who had sent nudes whether they regretted it. About one in four felt regret or worry about the decision; most did not. Young women in the study (though not men) were more than twice as likely to report regret when the pictures were sent to casual partners versus in the context of committed relationships.[20] Though not a focus of the college student study, privacy risks are amplified for people whose sexual identities are not public and would be revealed through sexting leaks.[21]

As we listened to teens' perspectives on sexting, we heard enough stories like Anya's to know that, for some teens, the calculus about sending nudes takes on board the possibility of zero bad consequences. These realities stand in stark contrast to what teens describe as alarmist school assemblies with *"condescending"* messages, *"shaming us"* through anxiety-provoking stories that leave them feeling *"exhausted [and] . . . ashamed for potential choices we might make,"* as one teen put it. Again and again when we asked teens to weigh in on sexting issues, they raised considerations about consent and trust. *"As long as sexting was consensual with both parties, it's cool"*; *"if it's two consenting teenagers at a decent age, it's okay for them to explore that kind of sexual connection"*; *"Maybe they are dating and have lots of trust towards each other."*

In a timely editorial published in the *Journal of Adolescent Health*, one of the leading researchers on sexting concluded a brief recap of sexting studies with an instructive parallel: "Adults often ask what can be told to youth to completely stop them from sexting. The short answer is probably nothing. In the short term, sexting appears to have a psychological profile similar to that of adolescent sexuality. *Like sexuality, with the right partner, sexting apparently can be a positive experience; with the wrong partner, it can be very damaging.*"[22]

Sexting is not an inherent evil: among adults in committed relationships, consensual sexting is even, in some cases, associated with positive outcomes like relationship satisfaction.[23] It's understandable to cringe at the thought of teens exchanging sexts of any kind. But consensual sexting is best understood as an extension of developmentally expected desires to explore sexuality and intimacy. The behavior undoubtedly carries a constellation of potential risks for teens—and, as with sex, the risks of negative experiences and consequences are certainly heightened for younger adolescents.[24] Crucially, when the sexters are minors, legal issues can arise, as we will touch on later in this chapter. Nonetheless, wanted and consensual sexting exchanges occupy a meaningful place on the spectrum of teens' sexting behaviors.

PRESSURED SEXTING

As reflected in several of the "9 Reasons Why," teen sexting isn't always consensual. Young people also send nudes as the result of pressure, one-sided persuasion, or worse. Data from more than eight hundred sixth to ninth graders who had been in romantic relationships revealed that roughly one in eight had been pressured to send sexual messages or photos.[25] As you might expect, girls were significantly more likely to be the ones pressured to sext, while boys were more likely to be the ones applying pressure. Still, this doesn't mean boys never feel or face pressure to send.

In our own data, the word "pressure" abounds.

I don't want to feel pressured into doing something that I know is not right. I also know that it will be on the internet forever so it could mess up my life later on. (eleven-year-old girl)

They pressure you and I would get in a lot of trouble. (thirteen-year-old boy)

I don't want to be pressured into sending something i don't want to send. (thirteen-year-old girl)

I do not want to be in a situation that pressures me to do something that could ruin my future. (fifteen-year-old boy)

Boys can pressure girls, [in my] *personal experience, to send photos of themselves.* (fifteen-year-old girl)

For some teens, just being *asked* is enough to evoke discomfort and a feeling of pressure. The request *"is very awkward and it makes me uncomfortable,"* one fifteen-year-old explained. Others concur: *"It just puts you in an awkward situation. You always have to be paranoid in the circumstance"* (twelve-year-old girl). Such feelings can stem from a worry that declining a request will damage a teen's relationship with the asker. If the asker is a partner or crush, the person might lose interest if nudes aren't shared. If the asker is a "friend"—for example, someone in their friend group who is interested in them but for whom feelings aren't reciprocated—the concern is different. As thirteen-year-old girl put it, *"If its someone I'm really close to, I don't want us to just stop being friends because I didn't send them a picture."* Another girl, also thirteen, echoed a similar concern: *"If you're pressured but don't want to, you might risk having someone as a friend or not."*

Recall that, developmentally, the adolescent impulse to protect and preserve peer relationships is strong. It's stressful to think that a relationship might be in jeopardy, and even more so if a teen feels like she could have done something to prevent it. Ideally, teens will recognize that a friend who pressures them is not such a good friend after all; in the wise words of one sixteen-year-old girl, *"I feel the peer pressure from the people that ask and when I say no, I worry that I will lose them as a friend. But, then I consider, are they actually my friend?"* And yet, another acknowledged that sometimes teens do feel *"it's easier"* to just acquiesce rather than *"ruin the relationship they have with the person by being like: no. And so they just send it."*

SEND, OR ELSE

Pressures to send can also stem from real or imagined fears about how the asker will react to being turned down. *"I get asked to send nudes a lot and it always makes me uncomfortable,"* one fourteen-year-old explained, *"I'm afraid the other person will hurt me when i say no."* These cases can cross a line into cyber sexual harassment.[26] And yet again, context matters:

where misogyny and sexual harassment appear rampant, teens describe how spurned requests spill over into aggression:

When boys get rejected, they turn into the most hostile, violent people you've ever known. I've known girls will get bottles thrown at their heads for rejecting somebody. I've known girls who get cussed out and get exposed on social media and get, like, the screenshot of their chat exposed . . . it can really turn out terribly for the girl. . . . [Boys] feel so entitled that it's like: how dare you say no to me? And so oftentimes I feel like it's nothing but violence and verbal assault that comes after that. Like that's pretty much all I've ever known it to be.

Girls' concerns also veer into fears about coerced sexting and sextortion: askers threatening to publicly circulate nudes to manipulate someone into activities like sending more sexts or engaging in sexual activities.[27] Some portray requesters as relentless: *"once you send it once, bruh, they never stop, they literally going to be coming at you back to back to back and forcing you like, 'yo, I'ma send this out if you don't send me this.'"*

Indeed, teens speak to tactics that range from manipulative flattery to direct threats or blackmail (*"Some people would send threats when I didn't [send nudes]. And I wouldn't send them"*; *"They always try to blackmail you into sending and it's just so annoying"*). Some girls worry specifically about being blackmailed into sending pictures by the asker threatening to *"hurt people I care about."* Even among teens for whom physical violence isn't a concern, the decision to turn down a request can cause considerable anxiety about potential harassment, name-calling, cyberbullying, or false rumors. Recent studies unsurprisingly show that coerced sexting predicts psychological distress.[28] Pressured sexting can be an aspect of "digital dating abuse," too, which is "a pattern of behaviors that control, pressure, or threaten a dating partner using a cell phone or the Internet."[29]

In short: while sending nudes can lead to consequences like public humiliation or getting in trouble, turning down requests can feel equally riddled with other near-term repercussions.

THE ULTIMATE BREACH: SHARING OTHERS' NUDES WITHOUT PERMISSION

Recall Josephine, the teen who shared a photo with her boyfriend and then had her pictures circulated. She initially shared her nude voluntarily (without direct pressure or any coercion). But then it was forwarded on and the situation changed instantly.

Sharing others' pictures without permission is a major violation of consent: it is a breach of trust that is understandably traumatic for the person whose picture was shared. Again, there is a gendered dynamic here: girls experience more social shaming and trauma in such scenarios.[30]

Data are at once reassuring and concerning. Though reports vary somewhat across studies, between 7–12 percent of adolescents say they have forwarded sexts.[31] This suggests that a minority of youth have forwarded others' pictures. It may, however, be an underestimation of current prevalence given that (1) sending, receiving, and forwarding sexts have all become more common in recent years; and (2) the focus on forwarding overlooks nonconsensual sharing that happens in other ways, like Peter (in the opening vignette) showing his friends nudes in person. Indeed, a 2018 survey of 800 Canadian young people aged 16–20 that asked about if people had ever shown, shared, or forwarded another person's pictures found that about one third had done so and that showing people others' pictures in person was the most common method.[32]

Who shares others' pictures without permission, and why? Sometimes the motives are malicious, as in the case of the girls who seized the chance to embarrass Josephine or a guy who leaks pictures as a form of "revenge porn" after a fight or breakup.[33] Pictures may also be leaked as part of ongoing coercion (recall the teen who described guys threatening to release pictures to elicit new nudes). Sometimes, money may even be involved—meaning, nudes are sold via peer-to-peer payment apps.

Pride, a desire for clout, and camaraderie building can all motivate nonconsensual sharing too. Josephine's boyfriend apparently wanted to brag about his hot girlfriend; we never interviewed him, but boys in our research explained that nudes are sometimes shared to show off a girl or because the nudes themselves are like "trophies." It's "an accomplishment" to get them and showing nudes to close friends can be a way to prove success. This idea is documented in prior research as well.[34] At the same time, teens also suggest that sharing can undercut the "value" of a girl's nude, which is relevant if the nude photo is of someone a teen is still talking to or dating ("You don't gain anything out of showing everybody what you *have."*) More generally, sharing nudes widely is described by some older teens as immature and *"childish."*

When Dame was in high school, one of his best friends routinely shared with Dame any nudes he got. They never circulated the images further; they had a mutual understanding that the pictures should be kept private between them. Still, Dame—now a college student—reflects that *"it was kind of messed up."* To be sure, their arrangement violated consent expectations from the initial sender. Sending nudes to a group chat—or even air dropping them to nearby friends—are similar practices that are routine in some teens' social circles. Such distribution can be a way to stake a claim over a girl, or it may be an invitation to assess and compare the nudes to a growing collection of photos from other girls. While teens may share photos with friends voluntarily, they can also face pressure from friends who request and, in some cases, even expect to see them.

BELIEFS → BEHAVIORS

Research finds a connection between teens' beliefs about traditional gender stereotypes and propensity to share others' nudes. In one study, adolescents (especially boys) who believed more strongly in ideas like "men should be more interested than women in sex" and "a woman cannot be truly happy unless she is in a relationship" were more likely to have shared another person's sexts without their permission.[35] Cultural beliefs about both gender and sexuality shape teens' ideas about sexting, which is likely why the prevalence of sexting varies in different countries and contexts.[36]

Unsurprisingly, teens' behaviors are also related to their views of broader peer norms. This is crucial to consider since those norms may also be changing. Teens' own sexting behaviors are influenced by how common they think sexting is among their peers. Teens are also more likely to share others' sexts if they feel their friends expect it. Moral disengagement appears relevant too: young people who shared others' nudes rationalized their decisions as either not harmful or "not as bad" as other lapses like cheating on a romantic partner.[37]

Because norms matter so much,[38] it's encouraging to see teen-driven efforts to shift them in positive ways—like a 2021 TikTok trend that featured teen boys rejecting the culture of sharing nudes. Each video showed a single teen playing dual roles of a guy sharing nudes and his friend's reaction: *"Damn yo, look at my girls fire nudes."* The response: *"Get that shit out of my face."* followed by *"Wtf is wrong with you."* One re-creation shared by "@jordanlicausi_" was viewed over 3.9 million times. The video prompted a series of mocking spinoffs, but still serves as a cultural artifact documenting the way some boys push back. We heard reactions of a similar sort from boys who were quick to label Peter's behavior (showing his friends nudes on the bus) as *"messed up"* and *"just rude, honestly."*

SEX(TING) AND GENDER

In the media, stories of sexting often portray a decidedly gendered narrative: boys are positioned as the askers and girls as the senders whose photographs are shared. Some studies indicate that boys are indeed more likely than girls to be the requesters, asking for sexts from others.[39] Interestingly, however, the large meta-analyses we cited earlier—including the most recent analysis of data from 79 studies and more than 184,000 youths—found no evidence of gender differences in the rates of sending sexts, receiving sexts, or forwarding sexts.[40] There are several possibilities for this apparent discrepancy between the research findings and dominant public narratives about sexting. As several authors of a large meta-analysis suggest, it's possible that the rates of sending sexts are similar because boys preemptively send sexts in the hopes of eliciting sexts in return.[41]

It's also possible that the behaviors occur with similar frequency, but the stories that garner attention distort our perceptions because girls are more severely shamed when their photos are leaked. There is compelling evidence that this may be the case. Peggy Orenstein's book *Girls and Sex* provides a powerful account of how girls experience a double bind related to their sexuality.[42] Girls are expected, even pressured, to be attractive, sexy, and responsive to male sexual desire. At the same time, they are vulnerable to being labeled a "slut" if they acquiesce. This is a lose-lose scenario for girls, whose own sexual desires are minimized or even irrelevant.

The themes Peggy Orenstein describes readily play out in how boys and girls experience sexting. Sexting researchers Julia Lippman and Scott Campbell describe boys as "virtually immune from criticism for their sexting practices" while girls are—as noted—"damned if you do, damned if you don't."[43] In our own data, we see that girls (especially middle school-aged girls, roughly ten to thirteen years old) are significantly more likely than boys to report that being asked for pictures is their top worry about digital life. What's more, a recent survey of nearly a thousand high schoolers conducted by Lauren Reed and her colleagues[44] also revealed that girls report feeling more pressure to sext, and more negative feelings related to sexting: girls were more likely than boys to say being asked for sexts and receiving them made them feel annoyed, creeped out, turned off, embarrassed, scared, and disappointed. In contrast, boys were more likely than girls to report feeling amused, happy, sexy, turn on, excited.[45]

In short: we think it's fair to say that girls are more pressured and shamed when it comes to sexting and nudes. However, it would be a mistake to assume only one of these roles (i.e., asker or sender) applies to adolescent boys versus girls. Of course many teens identify at other points on the gender spectrum. We have much more to learn about the opportunities and stresses nonbinary and transgender youth face related to sexting.

Our data do suggest that boys can feel distinct pressure related to sexting too. In addition to the kinds of social pressures already discussed, they may have their own body insecurities that are in tension with a perception that they should *want* to sext. Sixteen-year-old Pablo noted that some guys feel self-conscious about nudes because of penis size; Dante (also sixteen) acknowledged that musculature, hair growth, puberty stage—and considerations of girls' preferences related to all these things—can lead teen boys to worry, *"Whoa what if I'm not right?"* or *"What if I'm not good enough?"*

SEXTING HACKS: HOW GIRLS NAVIGATE A LANDSCAPE OF NO GOOD CHOICES

As our account reveals, the landscape of sexting can be a minefield for girls. If they decide to share nudes, protecting themselves requires inventiveness. Some girls use strategic moves to try to guard against damaging exposure. Teens told us that savvy girls know to crop out their heads, remove any identifying jewelry, and check the background of the shot for identifying details. Some even go further with steps like watermarking photos with the recipient's name in tiny text. This will be used as proof—if it's ever needed—of who is to blame for a leak. An age-old strategy, word of mouth also helps girls identify (and then warn each other about) boys who can't be trusted not to leak nudes. Girls learn: "*You don't send to that person, you don't, like, interact with them. Because they're creepy, they're kind of sketchy . . . you learn to stay away from [them].*"

Another strategy: If a girl feels especially uncertain whether the asker is trustworthy, she may find a body-only picture online that looks conceivably like it could be her. As Michelle explained, she'll want to take a screenshot that clearly shows the picture in a search result. Then, she needs to send the screenshot to a few trusted friends to ensure they can vouch for the picture not being hers. If the boy ever leaks the pic, she then has deniability: she can honestly say it isn't her. If people don't believe her, she and her friends have the receipts to back it up. This might seem like a lot of effort and admittedly involves duping the requester, who may be looking for intimacy and have no intentions of leaking an image. But when girls feel like they have no good choices, they get creative.

LEGAL CONSIDERATIONS

A further consideration is potential legal ramifications for minors, especially since some of the content we're talking about falls under the category of child pornography. The headline is: It's complicated and frustratingly unpredictable. As of this writing, there are no U.S. federal laws on sexting. Laws vary by state: about half of the states have laws on the books that explicitly address sexting, while the remainder do not.[46] To further complicate things, there may be discrepancies between what is technically possible to prosecute and what law enforcement officers are actually doing. For example, a given state's laws may be written in such a way that a teen taking a naked photo of himself and sending it to his girlfriend can arguably constitute creation and distribution of child pornography. Under current Massachusetts law, minors can technically be charged with a felony offense (distribution of child pornography) for sending nudes.[47] Much is left to the discretion of the investigating officers and the district attorney, which makes it hard to predict what will and won't land teens in legal trouble.

Nonconsensual forwarding of others' pictures is a bit of a different story, at least in terms of legislation. Almost all fifty states are considering or have already passed laws that recognize the seriousness of what is commonly referred to as "revenge porn" and provide paths for legal recourse.[48] In 2017, Massachusetts Governor Charlie Baker proposed a bill focused on distribution of explicit photos without the subject's consent and with intent to cause emotional distress. Penalties for minors include a mandatory "educational diversion program" and potential filing of felony charges, at the discretion of the district attorney.[49] With legislation like this either in place or on the horizon, distributing others' pictures is not only a moral issue, but also potentially a legal one. But how adults talk about these uncertain legal risks with teens—and to what effect—is key. Especially as sexting becomes more prevalent, heavy-handed messages about worst-case scenarios may amplify anxiety or regret without equipping teens to navigate the real sexting pressures they face.[50]

HOW ADULTS RESPOND WHEN SEXTS CIRCULATE

The messages that well-meaning parents and educators convey about sexting, and the ways we respond when sexting situations arise, often place emphasis on the person who sent a sext in the first place. Teens hear: "Sharing inappropriate photos with someone can have lasting effects if those photos are shared online." "Never, ever put anything online/send anything that you wouldn't want everyone to see."

These cautions are understandable since many parents worry about their own teens playing featured roles in a sexting scandal. Yet in so doing, we may unwittingly contribute to a "blame the victim" mentality. In our surveys of more than 3,600 U.S-based youths, most teens (59 percent) agreed with this statement: "If someone sends a naked picture to someone else, it's their own fault if the picture ends up getting shared with other people" (25 percent of teens disagreed and 16 percent were undecided). This aligns with multiple studies that suggest victim blaming is widespread in cases of sexting.[51] Perhaps teens who blame the sender reason that because creative strategies exist, senders who fail to use them are irresponsible. Or perhaps they reason that privacy is forsaken in a networked world and leaks are par for the course. Or perhaps they simply get caught up in the scandal. Importantly, young people who tend toward victim-blaming mentalities are also more likely to forward on others' images without consent.[52] It's not hard to see how the thinking goes: if it's your fault for sharing the picture in the first place, I'm not to blame for simply passing it along.

We also asked teens to respond to a dilemma about a parent who accidentally sees a series of private and sexual messages on a teen's phone, including whether it would be okay or not for the parent to tell the other teen's parents. Tweens were the most in favor of adult involvement but had a lot to say about how. We heard a plea for adults to slow down and clarify the situation before jumping to assumptions or rushing to alert authorities or confiscate devices: Was this consensual, wanted, pressured? If pressured, then what might be at risk and how could adult intervention help versus amplify teens' stress?

Many adolescents see a place for adults in helping them manage sexting. Middle school girls in our study described their inclinations to turn to trusted adults in the face of unwanted sexting requests. Understandably, the roles teens hope adults will play change as teens get older. Especially where tech and sex are concerned, older teens (appropriately) crave more privacy and autonomy over their relationships. But this doesn't mean there's no need for positive adult support.

Relevant here is a powerful set of insights from research by Jennifer Hirsch and Shamus Kahn. Based on their in-depth study of sex and sexual assault on a college campus, Hirsch and Kahn unpack the varied and often complex reasons for engaging in different sexual activities. Young people's sexual decision-making, they find, can have a fraught "trial and error" quality to it; at times it's pleasurable, at times it induces regret and shame.[53] Adults are implicated in the latter. The young people they interviewed described their parents as downright avoidant of conversations that acknowledged sex as a meaningful or valuable aspect of life. In so doing, these adults missed opportunities to discuss the moral dimensions of different sexual endeavors and how they might fit or depart from personal values.[54] Young people turned to other sources of information to fill the gap, namely peers and pornography. Hirsch and Kahn offer an expansive vision of how peers, parents, educators, schools, and policies can support "sexual citizenship: the recognition of one's own right to sexual self-determination and an equivalent right in others."[55] This vision is all about both respecting rights and creating a sense of agency, which applies to sexting and more.

Understanding that teens' sexting decisions are made amid a complicated mix of desires, tensions, and pressures is crucial. Even in cases where a teen's sexting is consensual and wanted, there may be good reason for conversation—at a minimum to discuss the many ways the digital context can undercut their ability to control and consent to who sees the pictures. For example: even if they trust their partner implicitly, a picture might be stored indefinitely on an app's server or accessed and leaked by another person without their or their partner's permission. Acknowledging both inherent digital risks *and* the reality that teen sexting may happen regardless has prompted some experts to advocate teaching safe sexting practices. Echoing what we heard from teens: avoid sending photos with your face or identifying information; turn off location and delete other metadata that might attach to photos automatically; and collect evidence of being pressured or blackmailed if possible.[56]

"THE PORN CRISIS"

When we initially wrote this chapter, we mentioned porn only in passing. Largely due to our study design, we had little direct data from teens on the topic. One discussion with our teen advisory council surfaced the view that pornography can fuel an interest in sexting: "*It's an addiction from adult videos. So from watching those so much, they get bored of it. And they're just like, 'I want more. I'm bored now, like this isn't interesting no more.' So, then they go and they start asking for nudes or sending theirs.*" But we had little else to share about teens' perspectives, and we worried about speaking beyond our data.

Then, we had a wakeup call. We attended a virtual conference where pornography expert and researcher Gail Dines spoke about the landscape of Internet porn and how it's changing teen sex.[57] Frankly, we were stunned at how much we had missed by not more intentionally exploring "the porn crisis."[58] Kids and teens have easy access to free, hardcore porn and many find this content for the first time by accident.[59] What they see is dominated by violence and aggression. Content analyses of porn scenes reveal that nearly 90 percent contain aggressive acts toward women.[60] Dines pointed to research that found gagging, strangulation, rough anal sex, spanking, hair pulling, and more as routine features of porn.[61] Women are typically the targets of physical aggression, and they rarely exhibit negative reactions to it on screen.[62] Consent is portrayed as murky, often nonverbal, and assumed in the absence of explicit resistance or a verbal no.[63]

Practically, this all means that curious teens who are seeking content like naked bodies or breasts may quickly become audiences for violent depictions of sex and ambiguous messages about what counts as consent. Watching porn can distort sexual expectations and shape perceptions that aggressive behavior is just part of sex.[64] At age nineteen, singer Billie Eilish offered a poignant personal reflection about this very phenomenon. In her words: "I started watching porn when I was like 11. . . . I feel incredibly devastated that I was exposed to so much porn. . . . The first few times I, you know, had sex, I was not saying no to things that were not good. It was because I thought that's what I was supposed to be attracted to."[65]

Pornography is a notable feature of the digital landscape. Teen interest in sexting and the way it plays out—pressured, consensual, or nonconsensual—may be shaped by messages absorbed from their own (or their peers') exposure to porn. This amplifies the importance of intentional sex education that incorporates media literacy and explicit conversations about consent, respect, and agency. Don't overlook porn in conversations with teens: they need to know about its lasting, distorting impacts on their sexual expectations.

TEENS WANT ADULTS TO KNOW

Teens want from adults a recognition that sending nudes is, in some contexts, *"part of teen culture."* They need us to acknowledge the difference between consensual and nonconsensual situations, and to recognize that sexting becomes nonconsensual the second a picture is seen by an unintended viewer.

Teens want us to know that they find it *"ignorant," "not practical,"* and *"not realistic"* when adults say, "Just don't sext!" It's not that they want adults to leave it all alone—to the contrary their advice to adults on this front is clear: *"just ignoring it—that's not going to help anything."* But they need adults to enter these conversations with an openness to seeing the real complexities they face. This includes how vexing it can be to say no, and how real the consequences might be for them when they send *and* when they don't. Girls especially want us to appreciate the no-win situations that can leave them feeling trapped. They want parents of boys to emphasize the unacceptability of asking girls for nudes.

Teens want adults to know that the social consequences of leaked nudes are bad enough without adults layering on further punishments for the person whose picture was shared; what that person truly needs is support. As one teen put it: *"the focus should be on why would [someone] send around somebody's pictures? Why would you do that? Because that is, I think, a greater evil."* In that spirit, teens want *"better privacy laws"* when it comes to pictures forwarded without consent.

In the meantime, they ask that we go beyond alarmist "don't sext!" school assemblies and provide more comprehensive interventions. In their view, it would help for all teens to understand legitimate risks *and* learn strategies that build agency for responding to real sexting dilemmas.

6

THE POLITICAL IS (INTER)PERSONAL— AND VICE VERSA

In mid-June of 2020, a viral video trend surfaced on TikTok: teens and young adults doing the Macarena in front of screenshots of ticket confirmations to a Trump campaign rally. "I just registered for Trump's rally, and I'm so excited—to not go," one TikToker declared. Another posted, "Oh no, I signed up for a Trump rally, and I can't go." The grand prank sought to mobilize a mass audience to register for tickets to the rally with no intention of attending, leaving Trump to speak to a largely empty auditorium. In the end, while Trump's campaign manager declared that one million tickets were requested on their website, Tulsa city officials reported that fewer than 6,200 people attended the event in a stadium that seats 19,000.[1] Notably, the TikTok prank was organized and carried out by a perhaps unexpected group: young K-pop (Korean popular music) fans and others whose content comprises "Alt-TikTok." (Alt-TikTok is used colloquially to refer to pockets of the app where alternative content circulates: this is *not* where verified TikTok stars like Charlie D'Amelio are dancing.)

Whether or not you consider the TikTok Tulsa caper a political win, the story points to the savvy and creative ways teens leverage social media to participate in and even lead civic actions.[2] It stands as a signature example of how popular culture, social media, and politics can collide in unexpected ways, highlighting how online communities—even those like K-pop that are not explicitly civic—have power that lies in wait to be tapped via the right (or wrong) digital invitation, meme, or trend. In this chapter, we use the term "civic" in a broad sense to reference any issues that are relevant to public life. We see civic *actions* as inclusive of political participation (e.g., voting) as well as efforts to discuss, raise awareness about, protest, and propose solutions to community concerns and societal issues.[3]

While some might dispute the idea that the TikTok prank constitutes civic engagement at all, it points to a kind of participatory practice that warrants attention. A decade of research on digital life highlights new potentials for youth civic agency but also new puzzles. Our own studies on this topic have surfaced an array of digital civic opportunities that youth acknowledge to be meaningful, powerful, *and* vexed.

Consider another way electoral politics and polarization unfold in teens' online worlds—through online polls. Quizzes and polls are a common feature of social media life, often used for entertainment ("Which *Games of Thrones* character are you?") and feedback ("Which dress should I wear to the prom?") Polls are also used by teens to take a pulse of their peers' attitudes, including views on political candidates. In the fall of 2020, polls asking "Who are you voting for (or supporting): Trump or Biden?" circulated on Instagram and Snapchat and teens and young adults collected votes from their audiences.

The way individual followers vote in an Instagram poll is generally viewable only to the person who created the poll. Poll results are typically revealed to others as a high-level summary with votes and comments anonymized. For example: results from a "Nicki Minaj or Cardi B?" poll would be displayed in aggregate, as something like "Nicki: 65 and Cardi: 35," perhaps with added commentary like "Nicki slays!" But data from polls can sometimes have a second, more public life.

In the lead-up to the 2020 presidential election, sixteen-year-old Ruby saw videos popping up on TikTok that used poll data from Instagram to expose people who supported a certain candidate. For example, after teens created and posted polls asking questions like "Biden or Trump?," they used the data to create video mashups. The mashup videos would begin, "Here are the people who support Y," followed by strategically curated, rapid-fire photo compilations of candidate Y supporters. The strategy was typically something like this: screenshot and use only unflattering pictures of candidate Y's supporters, and only flattering pictures of X's supporters. The resulting compilation made teens' stances public with a clear message that those who support the creator's preferred candidate are superior and attractive, and those who support the other candidate are comparatively ugly or uncool—or both.

Ruby shared the strong majority view in her community, so it wasn't that she feared her personal candidate preference would evoke backlash if made public through a mashup. Rather, the weaponization of social media in this way—and its contribution to what felt like growing polarization among her peers—made her uneasy.

This story is another example of how social media is a dynamic and contested space for youth engagement, including with electoral politics. It also begins to surface tensions that today's teens give voice to as they navigate contexts where the personal and political are increasingly, often painfully, intertwined.

The powers to copy, paste, remix, and spread content across platforms and audiences are now well-recognized.[4] Yet these affordances intersect with new social expectations linked to current civic realities. At the time of this writing, a global pandemic has gripped and, in many respects, paralyzed the world. In the U.S. context, we see heightened attention to racism and racial injustice. In January 2021, we also bore witness to a volatile presidential election and the storming of the U.S. Capitol building by insurrectionists. Then, in August of the same year, the world watched the Taliban's takeover of Afghanistan. These realities played out with social media as indispensable venues for documentation, mobilization, and collective processing.

SLACKTIVISM AND HASHTAG ACTIVISM

The big idea that social media are civic and political spaces isn't really contested at this point, especially as a recent U.S. president used Twitter as his main communication channel. What is contested is how these channels contribute to civic life and their impact.

In the late 2000s, the term "slacktivism" (or slacker activism) came into parlance.[5] In 2009, writer Evgeny Morozov described it as "an apt term to describe feel-good online activism that has zero political or social impact. It gives those who participate . . . an illusion of having a meaningful impact on the world without demanding anything more than joining a Facebook group."[6] In a subsequent *New Yorker* article in 2010, Malcolm Gladwell proclaimed that "the revolution will not be tweeted," casting social media posts as lightweight and inconsequential, especially compared to high-burden and high-risk forms of protest of the past. (The 1960s lunch counter sit-ins protesting racial segregation in the South were Gladwell's case in point).[7]

As researchers (including us) took up studies of online civics in earnest, it became clear that the story is much more complicated. First, political context is hugely important. As Zeynep Tufekci's research on networked protest in Egypt and Turkey shows, in repressive countries, tweeting can be "very brave" given the dangers of public political expression.[8] More generally, the role of the Internet in sharing information and mobilizing actions (even "thin" actions[9] like reposting information) is hard to dispute. An obvious example is use of e-petitions to mobilize mass support for civic causes ranging from "Stand with Law Enforcement" to "Stand with Our Teachers."[10] Even Morozov acknowledged that social media campaigns can raise awareness and, in some cases, considerable funds that can be deployed toward impact.[11]

The distinction between "voice" and "influence" offers a helpful, even if not precise parsing of recurring questions about online activism.[12] Indeed, influence or concrete impact often requires more than a compelling viral video, whether it be a poignant narrative about growing up in a racist world or a more explicit call to action to protect or limit gun rights. Specifically, achieving impact requires identifying the right levers (whether they be law or policy shifts or changes in social attitudes), sorting out how to apply strategic pressure, and mobilizing others to participate.

Yet, voice does matter—and in ways that go beyond the vital and empowering effects for individuals of "having a voice." In their book *#HashtagActivism* (2020), Jackson, Bailey, and Foucault Welles document the significance of social media—especially Twitter—for historically marginalized groups' efforts to build powerful "counterpublics." Key to this is the hashtag (#), an important platform feature that allows users to tap into broader audiences and contribute to "a larger collective storytell-ing."[13] While there is much work to be done to address racial profiling, identity-based discrimination, and sexual violence, hashtag activism has brought important voices and stories "from the margins" to the center. Even as racism and sexism persist in various forms, the #BlackLivesMat-ter and #MeToo movements drove visible shifts in public discourse if not some policies.[14]

Early critics cast online civic posts as "clicktivism": thin and "easy" moves that merely give the poster a sense of self-satisfaction that they're doing something. But it's always been more complicated than it seems.

YOUTH AND PARTICIPATORY POLITICS: NEW POWERS, NEW PUZZLES

One need not look far to find inspiring examples of how young people leverage digital tools for voice and influence. You may think of Greta Thunberg: the teen climate change activist named *TIME* magazine's 2019 Person of the Year and who, at the time of this writing, has five million-plus Twitter followers. But Thunberg has plenty of company from smaller players who are engineering big impacts. Examples of digital activism aimed at protecting the Arctic National Wildlife Refuge (ANWR) offer an illustrative case (see the "'Give the Animals and People a Voice!!!'" box).

Such examples of youth digital activism are captured by the term "par-ticipatory politics." These are "interactive, peer-based acts through which individuals and groups seek to exert both voice and influence on issues of public concern."[16] Digital media lower barriers to the public sphere, offering interactive and creative entry points for participation. Informal avenues for changemaking are especially relevant to youth who are not yet of voting age and whose voices may be sidelined in institutional poli-tics and policymaking.[17]

Naming the particulars is important. Specific participatory practices include opportunities for civic inquiry, voice, dialogue about public issues, and mobilization of audiences to act on a given cause.[18] These practices are longstanding components of civic action to which digital technologies lend new powers. Opportunities for voice are especially notable in a context where youth can express themselves in authentic

"Give the Animals and People a Voice!!!"

In the fall of 2020, Alex Haraus, a twenty-three-year old climate activist and TikTok user, created a toolkit of digital content, pulling together images, video, and essential information about the Arctic National Wildlife Refuge (ANWR) and a key threat to its future: oil development interests.[15]

Table, if you can, your personal views about oil exploration. Our aim in highlighting this story is to show how social media creates a powerful context for young people to engage in public life via informal, yet impactful channels.

Haraus invited other TikTok users to draw on the digital content in authentic ways to further the campaign. The goal: mobilize a mass audience to flood the U.S. Fish and Wildlife Service (FWS) with letters during the official public comment period on the Trump administration's proposed oil exploration plan. Haraus's resources were ready-made with action steps laid out.

Sixteen-year-old Noah Dulay jumped right on it, creating a TikTok that asked viewers, "Want to see one of the most beautiful places on earth?" before cutting to images and video of polar bears, caribou, and other animals whose survival is at stake. Accompanying the images were his statements:

This is the ANWR (Arctic National Wildlife Refuge)!!!

It is being leased for oil drilling very soon!!!!"

We can save it, but here is why this place is so valuable!!!! It is home to hundreds of animal species including the 200,000 porcupine caribou that return to the coastal plains early for calving!!! It is also home to the indigenous people who have called ANWR home for so long!!!!

And here's how you can help!!! We need to send as many letters as we can!!!! In my bio I have the simplest way to send yours, so go write one and give the animals and people a voice!!!

Dulay's first ANWR TikTok received more than one hundred thousand views, which motivated him to make more. As a result, he was seen as "single-handedly responsible for tens of thousands of letters." The FWS ultimately received 6.3 million letters—far too many to process before Trump left office, effectively thwarting the oil exploration plan.

ways, producing and circulating meaningful content in formats ranging from punchy tweets to pointed memes and infographics.[19]

But the opportunities for civic voice are far more complicated than most adults realize and are relevant in everyday life, not just in extraordinary cases. This is the message we heard from today's teens again and again: the current context is riddled with social tensions that make online voice both an unavoidable consideration and unequivocally fraught.

REWIND

A brief rewind to an earlier state of play sets the stage. In 2011–2012, we set out to understand how civically engaged youth were tapping social media as part of their activism. We interviewed seventy young people (ages fifteen to twenty-five) who had varied civic interests and political views. We met teens like Gavin and Chen, both sixteen at the time. Gavin was involved in Organizing for America and a suite of other youth democracy initiatives. She also cohosted a cable TV show about politics. Chen was serving on a local politician's youth advisory council and active on the jobs committee. How, we wondered, did young people like Gavin and Chen who already had strong civic commitments navigate social media?

We coined the terminology of "blended," "bounded," and "differentiated" to capture what we found. Most used social media to share their views and signal commitment to their chosen causes. *Blended* described young people like Gavin, whose civic lives were an integrated feature of their online identities. Chen and others instead *bounded* their civic and political views, keeping them entirely offline—in effect, setting boundaries around this aspect of their identities. A third group adopted *differentiated* strategies that varied by platform. They might be unabashedly political on Twitter, but never on Facebook.

Young people weighed a variety of considerations as they decided how much, and where, to be civic online. Some of them were involved in civic organizations that required them to post as part of their organizational roles or instead prohibited from expressing anything potentially political online. Audience and reputational concerns played a role, too, as they considered such questions as: "How will my followers react if I post about this particular issue?" "Will I be praised, attacked, or just muted for trying to advance an agenda?" Some reasoned that social media is a powerful PR tool for civic action; others worried that their posts would be seen as self-promoting.

Overall, our most striking finding was that even those with deep civic involvements adopted quite different approaches when it came to social media.[20] Youth made this clear: blending was an option, and so too was bounding. Most young people chose to raise their civic voices online. Some did so unreservedly, while others limited their political posts to controlled audiences on specific apps. Still others remained silent on civic matters on social media despite their unambiguous civic commitments offline in school-based or community organizations.

When we followed up with the same people a few years later (specifically, in 2013), all were past high school, and some were well into the early years of their careers. Notably, their online civic expression had become quieter overall. Concerns about both online toxicity and leaving behind a politicized digital footprint were key drivers in what we referred to as a "hush falling over the crowd."[21] Other studies found similar dynamics, adding to a growing perception of social media as a "risky" space for political talk.[22] Choosing not to speak up seemed to offer a safer course.

WHAT DIFFERENCE DID ONE DECADE MAKE?

Fast forward to 2020–2021. Our original interviewees are now well into adulthood, but our research has continued, and other teens have stepped up as our tour guides through the landscape of digital civic expression. We can see what's endured, including anxiety about navigating a networked public sphere that is starkly polarized and often toxic. Scalability (the capacity to reach potentially large audiences via social media content) remains a game changer for civic agendas. The opportunities to share information and learn about issues are ever-present. And reckoning with the "digital afterlife" of online expression, civic and otherwise, is still a noted concern.[23]

Yet there is also something new: a widely felt set of social expectations means that being quiet online is difficult. The age-old expression "between a rock and a hard place" has a particular resonance as we listen to today's teens. There's a consensus among them that civic and political life has a clear, unavoidable digital dimension. And at once, digital life has an unavoidable civic dimension. Even teens who aren't civically active feel subtle and not so subtle pressures to take a public stand on current issues. What, when, and where they post—and, importantly, don't post—are all charged.

SILENCE IS TAKING SIDES

Teens feel pressured to signal awareness and support for timely issues on social media and even evidence that they're taking action on some level. The particulars of their experiences are unequivocally shaped by their identities, contexts, and the civic topic at hand. Yet the notion that social media creates pressure, and a sense that there are countless ways to "get it wrong," has broad resonance.

Case in point: Black Lives Matter.

The Black Lives Matter (BLM) movement intensified discussions of race and racism across the United States. Though the movement began years earlier, the 2020 murders of George Floyd, Breonna Taylor, and other unarmed Black Americans refocused attention to the long history of racial injustice and reenergized calls to action. This cultural and political moment is significant in its own right; it also provides an illuminating window into current complexities behind teens' screens. Instagram, TikTok, Snapchat, Twitter, and Facebook all offered crucial spaces for learning, voice, dialogue, mobilization, and coordination of actions ranging from fundraising to in-person protests. And teens from all racial backgrounds were active participants: liking, posting, or reposting expressions of outrage and impassioned calls to action often punctuated with strategic hashtags (for those supporting the movement, such hashtags included #BlackLivesMatter, #ICantBreathe, and #DefundThePolice). But behind these digital acts, big and small, teens grappled with a range of worries from the civic to the personal and social.

Being vocal on social media is a pressure felt across the board, but teens of color face particular burdens. Allahna, a high school senior who is a leader in her school's Black Student Union and identifies as Black/Haitian, recounts being caught up in the work of organizing protests and programming for her school. As a leader, she felt an implicit but distinct pressure to post on social media too, which frustrated her because many of the BLM social media posts that flooded her Instagram feed from her peers felt less than helpful and, in some cases, wholly disingenuous. She didn't really want to post, but others seemed to expect it.

Ashlyn is a Sri Lankan American teen with a keen interest in understanding the psychological roots of social injustice. Over the past year, Ashlyn developed a palpable sense that she needed to be "woke" to every injustice and post about every issue. This caused personal stress; plus, she wondered about the potential civic impact: "*I felt a pressure to post and use my platform like big or small to spread awareness about these issues. But later on, I felt like it was just not impactful.*" It also took a toll: "*[It started] impacting my mental health . . . it just felt like too much pressure.*" In a world where information is so easily accessible, teens repeatedly voice a sense that knowing everything about everything (and having an opinion on it) feels expected.

Oshun, who identifies as Ghanaian, is a natural leader and the eldest of nine in her family. She found that her Black peers were quite explicit about the obligation to post. "*Their little comments, their little captions would be like, 'If you don't post, you really aren't a Black person.'*" For Oshun, this pressure was productive and "*for a good cause, like the things that they pressure you to post are things that matter . . . life and death situations.*" And yet, she weighed a range of risks and considerations, amplified by the context of her largely White community. She explains, "*People in oppressed groups, people of color, in a White area, often think: 'Am I ready to post this?' knowing that I might get some backlash.*"

Oshun navigates a distinct sense of stress when she posts about BLM. She grapples with questions like: "*Are my friends gonna be offended by this? Am I comfortable losing those friendships about this? Am I comfortable being the person who speaks out for everybody else on this? . . . It will get to the teachers because someone will take a screenshot and send it to a teacher. The principal may talk to you about it. Am I ready for all that to come down for one post about Black Lives Matter?*"

Beyond the interpersonal risks, Oshun fears potential consequences that spill over to her school life and to adults in positions of authority. This worry has an even higher-stakes corollary in how youth of color are often subject to racialized digital surveillance by law enforcement officers who can now imperceptibly monitor teens' posts for possible signals about criminal activity. Officers can make judgments about *whose* social media activity warrants their monitoring.[24] The ways in which social media posts are subject to "policing" by both peers and adults clarify the stakes of online participation.

Oshun *wanted* to post—and ultimately, she did again and again because of her core commitment to the movement. Still, she had to calculate the risks. Other teens, like Allahna and Ashlyn, felt a shared and deeply personal commitment. Still, they would have preferred to stay quiet online but felt pressured to post.

White teens also experience pressures to signal that they care about and are acting on racial justice issues. And their White racial identities matter in how they proceed. Some prioritize civic impact and a sense of responsibility to speak out. As Maeve shared, "*I think if you have a platform, then it's really important for you to use it, especially if you're someone with privilege. I have a very small platform but as a White person, I think it's important to speak out [against racism].*" Other White teens struggled to find their footing, posting with a keen sensitivity to the risks of misstepping and being called out for it. Ruth Joy explained, "*It's almost like people are just ready to jump down your throat and tell you you're doing it wrong any way you do it. And it makes it hard to be like a good ally and be supportive and know what to do sometimes.*" Still others grappled less with the civic import of issues at hand and more with the immediate repercussions of posting and of not posting. As Jack put it, "*I think it goes both ways, you know, feeling scared to post something or feeling obligated to post something.*"

Winter (who identifies racially as Black and from a Latinx/Hispanic background) shared, "*I think if teens don't post, especially if you're White, it's a red flag because why wouldn't someone want to support people getting justice?*" In 1967, long before social media posting was a consideration, Dr. Martin Luther King Jr. proclaimed, "There comes a time when silence is betrayal." Adults may consider social media a distinct domain, optional and "extra credit" as a context for speaking up, at least as compared to in-person activism. A decade ago this may have been the case. But no such distinction exists for today's teens. Social media is a key venue for voice about all things. Silence on pressing issues can indeed feel like a betrayal.

And yet, finding the right balance between showing support but not grabbing the mic, so to speak, is crucial and again vexed. Jade, who is Indian, expressed frustration about posts by White teens that signal support but are ultimately "self-centering" or suggestive of "White saviorism" rather than uplifting the voices of people of color. For all teens, the under-a-spotlight quality of public social media posts and a larger cancel culture adds to the stakes. The proximal, interpersonal threats are especially front of mind.

FRIENDSHIPS ARE ON THE LINE

Based on our earlier studies of youth online activism, I (Emily) published a paper in 2014 titled, "The Personal Is Political on Social Media." The title played on a well-known saying about how one's personal life and choices have political significance. This remains true *and* teens' experiences in today's digital public sphere suggest that the inverse is also true: the political is interpersonal on social media.

Friendships have long been recognized as complicating factors in, if not an impediment to, discussion of political issues both in person[25] and in digital spaces.[26] But current social pressures to speak out about timely civic issues are palpable, putting friendships literally on the line. Teens judge and feel judged by friends and peers for the presence and absence of posts on trending civic topics. The when, what, where, and frequency of posts about civic issues are all under the microscope—and what is said and unsaid can reaffirm, strain, or break friendships.

Earlier, we quoted Oshun who puzzled about her friends' potential reactions as she crafted her own posts. Nanaa describes how some teens actively monitor their peers' posts—and what they see, or don't see, determines friendship status: "I had a lot of friends who are minorities and this summer, they were like, 'I'm watching . . . which one of my friends are reposting things and . . . if you haven't said anything about BLM, then you don't care about me and you're not my friend.' . . . people genuinely will break friendships over someone not like using their platform and like posting about it." While Nanaa doesn't monitor her friends in these ways, she understands the motivation. Echoing the theme of "silence is taking sides," she believes that "not picking a side is not an option because that means that you don't care."

The dominant beliefs in a teen's community (liberal, conservative, mixed) determine reception of posts and associated social consequences. Genevieve, a White teen who lives in an ideologically mixed community has publicly *"picked a side"* and suffered the (interpersonal) consequences. She lost not only thirty-plus followers, but also at least one friend. She explained, *"I never really spoke about human rights issues . . . and then when I did, I started to lose followers. . . . I've also had my stuff posted on other people's Private Stories and then they're saying mean things about me."* She recounted people who responded to tell her they disagreed with her or even to inform her their friendship was over: *"I posted something supporting Biden and this girl on my swim team swiped up and she was like, 'oh, like, I'm not gonna be friends with you anymore' . . . and I have not talked to her in months because this happened like a while back, and she just hasn't talked to me."*

Ruby's story about TikTok posts to expose people's political beliefs was part of a broader climate of intolerance for peers who weren't politically liberal; in Genevieve's case, it was her liberal views that were out of step with her peer group and caused interpersonal issues. Despite the obvious social costs, Genevieve persisted, sustained by the belief that the issues are bigger than her: *"I have to post . . . because, like, I feel like things need to be said . . . things need to be shared. . . . Things need to change in the country."*

PERFORMING FOR (LIKE-MINDED) OTHERS: BEING WOKE AND BEING GOOD

The same kinds of posts that cost Genevieve friends and followers have a different reception and meaning for teens in less ideologically diverse contexts. This ties into another social fact: posting that is controversial in one context can be performative in another.

For example: Jack's Instagram followers largely share his views so when he posts, he says, *"I'm not expecting any controversy . . . zero pushback."* Graham describes his community and his audience as similarly ideologically homogeneous, which is why he sees political posts as simply *"feeding a fed horse."* In these cases, whether online posts will impact the issue they care about is not the material question. At the end of the day, their digital posts are about creating or maintaining a public image as *"a good person"* with the *"right"* views in front of a vigilant, like-minded audience.

Strategic curation of teens' online identities for peers and other audiences is ongoing[27] and alertness to one's civic self-presentation is now an essential component. Among the qualities teens feel pressure to perform is being up on the news and more generally woke. Recall Ashlyn, who expressed how a need to be woke to *"all the situations and injustices that are happening"* and post accordingly ultimately affected her mental health. Posting is a way for teens to signal awareness and moral goodness. As Jack explained: *"You have your political opinion public and everyone's like, 'Oh yeah, you're a good person and you know what you're talking about.'"*

PERFORMATIVE ACTIVISM

It may be unsurprising, then, that the term "performative activism" is well known to today's teens as a common allegation and ongoing source of struggle. It goes both ways. Teens interrogate the authenticity of peers' civic posts while puzzling over how they themselves can be authentic.

Knowing what's authentic versus performative on social media can be hard to pin down. Teens nonetheless often feel, rightly or not, that they can decipher the authenticity of peers' posts.

Easy forms of digital activism are quickly labeled as performative, and at times they are. "Tagging chains" are a prime example. Participating in an invitation to "tag six of your friends who also believe in Black Lives Matter" requires minimal effort and shows little evidence of further commitment to a cause. For Jade, these tagging chains both *"trivialize the movement"* and are ultimately self-centering: *"it's a way to subtly bring attention back to yourself rather than truly to the movement at hand."*

The presence or absence of actionable information in a post can be seen as a further indicator of authentic commitment to an issue versus paying lip service. Teens take notice when posts express outrage about an issue or indicate moral support but don't include links to news, information about a rally/protest, an e-petition, or a site to collect donations for the cause. As one teen put it: *"If you're not posting to, like, actually help those situations then are you really even doing anything?"*

As teens read peers' posts for signs of performativity, they triangulate with other data, both from their in-person interactions and the person's posting history. Who continues to post about issues? Who shows up to post when a topic is hot but then exits once the moment has passed and they *"stop caring about looking good"*? Lil Ronny says he can tell *"who are the people who fake it"* versus those who are committed. *"Because there's people who would show up [to the protest], take a couple of pictures, be like, 'oh yeah everybody pop out' and then they leave. And then there's . . . the people who walk at least over two, three miles for a cause and actually go ahead and pursue that change."* Teens take quick notice, too, of misalignment between how some people act in school (*"who's standing up for oppressed groups?"*) and what they're posting online. Other studies of teens' experiences also suggest sensitivity to "fake wokeness," meaning posts shared mainly to impress others.[28]

Attempting to suss out performativity online seems almost reflexive, and it likely has roots in identity development.[29] In a pre-Instagram world, Nakkula and Toshalis described the friction between adolescents when peers observe what they see as differences in behavior across contexts: "Why are you like that with them but like this with me? Which is the *real* you?"[30] Social media is yet another context where adolescents are under the watchful eye of peers who take quick note of any potential inconsistencies. And yet, this is a puzzle for teens who are in the very process of developing their own views and civic identities, still learning about new issues and finding their footing as they learn to articulate personal stances.[31]

In the digital public sphere, it doesn't seem to take much to create friction. For example, posting about a civic issue if one hasn't before might be judged by peers as discrepant and inauthentic. What seems inauthentic may indeed be a shallow attempt to avoid social censure. Or, what appears like a random jumping "right on the bandwagon" may instead be first steps in a young person's trajectory of building a civic identity.

POSTING OUT OF TURN

Today's teens confront two truths: posting can be a must and there are countless ways to get it wrong—being seen as inauthentic or performative is just one way. Again, the particulars vary based on teens' identities and contexts, yet the sense that both risks and pressures abound is cross-cutting. This tension is heightened by observing, if not directly experiencing, fallout from misposts. Teens name several distinct ways in which they or their peers have stumbled.

Timing (*when* teens post certain content) is crucial and complicated. Flagrant missteps include posting of frivolous and self-focused content when urgent issues are unfolding. Here, the person who misposts is (or at least appears to be) completely oblivious to events in the wider world. One teen at a large, suburban high school posted a selfie at the beach that would have, on any other day, received just a steady stream of likes and even over the top praise. But the beach selfie was posted just a few days after George Floyd was killed.

The blowback was severe and highly public. The post caused a full-blown *"scandal"* among students that unfolded largely in the Instagram comment thread where critics of the post clashed with close friends of the teen. A vocal group bashed the post for being disrespectful and simply wrong, while others defended the post and pushed back on critics' harsh tone and personal attacks. This incident makes visible the undeniable relevance of civic life to teens' social media lives in general. It also points to shifting norms about when it's appropriate to post certain content and the role of technological affordances. The timestamp affixed to online posts serves as a visible and persistent record of the misstep. And deleting the post does little to expunge the evidence in a context where screen-shotting and reposting is easy and a go-to strategy for accountability.

Even when the content of a social media post is decidedly civic, teens can stumble by posting about the wrong issue at the wrong time. Nanaa shared how this plays out in her networks: *"There's always an argument about like, 'Oh, why are you focusing on that issue right now? Because this like this [other] one is more pressing, and this is what we all need to be focusing on and putting our resources towards.' . . . People punish each other when what they're passionate about isn't on trend. So activism for issues which might not be as mainstream is much harder to achieve because people feel like they're not supposed to be speaking about that right now."* Here, Nanaa points to individual and civic costs associated with a world where myriad civic issues compete for attention and—in certain contexts, at certain moments—there are "right" and "wrong" issues to give voice to.

Even when a post hits the marks of being the "right" content at the right moment, dilemmas abound and it's easy to slip up. Posts can intentionally or unintentionally trivialize movements, can be read as self-indulgent or self-centering, can hint or even strongly suggest White saviorism, and more. And yet, again, being silent on a burning issue is seen as taking sides.

Teens observe, and express varying levels of dismay about, the public shaming and social outcasting of peers who misstep or just hold views that are out of step with their peers. Online bullying and even physical violence like getting "*jumped*" are cited outcomes for voicing the "wrong" beliefs on social media. As teens contend with a range of pressures and risks, a broader cancel culture looms.

THEY'RE CANCELED

Cancel culture or "call out culture" refers to a dynamic by which individuals are canceled, in effect socially exiled, for stepping out of line in some manner. Whether the infraction is online (an offensive tweet) or "in real life" (a verbal rant toward a neighbor or stranger that gets recorded), digital and social media are central to cancel culture. The same technologies and participatory practices that facilitate broader civic actions are leveraged to call out the perpetrator. Digital evidence is often circulated far and wide. It gets reposted in comment sections on the person's latest posts. The canceled person's infractions may even be compiled into videos or detailed on designated accounts.

Public figures, influencers, and celebrities are common targets of cancellation. Their social media blows up as they are shamed for offensive conduct, past or present, along with implicit or explicit calls for others to unfollow or "deplatform" them (i.e., mass unfollowing as a means to cut their audience). Examples abound. In late 2019, popular author J. K. Rowling faced a backlash for tweets identified as transphobic. Harry Potter book sales subsequently dropped precipitously, and some fan fiction sites scrubbed the author's name from their forum.[32]

In this way, cancellations can be seen as a "cultural boycott" and a mechanism for holding elites accountable.[33] As Zeynep Tufekci argues, a "social-media fury" is sometimes "protesters' only tool of deterrence against wrongdoing by the powerful."[34] Some teens agree and endorse the idea that cancel culture is a valuable tool or at least "a necessary evil." It's *"a way we can hold celebrities accountable. . . . There are some social media influencers/celebrities who I think have actually learned and improved . . . without cancel culture they would have continued with their other beliefs."*

Although such cancellations have a clear civic agenda, the phenomenon of cancellation has also drifted toward infractions that may be better characterized as drama. A high-profile example: In the spring of 2019, beauty influencer and "CoverBoy" James Charles was declared canceled by fellow influencer Tati Westbrook after endorsing a rival vitamin product. An online feud ensued that included damning personal attacks and false allegations. In the drama, Charles lost millions of followers, although once the dust settled, his platform recovered.[35] This kind of mission creep leaves some teens skeptical. Seventeen-year-old Michelle explained, *"Cancel culture started with maybe good intentions of trying to call out people that have done wrong things but [now] it's, like, confused. It's diverted from its original purpose. Now there's like people who are getting canceled for very minor things."*

Whether cancel culture is an effective tool for accountability and justice, a reasonable way to motivate real change, or simply a drama machine is subject to debate. Yet its relevance to digital civic life is not. Although some teens perceive cancel culture as only relevant to influencers and others with massive online platforms, the phenomenon is observed among everyday people, including teens.[36] A number of teens in our research recounted attempts to cancel peers for offensive speech in class or online. Some raised questions about the efficacy and value of such efforts: *"How does that help in the long term? How does that help them understand?"*

Whether teens risk cancellation on a large or small scale, the threat can amplify the stakes of online posts that, as noted, are already pressured as is. More generally, these realities complicate once again the broader claim that online activism is easy.

THE THIRD RAIL: IS IT OKAY TO LISTEN TO THE OTHER SIDE?

As we were working on this chapter, we used our typical approach: drawing on our own recent data, past research, and the literature, and then circling back to review our interpretations with teens. One of these conversations—with four teens who were part of our advisory council—grew so heated that when it ended, we called an impromptu, late-night research team meeting to debrief. Perhaps because we knew that the four teens shared similar (liberal) political views, the intensity of the exchanges caught us off guard.

This was the crux of the conflict: is it okay to listen to the other side? As we continued to explore this issue, it proved such a volatile faultline that we started to think of the question as a third rail.

The sense of urgency around certain identity-based civic issues is certainly at play here. Some teens are of the mind that hearing out the other side is risky when human rights and lives are at stake. Maeve put it this way: *"It's hard to have conversations when their side is that you don't deserve rights. It's hard to hold a dialogue when the other side is just against you as a person."* Adrian couldn't bear the thought of it: *"Why should I take anything they say into consideration if they don't consider other people's lives? If they're not respecting other people's lives, then why should I respect what they say?"*

Still other teens expressed dismay about a felt climate of intolerance that social media can exacerbate. Diego described a climate at his school whereby *"If you don't agree with us, then you shouldn't have a voice."* He saw this dynamic reflected online where *"a lot of voices are suppressed. . . . I know people who are conservative and don't post because I think they're kind of afraid to be shut down and canceled. Personally, I'm someone who's on the left but I also want to hear from other people's perspectives and I don't get to."* Graham echoed this concern: *"I just feel like we shouldn't shut people out just for their beliefs and I feel like my experience on social media has kind of made me shut others out."*

Teens' polarized perspectives on the acceptability of listening and dialogue play out among adults too. Features of the current political moment (particularly the stakes associated with issues like racial justice) may be relevant to some teens' reluctance to talk across perspectives. Interestingly, studies show that listening to the other side comes at a cost: it can sap motivation to go to bat for one's own side.[37] From a civic development perspective, dialogue across perspectives *and* experiences with civic action are both important.[38] But they don't always mix well.

Filter bubbles are created and reinforced by algorithms that personalize digital experiences, including newsfeeds, ads, and recommended content.[39] These algorithms can pull teens into insular pockets of the Internet based on budding beliefs and interests. The downsides of being stuck in an echo chamber or pulled into a conspiracy theory are self-evident. Some teens who recognize them try to strategically outsmart, reeducate, or hack the algorithms behind their feeds (searching, for example, for different kinds of content to reshape what they see). These efforts to hack the algorithm have limited success. At the same time, teens acknowledge upsides of echo chambers, including the ways that going deeper into an issue sharpens one's understanding and stance in a community of like-minded people. For teens like Maeve and Adrian, the echo chambers are almost a source of self-protection since seeing what feels like personal attacks on their feeds seems to erode a sense of well-being. And yet, the algorithm acts as a consequential Harry Potter–esque Sorting Hat, using an invisible logic to send people in different directions that have profound implications for what they see and what they don't.

TEENS WANT ADULTS TO KNOW

The breaking news for us in our latest round of research is that avoiding politics is no longer an option. Listening to teens, we heard a lot about what's hard: about pressures and challenges, about interpersonal tensions and consequences, about being authentic versus performative, about echo chambers and intolerance.

We also heard the same questions adults often weigh in the current polarized context: How can social media enrich versus undercut civic life? What information can I trust? How much of an echo chamber am I in? Is it ok to listen to the other side and on what issues?

But, make no mistake, we also heard about the positives. These emerge loudest and clearest when we asked teens, "What do you wish adults understood about teens' civic and political lives on social media?" Here are a few examples that encompass themes we heard repeatedly:

I wish that parents knew that a lot can be learned and good conversations can be had online. (sixteen-year-old)

I am certain that if the internet did not exist, I would not be even close to as informed as I am today, nor would I be as intellectually curious. (seventeen-year-old)

I love having access to social media because it gives me a window into pieces of society, ideas, and people that I wouldn't otherwise have. (sixteen-year-old)

Adults need to understand our activism holds major significance in our lives. . . . If you choose not to care, you're living a life of privilege. Adults, in my opinion, should . . . uplift our voices and use their platforms to support the new upcoming generations— virtually and non-virtually. (seventeen-year-old)

But acknowledging the positives is just one step. Also on teens' wish list for adults to understand: the pressures and complications they face as they explore and express civic issues online.

I wish adults saw the transformation of activism [and] how it has manifested into peer pressure to validate your morality. A lot of parents encourage us to think for ourselves but the social climate does not always allow for that. (seventeen-year-old)

Adults need to understand the underlying pressures teens experience when trying to navigate politics/civic expression on social media. . . . I think adults need to acknowledge that it's difficult for us to feel informed and knowledgeable about topics when there is so much misinformation out there. They should also understand . . . the fear of posting about controversial topics that could potentially spread hate towards you. There are the pressures of not trying to be performative, but also trying to voice your opinion. I know a lot of people have stepped back due to their fears of being seen as a performative activist. Finally, I just think that adults need to recognize the impacts of this form of social [media] on our mental health and how we sometimes just need to take a break from it all. (fifteen-year-old)

This is their world: digital and civic, powerful yet pressure-filled, rich with information and misinformation. The personal is political on social media. The political is also profoundly interpersonal in today's networked world.

7

DIGITAL FOOTPRINTS THAT (MAY) LAST A LIFETIME

On a Friday afternoon in March of 2021, I (Carrie) received an inquiry from a reporter. The request was familiar. She wanted my insight about the latest public fall from grace prompted by digital evidence of a past indiscretion. In this case, a young rising star and impending editor in chief at *Teen Vogue* was compelled to resign before she even started. The offenses: racist and homophobic tweets from a decade ago.[1]

Flash back to the summer of 2017. We received an email from Harvard's Office of Admissions seeking guidance. It was just a few months after that office had rescinded offers of admission from ten accepted students for content posted in a "closed" (semi-private) Facebook group.[2] The group, dubbed "Harvard memes for horny bourgeois teens," contained disturbing memes shared by the new admits. The memes trivialized pedophilia, sexual violence, and genocide and featured explicit racist and anti-Semitic language. It was just the latest incident where digital evidence had called admissions decisions into question.

When we met their team, the admissions officers struck us as uniformly thoughtful, even if not all on the same page about how best to navigate such cases. They were genuinely perplexed by a core dilemma for competitive admissions in the digital era: How (if at all) should they be thinking about a young person's online presence as part of the admissions process? And what should they do when digital evidence is at odds with the character strengths they've tried so hard to assess through an applicant's recommendation letters, essays, and interview?

In this chapter, we dig into dilemmas of digital footprints, which arise in job decisions, admissions decisions, and more. Digital footprints are trails of content and information about each of us that exist and persist online. Because so much of teens' social lives and interactions is digital, there are enduring artifacts that document everything from casual banter and offhand remarks to momentary lapses of judgment and major missteps. Sometimes those major missteps feature language that veers into moral and ethical territory, as in the Harvard examples.

Digital artifacts of speech and behavior—transgressive and otherwise—are readily shareable with others. Posts can persist on the web for long periods of time. Screenshots of Instagram Stories, snaps, or text exchanges can be stored on others' phones indefinitely. In truth, no one knows whether, when, or how teens' digital posts will come back to haunt them. But the ever-present possibility looms large.

RUINED LIVES

Regardless of the soul searching we saw underway at Harvard's Office of Admissions, news outlets came to their own conclusions about the 2017 scandal and its upshot. The most cautionary of them was headlined: "Meet the 10 Harvard Students Who Just Ruined Their Lives: The lessons? Don't say racist, sexist, misogynistic stuff—and especially don't say it on the Internet."[3]

The possibility of such dire consequences is a key reason why adults give digital footprints so much airtime when they talk with teens. The potential of a revoked offer of admission to a prestigious college or "ruined lives," as that headline put it, hovers. It's obvious why we need to address the moral gravity of hate speech. But also important is the question of whether and how we, as a society, navigate digitally documented transgressions from the adolescent years.

This was one of our most difficult chapters to write because nearly every stance has implications that feel unsatisfying, if not unsettling on some level. To that end, we make this acknowledgment up front: we don't provide decisive answers so much as what we hope will be a useful reframe of digital footprint dilemmas grounded, once more, in teens' perspectives.

THE TROUBLE WITH "YOU ARE WHAT YOU POST"

More and more, children begin to hear about digital footprints starting in elementary school. As they move up through middle school and into high school, adults' messages become more pointed, even panicky. In the classroom, many of the strongest messages educators share about digital life emphasize the long and pernicious shadow of digital footprints. Just a few examples that we've captured in our research with teachers:

What you do online CANNOT BE ERASED.

Posting comments online is like shouting them on the town square, except that they NEVER go away.

You are what you post; now, tomorrow, and in the future.

These well-intentioned cautions are echoed at home by parents who double down on the warnings. Parents may relate to the mom who told us she emphasizes to her son that "he can get in HUGE trouble and ruin his entire reputation and future with one inappropriate text."

A core belief that is often behind these messages is that young people are oblivious or apathetic about the risks of their online posts. Ideas abound that "kids these days" have no concept of privacy, no understanding that their actions might have future impacts, and no sense of responsibility. In our own research, we hear adults lament that teens "don't think of the permanence" and "do not care about the future—they live in the now!"

Some adults blame themselves when teens misstep; it's seen as a sign that adults haven't been clear, loud, or forceful enough. And because digital misfires can be so very consequential, doubling down on messages about risks and repercussions therefore feels both rational and "right."

Such warnings are rooted in good intentions: above all, to protect young people. But good intentions are destined to fail when based on flawed assumptions. In this case, it's a house of cards built on the faulty belief that teens would act differently if only they truly understood the stakes.

"THERE'S NO GOING BACK"

In chapter 2, we revealed that teens' worries about digital habits and device dependence can sound surprisingly like adults' concerns. The same is true when we consider fears about digital footprints. Again and again, teens in our research articulated concerns about the digital after-life[4] of their online posts:

If you post one thing on social media, you can't get it back. If you mess up, you can't get it back. (sixteen-year-old)

Once something is said, posted, etc, it NEVER goes away. Even if you think it does. (twelve-year-old)

If you make one wrong move, u could destroy your life. (fourteen-year-old)

We couldn't help but wonder: is it just a few exceptional teens who happen to be alert to their digital footprints? We had amassed more than two hundred similar comments across our dataset. Still, we found ourselves wondering whether the teens who voiced this worry were qualitatively different from those who misstep. Is the young person who shared *"If you post one thing on social media, you can't get it back"* certain to avoid their own digital misstep?

We don't think so. As we dug deeper into the issue of digital footprints with teens, we started to grasp why even awareness about the permanence of posts and anxiety about misposts won't inoculate them from risks. Powerful forces are at play and often in tension. Teens are changing and the world is changing. Yet their online posts are poised to linger in ways that are often out of their hands.

A SCROLL DOWN MEMORY LANE

What will today's teens think later in life, when they are confronted with digital artifacts of their teen years? Researchers Brady Robards and Siân Lincoln were curious about this very question.[5] They interviewed twenty-somethings who were part of the first generation of young adults to grow up with a single social media site (Facebook) archiving their individual journeys coming of age. In each of these forty-one interviews, Robards and Lincoln used an original "scroll-back method" whereby young adults scrolled back through their Facebook timelines and narrated their reactions as they rediscovered old posts and tags.

Chief reactions included a sense of "panic," "urgency," and/or "anxiety" as people found that posts they had long forgotten (like pictures from nights out drinking) remained public or otherwise viewable to others. Scrolling back also at times resurfaced painful memories of traumas or difficult events. Yet for some participants, the process was profoundly positive—even "therapeutic"—as old posts created "memory 'sparks'" for revisiting joy or milestones.

It was evident that Facebook timelines served as important personal archives. Robards and Lincoln also came to appreciate how expectations that young people should take care of their digital histories by untagging and considering future ramifications can generate "intense pressure . . . and an implicit call to erase and sterilise normative youthful experiences of experimentation, celebration, rebellion, and figuring out their own boundaries."[6]

THE LIABILITIES OF LEARNING AND CHANGING

Even before they are adults scrolling back through artifacts of their adolescent years, teens describe a sense of stress about inevitable mistakes they've made in the past or are destined to make in the future. A high school senior lamented to us: *"Things I've said in the past don't define who I am now."* Another, younger teen (thirteen years old) voiced more anticipatory regret: *"I might say something accidentally ignorant and that will carry into my future."*

The collision of past, present, and future selves feels to teens both likely and worrisome. Imagine being a fourteen-year-old grappling with this reality: *"If someone posted something like three years ago and it gets pulled up—and the person gets blamed but is a whole new improved person—they get judged for something they did when they were younger [even though they] had no idea what they were doing at that age."*

Or consider feeling, like another thirteen-year-old does, that you are coming of age in a world where documentation is a given and development is itself a liability: *"If you are young and make a post that the older you would regret, it's too late. Especially if that post contains sensitive information. Someone or something has already saved it and stored it so that you have no way of deleting it."*

Teens acknowledge people's beliefs, values, and identities evolve over time. But they also recognize that one-off remarks or illicit photos leave lasting impressions. This engenders a fear that *"you will be remembered in a bad way forever."* The notion that life gets better after high school and painful experiences will be left behind seems implausible in this kind of digital world.

On one level, it may be comforting to hear that at least some teens have internalized adults' cautions about digital footprints. And yet, we know that teens still post things online that they shouldn't. How can teens be so clearly aware of risks and yet so vulnerable to taking them?

THE (DEVELOPMENTAL) DRAW OF THE DIGITAL

Part of the answer lies in the ubiquity of ongoing, rapid-fire exchanges on digital platforms. Reliable stats are hard to come by, in part since messages are exchanged across multiple platforms. But anecdotally, we hear that teens routinely send one hundred or more messages each day, many sent with immediacy *because* they are part of real-time conversations. With that many messages, it's just impractical to assume that every text will be carefully evaluated for all the ways it could be interpreted by anyone, anywhere, anytime. This kind of reflection is a high bar for anyone, but especially for adolescents who are primed to prioritize the chance for immediate peer connection over longer-term potentialities.

Plus, the opportunities for self-expression online meet the developmental impulse toward identity exploration.[7] As we've discussed in prior chapters, identity formation is a primary job of adolescence.[8] Sorting out who one is, could be, and wants to be happens through trial and error, by fits and starts. Since long before tweets and snaps, teens have found ways to openly express their emerging ideas about all things from pop culture to fashion to politics. Now, social media apps offer choice venues.

In the Internet's early days, chat rooms and forums lacked slick design features but offered opportune spaces for identity experimentation. They were also largely anonymous. As Sherry Turkle wrote in *Life on the Screen* in the 1990s, such "virtual communities . . . offer permission to play, to try things out."[9] In such spaces, young people could experiment with more assertive, flirtatious, or even offensive selves with no enduring consequences or trails.[10]

Today's apps (perhaps especially Snapchat and TikTok) similarly offer compelling and fun outlets for self-expression. Among the very best parts of growing up with today's technologies, teens say: *"being able to express yourself more, you have more of a voice"; "You can show your feelings through social media"; "We get to express ourselves to a world of people who may have the same interests."*

But the stakes have changed. Online anonymity is largely a thing of the past. As our colleague Katie Davis and I (Emily) have written about, the free-wheeling nature and low stakes of the 1990s Internet no longer exist in the same way.[11] For better and for worse, the current digital context is largely identifiable: online posts are now typically tied to one's "real life" name and identity.[12] To be sure, some people take pains to try and set up accounts anonymously, whether for positive reasons (like staying behind the scenes of a "Random Acts of Kindness" account) or malicious intent (like wanting to troll another person's Instagram posts with mean comments). Yet there's no guarantee that such accounts will stay anonymous: *"people know that it's so easy to find whoever started an account now."*

Even when teens are *offline*, there is an ever-present possibility that their behavior will be digitally captured by a peer with a smartphone. The result is a major shift. The inevitable ups and downs, awkward and even regrettable moments of development are documented with unprecedented thoroughness. Periodic changes to the design of social media platforms can make old posts even more readily searchable. On Facebook, for example, the shift to timelines made it easier to access old posts that would have previously required more time and "digging."[13]

Importantly, risks associated with identifiability aren't equitably distributed. The rise in "social media policing" and disproportionate surveillance of social media posts of Black and Brown people has been described as a digital version of racial profiling.[14] Although teens from all racial backgrounds may experience risks associated with their digital footprints, systemic racism amplifies threats for teens of color.

EFFORTS TO FLY BELOW THE RADAR

As teens try to balance the opportunities for self-expression with the risks of networked publics, some find ways to fly below the radar. We wrote in chapter 4 about danah boyd's concept of "social steganography" or teens "hiding in plain sight" by posting public messages with layered meanings.[15] To illustrate the concept, boyd shared the story of a teen who posted lyrics from an upbeat song. The lyrics were interpreted by her mother and broader Facebook audience as a sign that all was well. But the teen's close friends grasped the hidden meaning: she had broken up with her boyfriend. Such coded language can be protective. It facilitates audience segmentation (making posts interpretable to one's target audience but not to others).[16]

Teens hide out of plain sight online, too, with duplicate accounts and stratified audiences they use for self-expression. Not so long ago, teens talked often about Finstas. Short for "fake Instagram," Finstas are pseudonymous, secondary Instagram accounts. (To be clear: Finstas are *not* a formal feature of the platform as U.S. Senator Richard Blumenthal suggested during a 2021 congressional hearing. His question to Facebook's Head of Global Safety—"Will you commit to ending Finsta?"—was seen as a sign that politicians are woefully out of touch with the tech platforms they may well need to regulate. It quickly became fodder for memes.) A teen might set up a Finsta for the purpose of evading adult oversight and scrutiny. Or, a Finsta may be a space to post more freely for a circumscribed group of close friends, thus avoiding the judgment of a wider peer group. It can even be used to vet potential posts with a preliminary round of feedback before posting more widely on "main stage" accounts.

Adults can misinterpret any efforts to fly below the radar as a sign that teens are necessarily up to no good. But these practices aren't just about creating ways for inappropriate or problematic sharing. As in the song lyrics example, there are times when teens want to update only their closest friends. They recognize, as these examples showcase, that audience and privacy matter. Some teens use Finstas to share more playful and less performative slices of life with a trusted circle. Some have aspects of their identities that they share only with certain audiences or friends, and segmenting can help them differentiate self-expression. In 2016, I

(Emily) interviewed fifteen-year-old Lily for my dissertation research. Lily described her Finsta as a place where she could *"express myself more"* because there was *"definitely less judging."* While she took care about what she posted on her *"real"* account, her Finsta offered *"a safe place to rant about life 'cause it's all your friends."*

We heard about the same kinds of tactics from teens in our most recent research. But they talked mostly about strategic uses of Private Stories on Instagram and Snapchat. In these tightly curated inner circles (see chapter 3), teens similarly create a semblance of privacy and space for more authentic self-expression than feels possible in view of a larger peer group. Private Stories are thus the latest tools for creating a *"judgment free zone"* where teens can vent to friends or share random musings like *"how much I liked the taco I just ate."* Some sharing is benign but limited to close friends out of a desire to avoid *"polluting"* others' feeds with minutiae. The opportunity to share with close friends can also embolden more rant-y expressions that can cross a line. So, the featured content (and its consequences) may vary. But the overriding purpose—to speak to and with a circle of friends—is a constant. Even so, the privacy of private Stories is always tenuous given the ever-present possibility that any audience member screen-records or screenshots the content.

THE POWER OF PEERS

Both self-expression and peer connection are crucial to the process of identity development. Interactions with friends and peers aren't just a distraction or sideshow. They are central to healthy development, and adolescents are primed to seek them out. The possibility of gaining peer acceptance makes risky decisions more likely, which presents in the ways adolescents evaluate choices ranging from unsafe sex to cheating to stealing to reckless driving.[17] Research confirms a neural basis for this tendency, which is supremely relevant to digital contexts too. The sense of peer validation behind likes shows up in neural activity: specifically, the "reward circuitry" in the brain is activated when adolescents view social media posts with numerous likes.[18]

Adults often advise young people to look beyond the present moment and think about the future. A parent tells her teen, "Protecting your future is more important than a temporary 'like' on social media." This may seem like wise counsel. Yet, it trivializes what is more immediately meaningful to teens on a developmental and even neural level. Recall, too, that the prefrontal cortex (the part of the brain that handles self-regulation and thinking about the future) is still developing throughout adolescence.[19]

In sum: we know that peer influence plus normal brain development can fuel risk-taking. Add to this the expressive tools that social apps offer for sharing with an audience of peers and online misposts are to be expected. The chance to be seen as funny or to share something that might gain praise from peers is a strong pull. Even when teens are well aware of long-term risks, the power of peers is mighty. But we also need to face down a further complexity of networked life: teens' digital trails are not strictly of their own creation. This is another way in which adult warnings that focus strictly on personal vigilance miss the mark.

BEYOND THEIR FULL CONTROL

In their book-length exploration of Instagram, Tama Leaver, Tim Highfield, and Crystal Abidin emphasize the fundamental co-creation of digital footprints by other social media users.[20] A reality for adolescents today is that other people are coauthoring their digital footprints. As hard as a teen tries to project a certain image to the world (whether it be sarcastic, serious, or sexy) their friends and peers are ever poised to post a comment, picture, or video that portrays them in an entirely different light. This further complicates the task of managing one's digital footprint, as we heard from teens in our own research:

If someone posts something bad on my instagram, then it's there forever, even if i take it down. (twelve-year-old)

Someone would post something annoying and never delete it. (thirteen-year-old)

I could post something I don't want on the internet. Or a friend of mine could and I just don't like when things that have to do with me as a person are on the internet. (twelve-year-old)

Indeed, monitoring peers' posts for content about them is a key reason why some teens keep notifications switched on and devices within arm's reach.

Close friends may create codes, implicit agreements, or explicit pacts related to posting and tagging. These range from formal policies ("*My friend group has a policy where we always ask each other before you post a photo with somebody else in it*") to unspoken expectations that friends should know what their close friends would or wouldn't want shared. Such codes reflect sensitivity to the co-constructed nature of online identities. They also reflect a mindset that privacy is a deeply social matter in a networked world. Trust is key, but also fragile. When friendships go south, precarious pacts can be broken courtesy of leaked screenshots.

To be sure, the roles of friends and peers in co-constructing a teen's digital footprint are not always unwanted. Friends post pictures that can contribute to a desirable public image. And some teens proactively lean on their friends to project an image they *want* on view. Sharing embarrassing content may even be welcomed, as long as it's limited to a trusted audience (e.g., via Stories). "*I love to laugh at myself,*" one high school senior explained, "*and I trust my friends enough . . . where, like, they can post [embarrassing] stuff of me and I can post stuff of them.*" Our impression from years of interviews and observations is that this "*love to laugh at myself*" mindset emerges in the later teen years rather than in earlier adolescence. Though our data haven't enabled a formal assessment of age-related differences, well-placed trust in friends' judgments also seems to coincide with later high school years.

ADULTS AS (UNWANTED) COAUTHORS

With the very best of intentions, adults contribute to their children's growing digital footprints as they share both everyday moments and meaningful milestones. Parents may share ultrasound photos before babies are even born, like I (Carrie) did when I changed my Facebook profile picture to an ultrasound image of my second child. In one analysis of 289 #ultrasound images shared on social media, roughly one-third (34 percent) included visible information such as the mother's full name, baby due date, and location of scan. These personally identifiable details enable prenatal, identity-linked digital footprints.[21] Visual, digital personas thus start to form before a baby's first breath. Footprints are also co-constructed even past a person's *last* breath as others increasingly mourn by sharing stories, posts, and pictures on social media.[22]

In the interim, group affiliations can also produce an inevitable corresponding digital imprint. Adults from school and extracurricular groups participate in co-construction (typically with some form of parental permission). Sixteen-year-old Mary was frustrated when her school's account posted an embarrassing group photo of her and classmates in their costumes for a school play: *"My eyes are half closed and I was, like, half smiling. It was just so awkward and everybody else also was really awkward looking, you know, like eyes half closed. And they still posted it. And everybody was just like 'oh my goodness, please take this down' and they wouldn't. So definitely adults don't think about how those kinds of posts, you know, can influence kids and it's just like, 'Oh my gosh, that was so embarrassing.' It's still up on Instagram to this day."*

This may not seem like a big deal. But to teens, adults posting without their permission (even if it's just an unflattering photo) feels hypocritical. Adults often tell teens to take care about what is posted online, and to respect others' wishes about what is and isn't shared. When we promptly disregard their wishes in our own posting and sharing, it sends a mixed message. Echo, also sixteen years old, had plenty of experiences like Mary's: *"I've had like many, many instances of adults or my school post pictures of me that I would never post myself."* The irony isn't lost on her: *"I just think it's really funny when adults say, like, 'Be careful what you post' because like they're the ones who are posting the stuff that I don't want the world to see. Because I always think about, like, 'If I post this—is it going to hurt anyone?,' and 'Is it going to make anything worse for anyone?' And I just don't think the school or like the adults really consider that as much, in my experience. Other adults are posting stuff that I might not want online."*

COLLECTING RECEIPTS

Digital footprints can be co-constructed in other unwanted ways too. Consider a teen who rants to a small circle of friends or classmates in a group chat or Private Story. The rant might be about a peer, a teacher, or a political issue. It might contain language that is passionate but also offensive and hateful. It might be a "joke"—at least to the person sharing it. And it might be a source of immediate regret. Regardless, a small audience has seen it. Any one of them stands poised to leak it to a much larger, or at least unintended audience. Sometimes the stakes are considerable.

We touched in chapter 4 on the idea of receipts. Graham explained it like this: receipts are *"proof screenshots, screen recordings, [or] messages saved on Snap[chat]"* that provide evidence of an indiscretion. Digital affordances make such receipts possible. Routine screenshotting and recording make their collection likely. As one teen shared: *"Once you post something or do something, there's no going back. Usually there is one person who captures it, and then once it is online it can never be taken [back from] the hundreds of people who have possibly screenshotted it."* Another teen put it bluntly: *"Everything gets recorded."*

Consider fourteen-year-old Sarah's impulse to create a receipt of a peer's hateful speech *and* her hesitation share it, which are detailed in the "When Peers Hold the Cards" box. Both instincts are worthy of consideration. Digital technologies afford the creation of a persistent record of speech and behavior, both good and bad. This creates new opportunities for accountability following offenses but also new dilemmas. Indeed, the "right" course of action is subject to considerable debate—especially in cases involving adolescents.

Both teens and adults are often divided among themselves about the ethics of holding someone accountable for online posts created at a young age. We studied this very topic, including through survey questions that tap knee-jerk reactions to different issues.

In our research, we often ask people to signal agreement, uncertainty, or disagreement about statements like "It's fair for college admissions to consider applicants' social media posts" and "It's reasonable for people to face consequences later in life for posts shared in middle or high school." In 2018–2019, teens we surveyed were polarized; on both statements, there was no majority stance. We also asked about the statement "If someone makes an offensive comment on social media, people have the right to call them out—even if it hurts their reputation." In this case, a majority of youth (63 percent) tended to agree.[24]

Such scenarios surface questions about accountability and privacy rights, and tensions between them. Sarah was weighing this very tension:

When Peers Hold the Cards: Sarah's Story

Sarah, age fourteen, had an ongoing group chat with some eighth-grade class-mates who shared her interest in politics. She both enjoyed and was outraged by exchanges in the chat—especially with one boy whose ideological views consistently provoked her.

One day, he crossed the line, sharing a picture of himself smiling in front of a swastika. Incensed, Sarah saved the photo to her phone and weighed her options. Knowing that the boy had just been accepted to a prestigious high school, her immediate thought was to send the incriminating photo to the school. Shouldn't his new school know more about the true character of this student before he officially joined their community? Sarah showed her mom the thread and the picture and asked for her advice.

Ultimately, Sarah didn't end up sending the picture to her classmate's new school and the admissions committee never learned about the offensive behavior. But she still has it and is poised to bring it to light if and when it suits her. At best, the boy—only fourteen at the time—will come to under-stand in time the moral gravity of taking a selfie smiling alongside such a pernicious symbol of hate.

Of course, it easily could have gone another way. Had Sarah sent the photo to the admissions committee, her classmate may very well have lost his offer to attend the school—as the ten students accepted to Harvard did in the case opening this chapter. And still it might: what will happen if Sarah resurfaces the photo in the future? How could it impact him if, in twenty years, he is a beloved teacher, a religious leader, or a candidate for city council?

A Virginia teen sat on similar evidence (a Snapchat video) of a classmate's racist speech until he felt the moment called for its release: specifically, after the police killing of George Floyd sparked protests and widespread calls for racial reckoning. By that time, the featured student was a college-bound high school senior who swiftly lost her spot on the University of Tennessee cheer team and then withdrew from the university altogether.[23] The longer-term impacts for her future are a story that is yet to be written.

where and when is a right to privacy forsaken based on appalling speech or behavior? And who gets to decide?

A FURTHER THREAT: BEING CANCELED

Teens' experiences with digital footprints today are shaped by threats that include and go beyond loss of jobs or school admissions. In chapter 6, we described how cancel culture is firmly on teens' radars as they observe celebrities, political leaders, and other influencers being publicly shamed for inappropriate behavior, past or present, and "deplatformed" via mass unfollowing that undercuts their audiences.[25] Although cancellations are often directed at public figures, the phenomenon trickles down to the experiences of everyday teens and more mundane causes.

Diego told us about meeting up with a group of friends after school. Noticing the group was missing one of its usual members, he asked, *"Where's Vera?"* His friend replied, *"Oh, she's canceled."* Apparently, Vera was *"being fake"* to another person, was called out for it, and was now shunned. Diego was puzzled by the apparent cancellation for what felt like passing drama: *"Why does that make her canceled? Like, are you going to talk to her or are you just gonna put a label on her and then never speak to her again?"* Diego's reaction taps into the question of whether cancellations are permanent or temporary. Teens' stories suggest that the intensity of social sanctions often wane over time—though just how much time seems to vary considerably. Diego's friends may reopen lines of communication with Vera within days. But, in some cases, stigma lingers in a peer group's collective memory ("that kid got canceled in eighth grade for ___").

In cancel culture, social media plays a dual role: people spread the word of an indiscretion via Instagram or Snapchat (*"Like they expose you. And then in real life, you get canceled"*) *and* digital posts and comments are sites for discrediting the person and their reputation. Adults' persistent warnings about the risks of social media posts convey a strong message to youth, essentially normalizing a culture of surveillance[26] where "the whole world is watching."[27] In a context where cancellation is an added threat, the stakes of missteps can feel even higher.

Whether it's directed at peers, school communities, or cultural influencers, teens are polarized on the place and value of cancellation. To seventeen-year-old Jade, the civic intentions behind many cancellations make it a net positive: *"Cancelling is just like holding accountable and taking away a person's platform. In that respect, I think it's positive. . . . Like there's a TikToker, Lil Huddy, who said the N word and a lot of people canceled him and said, 'We're not going to support him anymore.' . . . And I think that cancel culture works if we all can agree to de-platform someone. . . . We shouldn't be like idolizing people who are racist and doing things like that."* Similarly, for Maeve (fifteen years old), *"Cancel culture is about not letting hate speech and systems of oppression get passed on to the next generation."*

Other teens acknowledge the intentions behind cancellation but question its efficacy. Michelle (seventeen years old) offered: *"There's a lot of emphasis on, like, punishing those people, on taking away their platform . . . and that can be a good thing if they've done something absolutely terrible. . . . But I think it's so much more useful to be like, 'Oh, hey. Why would you say that? Why would you do that? What were the intentions there?' Like, just like getting context for it."*

Nanaa was even stronger on this point: *"We're holding people . . . at a standard that's like inhumane. Because we are imperfect. It doesn't really solve anything. . . . That one moment or that one post is being defined [as] someone's whole entire character."* And she worries about efficacy. *"It denies them of those other steps. By canceling them, you're limiting them to that access of education. And also you're continuing to close their mind. . . . You never want to dilute it or, like, minimize it. Like, 'What you said was wrong. But you aren't a bad person. So I'm going to take the time to educate you on this.'"* In a similar vein, Diego fears that cancel culture is *"just avoiding the problem."*

THE RIGHT TO BE FORGOTTEN?

Mistakes are inevitable and today's world doesn't readily forget. As one parent put it bluntly, "The digital footprint is, by design, unforgiving and everlasting." The cases of the would-be *Teen Vogue* editor and the ten Harvard hopefuls who lost their admissions offers are part of a growing repository of high-profile incidents where digital posts (past or present) go viral, leading to mockery, humiliation, and public shaming.

Efforts to support erasure of digital content have been discussed and, in some cases, codified into law. The "Right to Be Forgotten" was embedded in the European Union's (EU) 2016 General Data Protection Regulation (GDPR) legislation, requiring companies to delete personally identifiable data about private citizens when those citizens request it.[28] But the logistics are complicated, as Kate Eichhorn thoughtfully unpacks in her book, *The End of Forgetting*.[29] Who is a private citizen and who is not? Or, rather, *when* is one a private individual versus a public figure? Let's say a teen's publicly available TikToks go viral and she accumulates two million followers. Does she forsake her right to have her footprint erased if she comes to regret her social media celebrity in two, three, or four years' time? What about old online photos of a person who was a "private citizen" during adolescence and later becomes a public figure: are their decades-old posts fair game for scrutiny? What if someone becomes a public figure as a child, but for something they did not choose? (Eichhorn cites the case of the "Star Wars Kid" who is often referenced as the first meme, an important part of Internet history.)

Practically, what are the geographic boundaries of the EU's policy, given the Internet's global reach? A 2019 court decision went in Google's favor on one such question, ruling that even in cases when a company is required to remove online content in response to a citizen's request, the "delisted links" can still legally show up in search engine results outside of the EU.[30]

Beyond the EU, the for-profit world is getting in on the game. Acknowledging that persistent content is profitable, Eichhorn explores an emerging industry around the idea of "paying to delete." Indeed, digital reputation management has ballooned in recent years—and become riddled with corruption. Shady businesses that purport to remove slanderous or unwanted content gouge victims after contributing to the spread of this content in the first place.[31]

THE LIABILITIES OF A WORLD THAT'S CHANGING TOO

In an era when content can persist indefinitely and resurface unpredictably (at least outside of the EU), the question of what to do with it is consequential. Probing teens' perspectives on cancel culture surfaces fundamental puzzles about character, growth, learning, and forgiveness. Shifting social norms and sensitivities add to the complexity: it's not just teens who are learning and changing but the world too. Views have evolved over time on topics ranging from the acceptability (and legality) of smoking marijuana to views about gay marriage to the degree of impropriety and harm of cultural appropriation. Yet digital artifacts can be wrenched out of context and travel across space and time toward new meanings and interpretations.

To be clear, public condemnation and censure for past atrocities is arguably warranted on many fronts. But when it comes to living individuals who are or were adolescents when they misstepped, how far should condemnation go? In response to the takedown of the future *Teen Vogue* editor, one journalist commented: "I suppose a magazine aimed at teens and preteens would strain to acknowledge what every adult knows, which is that the entire point of being a teenager is to make and correct the most mortifying errors of your life."[32]

With stories like this reifying a larger cancel culture, the stark reality of an unforgiving, make-no-mistakes world seems clear. But is there actually no way forward? Can we collectively own the unacceptability of certain speech *and* still create contexts where teens can own their missteps, take responsibility, and move on in some manner?

Carol Dweck's work on growth versus fixed mindsets is especially relevant in a world in which mistakes linger.[33] In a nutshell, people who approach errors as learning or *growth* opportunities are poised to recover from mistakes and do better going forward. By contrast, those who tend toward a *fixed* mindset attribute mistakes to identity or character flaws. It's not hard to see how such a mindset can prevent one from moving on. Doing so almost always requires self-forgiveness as well as some form of apology (public or semi-public) to an affected individual or group.

Getting to an authentic and accepted apology may be no small feat.[34] This is further complicated by the perspective (common to cancel culture) that no apology is good enough. As Genevieve (fifteen years old) shared, *"Apology videos are so hard to make without getting further canceled. . . . Like, if there's one comment that points out [criticizes] one tiny thing they said, you'll see a whole chain of comments off that comment that are like, 'oh wait, yeah.' And then more comments start popping up. Like Every. Single. Person. has to be like, 'This was good. This was good.'"*

Pulling back from the individual transgressor's redemption (when that's even possible), it's also fair to ask about our collective responsibility. Naturally, people who have behaved despicably aren't always committed to growth. But in our zeal to hold people accountable for lapses through cancellation and deplatforming, are we overcorrecting? What would a *collective* growth mindset look like?

Loretta Ross has some ideas. A Black feminist, scholar, and activist, Ross is an advocate of "call in culture." As she describes it, "Calling-in is simply a call-out done with love. . . . Some corrections can be made privately. Others will necessarily be public, but done with respect."[35] Echoing the voices of several teens quoted earlier, Ross prioritizes learning and growth as a more effective path to accountability and restorative justice: "We can work together to ascertain harm and achieve justice without seeing anyone as disposable people and violating their human rights or right to due process."

In short: antidotes to cancel culture are circulating—even as efforts to cancel those proposed antidotes follow. It remains to be seen whether the future will bring more opportunities to forgive and recover. Until then, teens sit with a considerable dose of anxiety about the certainty that they will stumble and the limited control they rightly feel.

FEELING OUT OF CONTROL: PRIVACY RISKS ABOUND

Digital footprints are just one in a larger set of worries teens feel about online privacy. As we recounted in the introduction, the initial data that inspired the idea for this book came from teens' responses to the question: What worries you most about today's digital world? We first asked respondents to choose from a list of different options that spanned issues like screen time, cyberbullying and drama, and being asked for inappropriate pictures, or to write in their own reply.

We have generally shied away from statements about prevalence because most seem misleading or inappropriate as characterizations of the data. For example, we don't make claims like "60 percent of teens are worried about X topic" because we actually only asked teens to describe their biggest worry. Teens may be indeed quite worried about topics they didn't select—or not. We just don't know.

Still, we couldn't ignore that the #1 most common worry—selected by 786 youth or more than one in five of our respondents—was "risks to private information."[36] This took us by surprise in some ways. For one, many teens seemingly opt for publicity over privacy on social media (e.g., when they choose not to use privacy settings because they want peers to find them or their content to be viewed more widely). Often, teens quite intentionally post what adults might consider "personal" information about their inner lives and thoughts. We've encountered enough of these posts personally and professionally to share the common wonder about whether privacy norms have changed.

At the same time, research has for a number of years revealed that networked teens think a lot about privacy, even if in different ways from what adults might expect.[37] What we heard from teens includes fears about dramatic consequences, often perpetrated by unknown 'bad actors' (e.g., hackers, stalkers). We also heard a vivid sense that damage was hard or impossible to control, as the following comments show.

Strangers on the internet could find out who exactly I am, where I live, or even my SSN. This worries me because I could be at risk of having my identity stolen, being kidnapped, constantly watched, or even murdered. (twelve-year-old)

People can steal your identity and money which is really hard to clear up. (thirteen-year-old)

I've seen stories about hackers who blackmail people when they didn't do anything wrong. (fifteen-year-old)

If someone hated me they could find my personal information and spread it around. (fourteen-year-old)

I don't trust those people in the Government. (fifteen-year-old)

Google and Facebook are Ad based services that inherently don't give a fuck about your privacy and just try and sell you stuff through targeted advertising. (seventeen-year-old)

These quotes point to a range of privacy concerns on teens' radars. They also beg the question of what teens feel they can do to manage them. We take up this question in earnest in our concluding chapter on the "agency argument."

ANOTHER REWIND

Rewind to 2012. I (Carrie) was analyzing transcripts from interviews with teens and young adults for my book in progress, *Disconnected* (published in 2014). I was trying to understand: How do youth think about the reality that their actions could, at any moment, be made public to an unanticipated audience and persist online forever after?

I noticed that there were three distinct ways young people viewed online privacy issues. These mindsets weren't fixed or even developmental, so far as the data could reveal; rather, they seemed to shift based on different contexts and considerations.

The first way of thinking was captured by Jess, a young adult, who said, *"There isn't much privacy on Facebook, but it kind of is in your own hands."* The mindset that *privacy is in your hands* parrots the top messages that adults and Internet safety programs typically promote: youth must take responsibility for protecting their own privacy by creating strong passwords, managing privacy settings, and generally avoiding reckless sharing.

A second mindset that *privacy is social* reflected the realities of co-construction. This mindset holds that privacy is forged with one's social ties through compacts. This is akin to what we heard most recently from teens who vet photos with friends before posting and tagging, or who agree to avoid forwarding content shared in a semi-private chat. Such agreements were sometimes explicit but more often tacit.

Another mindset also took on board the harsh reality that individual strategies only take you so far in a networked world. But, in this third point of view, *privacy is forsaken*: once content is posted online, it's seen as out there and up for grabs. This "eyes wide open" perspective was arguably adaptive. Yet, it also at times contributed to an "anything goes" mentality. If privacy infractions are expected, why not post, tag, and forward with abandon?

From today's teens, we hear that privacy is forsaken in further ways. When someone engages in reprehensible speech or behavior—even in a private chat—their privacy rights can be forfeited (canceled) in service of a larger public good. Teens are ambivalent and often polarized about this reality. Accountability matters and yet some wonder: are we also forsaking learning, growth, and forgiveness?

The view that privacy is forsaken also connects to a more global concern that risks abound, whatever you do. Teens recognize that even if *they* do not post or leak information themselves, others may nonetheless share or access it. In their words:

Even though I am very careful about it, it could still get out. (eleven-year-old)

As a programmer myself, I know how easy it can be to obtain people's passwords, or mess with a Wi-Fi network. (thirteen-year-old)

It's terrible to know that anyone can get your information and ever year it gets easier for people to take it. (fourteen-year-old)

Safety, reputation, security—there's a sense among teens that these are all in jeopardy in today's digital world. Digital affordances in the hands of peers or strangers add to this vulnerability. Documentation of the good and the bad feels unavoidable. Teens vary in how actively they try to manage these risks, and in how alert they are to longer-term potentialities. But even those who undertake intentional efforts can feel rightly out of control. Researchers have called this "networked defeatism": "personal privacy management in itself seems pointless, [and] constructs a false sense of security."[38]

TEENS WANT ADULTS TO KNOW

Adults often assume that teens can control their digital footprints, if only they try harder or act more responsibly. Teens want adults to recognize that they cannot be solely, perfectly in control of their privacy or their digital footprints (*"Sometimes we don't have control over social media"*). Friends or peers can post pictures they do not want online and it's complicated, socially, to ask them to take them down. Plus (as adults are often quick to remind teens) once a picture has been shared, it's already out there in some form. This can add to a sense of stress as teens grapple with the reality that *"there's a lot of pictures [posted by friends/peers] that I just would never post. And that's like out of my control, obviously."*

They also shared more pointed messages for adults—specifically about our roles in creating teens' footprints: *"Adults really need to start asking us permission before posting photos of us. Even if they think you look fine, it might be super embarrassing for us."*

When adults double down on messages like "one post can ruin your future" it can amp up anxiety about past posts that are already out there, leading teens to wonder whether it's already too late. Former friends hold cards that may jeopardize their prospects in the near term or further down the line. Cancel culture can add another layer of anxiety, even as some teens acknowledge commendable and civic purposes of high-profile cancellations. The threat of cancellation feels real for teens who see it spill over from social media influencers into teens' everyday lives.

It *is* important, teens acknowledge, to be vigilant about things like *"good passwords."* And they do crave actionable information about risks that may not be on their radars, like unintentional consequences of location-sharing features (e.g., geotags and Snap maps). But personal vigilance is insufficient protection for the array of risks that networked life presents. Teens navigate proximal and more distant threats to their safety, reputations, and futures. They face risks that secure passwords, privacy settings, and even "thinking before posting" can't reliably eliminate. For all the reasons we unpacked in this chapter—developmental, digital, social—teens' alertness does not readily convert to control.

We need to teach teens about risks related to digital footprints. But we should also expect and anticipate missteps. We need to talk about careful posting. But we should also talk about apologies, accountability, and learning from mistakes. Crucially, all stakeholders need to take on board the precarious position we've put adolescents in by providing them with tools that document their lives and development.

This is an apt lead-in to our concluding chapter, where we tackle a looming question: What will it take to meaningfully support youth in this landscape?

CONCLUSION: THE DIGITAL AGENCY ARGUMENT

On a snowy winter day, we (Emily and Carrie) were in Portland, Maine, in the library of a charter middle school. It was the first of many school visits where we teamed up with teachers to try out classroom approaches for teaching thorny digital topics, from friendship challenges to civic dilemmas.[1] Before a few long days of teaching and observation begin, we gave a presentation about our research and how it has fueled our interest in the ways adults talk to teens about tech.

We started the session as we often do—whether the audience is teachers, parents, or tech insiders—by naming a collection of common messages adults convey to adolescents about digital life:

Think before you post!

Don't sext!

Stand up to cyberbullies!

Stand up for what you believe in (But also: Don't get involved! Online arguments are a waste of time!)

Be honest

Be kind!

Be there for friends in need

Get off your phone

You are what you post; now, tomorrow, and in the future

These messages are well intentioned and in many cases on point. They're shared with teens by adults who truly care about them and want to ensure young people are staying safe and on a path to a successful life.[2]

Still, these messages fall short. By this we don't mean they are inaccurate or wrong; we mean they aren't enough. Sometimes, they even backfire, amplifying anxiety without clarifying what teens can or should do when dilemmas or challenges come up. Today's teens need more than just broad principles and panicked warnings.

Our trip to Portland kicked off a search for answers to the obvious next question: What *do* they need? To be sure, schools that create space for digital literacy education. Tech designers who re-prioritize for youth well-being (and policies that ensure it). Caring adults who stay alert to digital dilemmas, set warranted boundaries, and offer empathy, connection and validation. This all requires that we address the fundamental ways digital life is undercutting teens' agency at a developmental moment when it really matters.

DIGITAL AGENCY

Psychologists have long recognized that we as individuals fare better when we believe our actions can influence what happens, when we can shape an outcome through our behavior—when we have *agency*.[3] Conversely, routinely feeling out of control can threaten our well-being.[4]

In so many areas of digital life, we see evidence from teens of a struggle to feel and to be in control. The struggle shows up as they fight to regulate digital habits amid powerful design pulls and developmental sensitivities. It surfaces when features like Snapchat streaks compel ongoing exchanges they may not want to keep up. But also:

When someone asks for nudes and they feel like every decision (including saying "no") is a lose-lose.

When they care about a struggling friend but also want to disconnect.

When they care about a civic issue but recognize perils of posting *and* of staying silent.

When they feel trapped in unwanted filter bubbles that determine what they see.

When they are told to take care of their digital footprints, but they can't prevent peers from posting things they would never want online.

When they fret about privacy risks but face a reality where many risks are out of their hands.

Looking across teens' worries reveals a persistent struggle for *digital agency*. This is a strong undercurrent as they describe worries that stem from not having skills, not having good choices, not knowing how to navigate hard social situations made harder by digital technologies. The struggle is complicated by the true benefits and upsides of digital life for adolescents. Social media meets teens where they're at developmentally: primed for self-expression, exploration of their interests and values, connection with peers, and curiosity about the broader world.

People are generally better positioned to cope with stressors when they believe that they can manage or control them in some way. This begs the question: If teens' digital stresses are often rooted in a sense of compromised agency and control, how can we authentically empower more agency and well-being?

IT TAKES A VILLAGE

There are at least three critical paths, and they build on the different types of agency outlined by psychologist Albert Bandura.

First, build *personal agency*. Personal agency refers to the things an individual can do to exert influence over situations. Our account in this book has called attention to myriad ways teens' personal sense of agency is strained, thwarted, or undercut. But if we've done our job, you also learned about inventive ways they create a greater sense of agency against the odds. You heard about teens who try to curate their social media feeds toward well-being by unfollowing or muting accounts that make them feel bad. You heard about those who set their own screen time limits or intentionally put their phones out of reach when they want to focus on studying. You heard about teens who strategically segment their online audiences to empower more intentional sharing to particular groups.

Building teens' personal agency means supporting skills and strategies they can deploy when digital stressors come up. For example: by anticipating and discussing different dilemmas *before* they arise, we can help lessen anxiety and create ways to scaffold communication skills or strategic plans that position them to feel more agentic when the moment calls for it. One of our favorite quotes from an educator we interviewed captures the spirit of what we're looking to support—specifically, teens' decision-making *"at ten o'clock on a Saturday night."* This can mean having go-to language to respond to a snap from a romantic interest asking for a nude or to kindly (but firmly) set a boundary with a friend whose texting has become overwhelming.

Collective agency is where people "provide mutual support and work together to secure what they cannot accomplish on their own." [5] A signature example: the ways teens form pacts to vet photos of each other before tagging and posting. Even amid dismay about a world in which privacy feels forsaken, some teens find ways to protect and respect each other's privacy and online public image. Collective agency is also at play when teen girls share intel about guys known to leak girls' nudes so that they can be on alert and avoid them. Yet another example came up in the descriptions of teens who create online study spaces over Discord or Zoom to help each other maintain focus while keeping other digital distractions in check. Because friends are often poised to make digital life more or less stressful, when teens work together to reshape burdensome norms, everyone stands to win. We support collective agency when we validate efforts by teens to have each other's backs in the face of digital age challenges.

Proxy agency is where adults often come in. This mode of agency acknowledges that on their own—and even when they collaborate with others—teens only have so much control over their circumstances. Proxy agents are typically those who hold more power and can wield it on others' behalf to support their agency. Because adults usually create the rules, policies, and relevant laws (not to mention the very technologies teens use!), we are critical proxy agents in a context of digital opportunities and risks.

Some adults are in positions that offer particularly relevant powers as proxy agents. Parents are perhaps the most obvious figures here, as they make day-to-day decisions that grant and limit teens' digital access (beginning, often, with the purchase of a first phone). Those who hold gatekeeping roles make decisions about whether to consider digital artifacts in school admissions, scholarship awards, and hiring. Adults may be the recipients of online receipts with evidence of transgressions. Those who work in education are often tasked with handling cases that unfold among students—where a teen is a target of persistent cyberbullying or where a nude a teen shared with one person was circulated around the entire school. Those who work at tech companies, designers especially, have the power—and the responsibility—to raise questions about whether features will hook and pull teens in at the expense of their well-being. Recognizing our roles as proxy agents means acknowledging our complicity in creating conditions that can unintentionally undercut youth agency.

Whatever roles adults are in, it's past time to consider: How do our decisions support or compromise young people's agency and well-being? Where, when, and how should we intervene and disrupt existing devices, apps, norms, policies, and laws? How can we design *for* more agency? And: how can we center considerations about differential susceptibility and equity when we do so?

THE ROOM(S) WHERE IT HAPPENS

Let's get more concrete about where (re)designing for digital agency can happen and what it might look like.

At home, building personal agency for teenagers means tuning into dilemmas. This can mean moving beyond rules that simply impose arbitrary screen time limits. To be sure, teens often need support developing healthy screen time habits and curbing unregulated binges. An important aim is helping teens recognize moments when tech use adds to or undercuts their well-being or personal goals. This requires focusing more on what a teen is doing during their screen time and to what end. By modeling intentional digital habits (e.g., "I need to turn off my notifications for a bit, I'm feeling so distracted by my phone today"), we can help teens do the same for themselves. In this spirit, Tom Harrison writes about the value of parents being "thick exemplars" who share with children times when we struggle with our own digital experiences, misstep, or puzzle over how to "do the right thing."[6]

Parents can also validate efforts that support collective agency, like when friends decide to keep phones in an untouched stack during dinners together. Or when they use location-sharing as part of a group effort to keep friends safe during a night out. Such approaches reflect a "digital mentoring" approach to parental mediation rather than simply limiting or permitting unlimited tech access.[7] While younger adolescents need more direct oversight, parents can support personal agency through a gradual release toward more age-appropriate independence and privacy as their children get older.

In classrooms and school communities, building digital agency requires doing more than mandating that students agree to a list of "don'ts" in acceptable use policies. Instead, educators can play the vital role of creating space for young people to explore true tensions and dilemmas about issues like sending nudes or collecting receipts. With Common Sense Media, we created free classroom materials (dilemma scenarios) and tools (thinking routines) that support both skills and habits of mind (self-reflection, perspective taking, communication skills) that empower personal agency. We've seen firsthand the power of these kinds of learning experiences. When educators lean into rather than shy away from complexity (a principle we will describe further), they create intentional space for students to think through digital dilemmas with real-world trade-offs. As one high school teacher reflected: *"I personally like the complexity of dilemmas because that's what they WILL deal with . . . I like that there isn't a clear take away because that's reality—that's the reality of the situations they're going to face. . . . [This] prepares them to . . . handle these situations."*

In admissions and hiring, gatekeepers can proactively adopt policies that take into account the complexities of digital footprints, co-construction with peers included. Digital posts etch moments in time from long ago that young people may have learned from and evolved past. This mode of proxy agency *doesn't* mean overlooking clear violations of community values, but it *does* mean inquiring about context and considering learning opportunities alongside sanctions.

For tech companies, designing for agency requires attention to the ways different features shape youths' experiences. How soon is too soon? An expert in development, Katie Davis argues that designers should build with attention to agency even when creating for toddlers and young children, and certainly for teens. She describes how design features like virtual trophies and autoplay grab young children's attention versus empower choice and self-direction.[8] Consideration must be ongoing, not only at the outset of product creation. Naturally, young people's uses of technologies can shift over time.[9] They may converge with the design team's intentions, or they may sharply diverge as teens start using features in ways that were never imagined. (An example here might be the close monitoring of Snapchat maps to detect evidence that one has been excluded from friends' plans.) Tech companies should have a responsibility to continually evaluate the ways their platforms are used and experienced by youth. Is a feature that was designed for practical value actually creating considerable stress for adolescents, as we saw in the case of alerts that a message has been Read but seemingly ignored?

Youth with particular vulnerabilities must get extra attention. Is an algorithm trapping a depressed teen in an unwanted content bubble, serving up dispiriting quotes and posts about self-harm? This requires going beyond light-touch user feedback. Admittedly, the Children's Online Privacy Protection Act (COPPA) can pose a practical challenge to collecting data on the tech experiences of youth under the age of thirteen. But ongoing research with youth and their families is necessary as a way to elevate their voices and experiences. In light of youth vulnerabilities, tech companies' sustained attention to how advertising partners leverage user data is also crucial *and* challenged by the data-driven business model of the Internet.[10]

CONVERSATION KEYS

No matter what your role or room(s) you are in, empowering digital agency may seem like a tall order. Even if you are on board with the mission, implementing new approaches is hard—whether it's disrupting parent-child dynamics at home or reworking deeply entrenched school procedures for digital mishaps. But there are a few guiding principles that you can take on board immediately. None is particularly mind blowing or new; these principles are tried and true to good teaching, parenting, and design. We've repackaged them here in the form of memorable "keys" to better conversations with teens about tech.

The first key is *asking over assuming*. Throughout the book, we've pointed to the many ways well-intentioned messages can fall short, often because they're rooted in simplistic if not entirely flawed assumptions.

In our research, we noticed a profound shift when we doubled down on listening to youth. We learned that open-ended questions are especially generative (e.g., What's your view of TikTok? What's great about having Snapchat, and what can get tricky? How do you decide who to follow on Instagram? What do you wish I understood about gaming? Is there anything you would change about Fortnite if you could?). If we want real answers, we also learned that we have to set a warm and nonjudgmental tone from the beginning. For parents and educators, this might mean making clear that a conversation isn't going to lead to immediate sanctions or new rules.

When we ask and listen, we may find that our initial assumptions were on the right track. In other cases, we will discover that things are "good" or "bad" in ways we hadn't seen. We may learn that a teen's time on TikTok isn't just wasted—because it supports their interests, learning, or self-care. Or, we may learn that a challenge isn't really what we thought, like when reluctance to unplug is rooted in concerns about a friend's mental health versus a phone "addiction." We may come to appreciate that advice we thought was helpful ("You are what you post, now and forever!") has some drawbacks.

The second key is *empathy over eye rolling*. As teens share their perspectives, there can be an understandable impulse toward judgment and even its visible marker—eye rolling. (Are you really telling me your friends can't live without your texts for one hour?) As we witness a teen's daily phone habits or observe their emotional reactions to a close friend's latest snap, it can be powerfully tempting to criticize. We offer empathy over eye rolling as a reminder to adults to press pause on knee-jerk judgments in moments when compassion is warranted.

We can likely tap into empathy when we recall our own adolescent missteps and perhaps feel a sense of relief that smartphones weren't around to record the damage. Empathy is constructive: it moves us past the stance that "they must not be thinking" and instead helps us attend to what teens are thinking about—often a web of social pressures from multiple sources. Empathy is also productive: it changes the tone and tenor of our responses in ways that lay the groundwork for teens to share, listen, and accept our support.

The third key is *complexity over commandments*. This becomes important when we need to shift from empathic listening to providing more active and direct guidance. Leaning on commandments is a go-to move. Be honest! Do the right thing! Don't send a text you wouldn't want grandma to read!

Yet, the right thing is not always so easy to sort out, especially in networked life. Teens often face situations where values we want them to hold are in direct tension with one another. Is what people do or say in public fair for others to record and post on social media? In other words, which is more important: privacy or accountability? If a friend asks for honest opinions on an anonymous app, should you respond honestly even if it might hurt their feelings? That is, should honesty be prioritized over kindness, or vice versa? These tensions—and the resulting lack of a clear-cut right/wrong path—are characteristic of the digital landscape. In this context, commandments based on values like "be honest," "be fair," and "be a good friend" are important, but alone provide insufficient guidance for the dilemmas teens face.

Better conversations lean into complexity over leaning on blanket commandments. In a context where there is often no one right answer, teens need support thinking through tricky situations and identifying possible paths forward.

Another feature of complexity is the way in which contexts, circumstances, and teens themselves differ. What is essential as an intervention for one teen is at times unnecessary or unhelpful for others. Complexity over commandments creates space for these differences. Likewise, as tech companies iterate their approaches (e.g., through A/B testing), attention to complexity requires ongoing awareness that what builds agency and well-being may differ based on people's ages, identities, and circumstances.

"I USED TO THINK . . . NOW I THINK . . ."

Up to the very last minute, discussions with our teen advisory council yielded gems. The council met regularly over six weeks, digging into data on various topics (digital habits, close friendships, sexting, civic expression, footprints, and more). Each week, teens exchanged and unpacked different perspectives. To wrap up our final session, we turned to a compelling prompt—a thinking routine created by our colleagues at Project Zero: "I Used to Think . . . Now I Think . . ."[11]

As they shared their reflections, we were particularly struck by a repeated theme: teens were surprised to learn that other teens shared many of their thoughts about growing up with today's technologies:

I used to think that I was alone in my thoughts but now I know that I'm not. Everybody here has just given me some good ideas and seriously, this has been really good.

I used to think that no one had a problem with social media and that everyone just saw it as like this perfect thing. And now I know that [other teens] realize that it has problems with it. They just don't want to talk about it because nobody's talking about it.

I used to kind of think that . . . I was the only one who had these kinds of opinions and thoughts. But now I see that it's shared by a large amount of people. And it's been really cool talking with y'all and, like, learning everyone's opinion and different viewpoints from different places.

I used to think that we were all similar, but now I really think that we have a lot in common. Especially like seeing everyone's opinions. You know, we all come from different backgrounds, you know, gender, religion, race, everything. Grades, age groups. And it's interesting to see how much we have in common [as] like just teenagers in general.

Surely, we had thought, teens must know they're not alone in their worries and struggles. But they hadn't—and recognizing throughlines across their experiences felt *"really good."*

This isn't to say that they walked away with a sense that teens' digital experiences are all the same. Their reflections also captured a keen sensitivity to the importance of identities and contexts:

I used to think that people's personal experiences were solely affected just by what stage of life, like what age group they're in. But overhearing people's opinions, I realize how much of a factor environment has. I used to think it was just like race [and] gender. But just where you grew up has such a shaping factor in what you believe in, and like what you're exposed to; what you see [and] what you don't see; what your opinions are and stuff like that.

I used to think that I knew the range of opinions on different topics. But then, through this group, I learned a lot more. There's a lot more, like, nuance to everything as well. And a lot of different perspectives and experiences that I hadn't factored into a lot of these topics. So I'm grateful for that.

I used to think that everyone had the same or at least a similar experience when it came to these topics. And I think I'm pleasantly surprised that that's not true. Like, everyone has very different experiences and I think that's dope that now I know that. And that is true.

The wisdom in these responses suggests the relevance of two additional keys for adults to bear in mind. First, the value of *normalizing without minimizing*. When teens hear that their challenges are shared by others, it both normalizes and validates their struggles.

Here's an example of normalizing *with* minimizing, and then one *without*. If Graham says that comparison on social media happens all the time and makes him feel crummy, a normalizing but minimizing response might be, "that happens to everyone, you just have to learn how to deal with it." Another response, "just delete Instagram," is minimizing in another way. Deleting it may well be a good step. But this stance denies that Instagram may be a gateway to friend support and positive content, alongside comparison-inducing highlight reels.

A response that normalizes *without* minimizing: "That happens to me too, and it's such a real struggle with social media. It's hard and definitely can lead to feeling crappy." Going a step further—toward agency building and empowerment—might involve brainstorming strategies Graham can self-employ like curating his feeds to follow more of the content he likes and less of what brings him down.

A further key, *normalizing without essentializing*, recognizes that while adolescents have commonalities by virtue of being adolescents, their experiences are powerfully shaped by their identities and contexts. Certainly, teens feel the pull to peers, alongside a need to express themselves. And yet, they experience the world (on screen and off) in important ways that intersect with their race, gender identity, sexuality, and more.

Recall our developmental and ecological lenses. Teens' needs, wants, and choices are informed by predictable developmental processes. When we normalize without essentializing, we acknowledge both shared aspects of teens' experiences *and* the real differences among them. These surface, for example, in the pressures they feel to post about timely civic issues, and in the differential risks they face when their digital content is surveilled or exposed. This means that our approaches to supporting youth agency need to take such inequities into account.

USED TO THINK . . . NOW WE THINK . . .

This is an apt moment to try our favorite thinking prompt on for size: How has engaging with teens' voices shaped or reshaped your thinking about their digital lives? What is something you "used to think" before reading this book, and what do you think now?

I Used to Think _____. Now I Think _____.

When we've shared the ideas from this book in workshops and talks, adults have offered responses like:

I used to think teens knew so much more about tech than older people. Now, I think they are actually seeking guidance from us.

I used to think teens were just using their devices out of habit. Now I think they use them for social-emotional reasons too.

I used to think young people didn't care about digital privacy, but now I think they do and it's pretty complicated.

I used to think digital well-being was just about scarcity of tech use, now I think forming healthy habits is essential.

I used to think talking about this stuff was important. Now, I think I have a better way to frame the conversations.

Our perspectives evolved too. After wrapping up this latest round of research, we have our own list:

We used to think adults would benefit from learning more about teens' digital experiences; now, we think teens need opportunities to hear about each other's experiences, too.

We used to think adults might be too worried about social media without cause; now, we think some worrying is well-warranted—though adults often misunderstand what's hardest and why. We also learned about savvy ways teens leverage apps for well-being, new dilemmas they face related to online civic expression, and intense expectations they can feel related to their friendships.

We used to think that conversations about teens would benefit from including their voices; now we think such conversations are inherently flawed when they don't.

If we thought our work would be done when we finished this project, we know now that it's far from over. A mapping of what teens are facing (and adults all too often are missing) tees up fundamental questions about how we can do better by them.

LOOKING AGAIN AND LOOKING FORWARD

We started this book with an optical illusion and a promise: when it comes to teens and social media, there is more than at first meets the eye. In the chapters thereafter, we looked anew at hot topics, digging into current incarnations including tea pages, highlight reels, cancel culture, effusive comments, digital receipts, performative activism, and the complicated calculus around sexting. The struggles we gave voice to in this book aren't relevant to every individual teen. What's more, there are certainly struggles we didn't name and haven't yet surfaced. The keys—beginning with *asking over assuming*—will help all of us continue to discover what we're missing.

Looking closely at teens' perspectives, we traced connections to developmental needs and sensitivities. At once, we identified the importance of teens' identities and contexts as they confer different kinds of risk, resilience, and vulnerability. We also looked through a digital lens. From the opportunities of mobile 24/7 access to one another to the realities of public metrics and persistent content, we saw how digital affordances shape and amplify teens' experiences.

Technologies (and the ways teens use them) will inevitably continue to change. Some changes are necessary and overdue, like recalibrating apps and policies with youth well-being in mind. Developmental, ecological, and digital lenses will remain essential. If we keep these lenses close, we're poised to keep seeing what teens are *really* facing behind their screens.

ACKNOWLEDGMENTS

The teens on our youth advisory council are amazing. Their insights and perspectives were essential to this book. Thank you to Amaiya Altamirano, Luis Baez, Zoe Brita, Hayden Brown, Luis Roberto Cortes III, Nate Dixon, Devren Edouard, Adyra H. Fine, Ashyah Galbokke Hewage, Ruiqi (Yuki) Guan, Eli Horwitch, Alex Hyman, Nicola Kachikis, Edna Kinyanjui, Marigold "Goldy" Lewi, Ria Lowenschuss, Emmaline Miller, Milan Moise, Priscilla Park, Ella Smith, and Zoya Unni, among others. We learned so much from each and every one of you.

We couldn't have carried out our multifaceted research project without the support of a fabulous, dedicated research team. We are especially grateful to Chloe Brenner and Sol (Peter) Lange. Chloe was close to all the details and her perspectives unequivocally shaped our data collection, analysis, interpretation, and writing. Sol is a natural connector who brought creative wisdom and positive energy to all our youth advisory work. Together, Chloe and Sol helped to facilitate discussions with our teen advisors that opened new lines of focus for our work. Daniel Gruner and Laurence Li provided key support for coding and quantitative analyses, and each played an important role in helping us explore our data. Andy Riemer and Damaris Altomerianos were key contributors to early data management and exploration, too, and we benefited from their careful work.

We were fortunate to have feedback on the manuscript in progress from an awesome group of critical friends and family members. We are especially grateful to Alexis Redding and Amanda Weinstein for their careful reads of every chapter. Each offered detailed comments, including celebration of where we hit the mark and frank criticism where we missed it. We are thankful too for Sophie Choukas-Bradley, Ariana Zetlin, and Abigail Feldman, for their sharp eyes and on point suggestions throughout the manuscript. Sophie also directed us to literature we were missing, and we were so grateful to have her expert eyes on the text. Liz Kline gave us invaluable feedback on our first iteration of this book—coaching us on ways to strike a balance between research and practical insights. We also appreciated opportunities to tap insights from colleagues in adjacent fields, including Jeff Temple and Justin Patchin who each generously responded to our questions about their areas of expertise.

We are thankful, too, to a group of critical friends who shared valuable comments on specific chapters of our manuscript: Tina Fetner, Wendy Fischman, Jessica Kauffman, Jen Ryan, Katy Sazama, and Jacob Watson, as well as Adrianne Billingham Bock, Lisa Utzinger Shen, and other members of the Democratic Knowledge Project research group.

Our Common Sense Media colleagues have been long-time, valued collaborators. We're especially grateful to Linda Burch, Kelly Mendoza, Rebecca Randall, Eisha Buck, Tali Horowitz, and, in earlier days of this work, Darri Stephens and Brisa Ayub.

Harvard Graduate School of Education has been a terrific intellectual home for each of us. Our Project Zero colleagues were enthusiastic supporters and sources of guidance who leaned into this interest with us, often coming by our office or sending us emails to share the latest digital dilemmas from their own lives and families. We consistently benefit from the support and guidance of wonderful colleagues, including Sarah Alvord, Tina Blythe, Liz Dawes Duraisingh, Shari Tishman, Rick Weissbourd, and Daniel Wilson. We are thankful for opportunities to share our research and ideas in progress with the Civic and Moral Education Initiative (CMEI) and the New Civics Early Career Scholars Program, and thank Meira Levinson, Helen Haste, and Janine Bempechat for their feedback on different aspects of this research.

Much of the work we do is in close partnership with educators and schools. We appreciate all the educators who helped support this work, especially Ron Berger and EL Education. One of the teachers who we interviewed a few years ago described her aim of preparing her students for decision-making that happens *"at ten o'clock on a Saturday night."* This became a guiding aim for much of our work. Thanks to all the educators who have continued to inspire and support our research.

We are grateful as well to our longtime colleague and advisor, Howard Gardner, for strategic advice on the final manuscript and general support for our work across the last decade-plus. We are lucky to have Katie Davis as a friend and a close colleague, and she shared relevant insights from her own work and expertise on youth development and tech design.

We feel fortunate that our editor, Susan Buckley at the MIT Press, saw the promise of this project and then viewed the pandemic as a good reason for more data collection rather than a stumbling block. She encouraged us to turn up the volume on youth voices as a key feature of the book, and we are so thankful she did. Comments from anonymous peer reviewers from the MIT Press offered a number of suggestions that strengthened the manuscript. We appreciate Julia Collins's careful copyediting and Kathy Caruso's editorial leadership. We are thankful to the artist Oleg Shupliak for generous permission to reprint his *Double portrait of Van Gogh* (2011) in the opening pages of this book.

Our agent, Jim Levine, has been a consistent champion of this project and provided wise counsel as we navigated our way through the process of finding the right publisher. We are thankful, too, to Courtney Paganelli at LGR for her helpful suggestions. Angela Baggetta joined our book team with full enthusiasm and we so value her wise counsel and publicity support.

The Susan Crown Exchange (SCE) shares our deep interest in digital well-being and our belief in the inherent value of uplifting youth voices. Kevin Connors and Haviland Rummel have become valued thought partners; we appreciate their sustained interest in our work at every turn. We are ever grateful to Susan Crown and to everyone at SCE for making this project possible.

Other funders supported this work along the way, and we truly would not have been able to launch this research program without their early support. Thanks, especially, to Anne Germanacos for her support of Emily's dissertation research and early postdoctoral work; the MacArthur Foundation, which funded our earlier research via the Youth and Participatory Politics Research Network and Digital Media & Learning Initiative; and the funders who supported our collaborative work with Common Sense Media, including the Bezos Family Foundation, the William and Flora Hewlett Foundation, and Niagara Cares.

We wrote and edited much of this book together over Zoom, during the COVID-19 pandemic. Our family members became accidental office-mates as we read and reread paragraphs to each other. We are enormously grateful to Ella, Carrie's teen daughter and our at-home, always-on-call teen advisor (even when we would interrupt a Zoom class to ask for her take on teen data about sexting). Thanks also to T for patience with Carrie as she spent long hours on this book when T would have preferred undivided attention. Emily's daughter Nina was born in the midst of this project, which gave Emily a new (and still growing) appreciation for the wonders of child development and the full catastrophe that is parenting.

We—Emily and Carrie—have loved being partners in this work. We also feel so grateful for the steady support of our other key partners: Jason and Perry. We love you so much, and we appreciate all that each of you do for our respective families. Tiffany was an unwavering champion of us and this book every step of the way; we especially value her pointed sarcasm and humorous commentary about our project aims. Carrie is thankful to her mother, Judith Lowitz, and her aunt, Carol Porter, for their loving presence and cheerleading. Emily also thanks Margot, Gary, Helene, and Michael for invaluable support—always, and through this book process especially. The opportunity for her own grandparents' close involvement in this chapter of Emily's life has been an incredible gift. Finally, Bob Selman's mentorship has been both professionally valuable and personally meaningful to Emily on many levels, and his focus on research grounded in young people's perspectives clearly had a reverberating influence.

APPENDIX: THE RESEARCH BEHIND
BEHIND THEIR SCREENS

The insights and arguments in this book emerged primarily from a large, mixed-methods study of tweens' and teens' perspectives on digital life that we carried out between 2017 and 2021. We launched this study, the Digital Dilemmas Project, with the aim of understanding young people's perceptions of the upsides and challenges of the digital landscape at that time. We also wanted to understand the ways adults were supporting them, and implications for new or revised supports.

Our broad questions were: How are young people navigating thorny digital issues and dilemmas that surface in networked life? How are adults supporting them? What more could adults do? Our inquiry included digital issues and dilemmas that spanned four spheres: personal well-being, close relationships and intimacy, peers and community, and the broader civic or public sphere.

When we set out to do this research, we envisioned our findings being mainly directed toward new or improved educational materials. Our home base is at Project Zero, a research center at the Harvard Graduate School of Education. Our longstanding partnership with Common Sense Media was key. Carrie first collaborated with Common Sense Media in 2006 to support development of their research-based Digital Literacy and Citizenship curriculum. Over fifteen years later, Common Sense Media is a leader in providing digital educational resources to schools in the

United States and, increasingly, around the world. In 2017, we partnered with Common Sense Media once again—this time, to bring fresh insights from empirical research to support updates to their curriculum.

As we collected our data, we saw immediate implications for the content of curricular lessons and pedagogical approaches. These insights were leveraged in short order to develop and pilot test new materials for schools. But we also came to see that our data had relevance beyond schools. The more we began to share selected insights from our survey, the more we realized that what we were learning had relevance for a broader audience, including parents, mental health professionals, youth development organizations, and technology companies. This book is one outcome of a quest to bring this research to a larger public stage.

Throughout the book, we've referred to our surveys, interviews, classroom observations, and youth advisory council sessions. Further details follow about these studies and our research participants. Because we have worked on these topics for over a decade, we've also had a steady stream of opportunities to have less formal discussions with teens, parents, and professionals who work with youth. These discussions often surface stories that corroborate themes in our more formal studies. They also showcase tensions through real-world dilemmas (Sarah's story, which we shared in chapter 7, is an example).

Our research with youth is the focus of this book. We first briefly describe the educator study because it was the direct precursor to the focal youth study.

PHASE 1: EDUCATOR STUDY

EDUCATOR SURVEY (PHASE 1A)
In the fall of 2017, we conducted online surveys of educators, recruiting participants via Common Sense Media's email listserv of educators interested in digital learning and citizenship. We received responses from more than 1,200 educators, although response numbers varied by question. Of those who reported race/ethnicity, gender, and age, respondents predominantly identified as White (80 percent), female (86 percent), and between the ages of 26 and 55 (79 percent). Open-ended descriptions of their school contexts and learner populations indicated that teachers

worked in a wide range of settings and with learners of diverse backgrounds, abilities, and identities. Of respondents who shared geographic
information, the majority (n = 715) reported that they live and teach in
the United States (although across different regions), while eighty-one
respondents were from other countries around the world (selected countries respondents were from included Australia, Canada, Jordan, Kuwait,
Malaysia, Mexico, Peru, Senegal, and Vietnam).

Our survey sought to understand educators' perspectives on the most
salient digital topics to teach students, those they had discussed with students over the past several years, their teaching approaches and takeaway
messages in relation to challenging digital topics, and memorable digital
dilemmas faced in their schools.

Educators' survey responses gave us important insight into adults'
views on the current digital landscape. We had descriptive data on the
digital topics these educators most often taught (#1 digital footprints, #2
how posts might make others feel, #3 talking with strangers), as well as
the topics of greatest concern to educators (#1 digital drama and cyberbullying, #2 screen time, #3 digital footprints, tied with pressures to stay
connected) and their stances on digital dilemmas. We conducted systematic coding and analysis of educators' strategies and takeaway messages
for teaching challenging digital topics. These data pointed to a tendency
toward protectionist messages about digital footprints, privacy risks,
and sexting that can amplify young people's anxieties about growing
up digital.

We also asked several questions that we included in our subsequent
surveys with students, including a version of our "worries" question
(though in the educator survey, we used the term "concerns"; i.e., What
concerns you most about today's digital world?). The response options
were the same as those offered to students, as well as: Why is [response]
your biggest concern? (See "Survey Details" under "Phase 2: Youth Surveys" section, following, for the full list).

Motivated by our particular interest in dilemmas that surface in networked life, our surveys of both educators and students included a series
of related questions. Respondents were asked to respond to a series of
short-form dilemma statements (example: "It's fair for college admissions
to consider applicants' social media posts"—again, see "Survey Details" for

a full list) with seven-point Likert scale response choices from "Strongly Agree" to "Strongly Disagree." We also included three dilemma vignettes on timely topics (doxing, or public shaming on social media; digital footprints and college admissions; and parental responses to sexting) with "Agree" or "Disagree" responses and opportunities to elaborate.

EDUCATOR INTERVIEWS (PHASE 1B)

We went on to recruit and interview a purposive sample of twenty-five educators from those who responded to our educator survey. These educators were invited for interviews based on survey responses that described compelling, novel approaches to teaching students about digital life. The interviews focused on the details of their pedagogical approaches and highlighted a number of effective ways of moving beyond simplistic messages and leaning into complexity. We describe key insights from these interviews in our previously published report, *Teaching Digital Citizens in Today's World: Research and Insights Behind the Common Sense K–12 Digital Citizenship Curriculum*.

DESIGN-BASED FIELD RESEARCH (PHASE 1C)

Drawing on insights from educator surveys, interviews, and emerging findings from our youth surveys (Phase 2, description follows), we developed pilot classroom materials in collaboration with Common Sense Media. Our design-based research process involved field testing dilemma-based activities with educators in sixteen different schools in eight different states (California, Texas, Arizona, DC/Virginia, Philadelphia, Maine, Massachusetts, New York). The resources we co-created are available for free as part of Common Sense Media's Digital Citizenship curriculum.

PHASE 2: YOUTH SURVEYS

Across a ten-month period between June 2018 and March 2019, we conducted online surveys of students at fifteen middle and high schools across the United States (three of these schools subsequently participated in the aforementioned pilot study of new classroom approaches to teaching digital citizenship). These schools include traditional public schools (n = 7), public charter schools (n = 7), and one private school, and they were dispersed across ten U.S. states in the Mid-Atlantic, Northeast, Southeast, Southwest, Midwest, and West.

At each school site, we worked directly with educators who reviewed study information with school leadership and pursued requisite school permissions in addition to our university IRB. The study used an opt-out parental consent process outlined in a letter sent home by educators to parents/guardians. During class time allotted to the survey (approximately fifteen minutes), assenting students completed the Qualtrics-based survey anonymously via school-provided devices. Students could skip any questions or discontinue the survey at any time. Per our IRB protocol, we do not have information on students who chose not to participate at all or whose parents opted them out.

PARTICIPANTS

Youth optionally reported gender identity, age, grade, and race and ethnicity. Of those who reported demographic information, approximately 48 percent identified as female, 44 percent male, and two percent nonbinary; 6 percent preferred not to specify. (A notable limitation of the question/response format: we do not know the percentage of gender minority youth in our sample given the binary/nonbinary response option invited self-identification yet did not distinguish transgender binary youth).

Participants' reported ages ranged from nine to nineteen but most were between the ages of twelve and eighteen. Youth could "select all that apply" in terms of race and ethnicity; of those who responded, 52 percent identified as White, 19 percent as Hispanic/Latinx, 17 percent as Black or African American, 8 percent as Asian or Asian American, 5 percent Native American/American Indian/Alaska Native, 2 percent Middle Eastern or North African, 1 percent Pacific Islander/Native Hawaiian, and 9 percent Other.

When we refer to differences by gender and by grade level (i.e., middle versus high school), we are limited by the information that respondents provided.

Student surveys: Self-reported demographic information

	Count	%
Gender (select one)		
Male	1425	44%
Female	1560	48%
Nonbinary	71	2%
Prefer not to answer	181	6%
Question total	*3237*	*100%*
Age (in years)		
Mean (Std. Dev.)	13.4 (2.0)	
Mode	13	
Range	9–19	
Race, Ethnicity (select all that apply)		
White	1678	52%
Hispanic/Latinx	614	19%
Black or African American	556	17%
Asian or Asian American	258	8%
Native American/American Indian/ Alaska Native	153	5%
Pacific Islander/Native Hawaiian	44	1%
Middle Eastern or North African	77	2%
Other (please specify)	297	9%
Prefer not to answer	213	7%
Question total	*3197*	

SURVEY DETAILS

The surveys sought to reveal young people's perspectives on different facets of digital life. Questions covered the social media sites/apps students
use across a typical week and their general perspectives about their digital
lives—including the upsides (example: What are some of the best parts
about growing up with technology like cellphones and social media?)
and the challenges (What are some of the most tricky or challenging parts
about growing up with technology like cellphones and social media?).

Across the book, we feature youth perspectives shared in response to
an especially revealing question: What worries you most about today's
digital world? Participants were offered ten options (randomized order)
that were (1) selected based on literature review about salient digital topics and prior fieldwork, and (2) pretested with youth. These options were:
Being asked for inappropriate pictures, Comparing to others on social
media, Connecting with strangers, Digital drama and cyberbullying,
Digital footprints or online posts lasting forever, Pressure to always stay
connected, Risks to private information, Seeing inappropriate content,
Too much screen time, and Other (please specify). All participants were
prompted for an open-ended explanation: Why is [response] your biggest
worry? At the time, this list of options felt like a comprehensive repre-
sentation of relevant topics. If we were conducting the study in 2022,
we would certainly include additional topics that we know are salient to
youth today (e.g., posting about civic issues on social media, echo chambers and filter bubbles).

This was just one of the shortcomings of our survey approach. We describe in the introduction other relevant limitations of the worries question:

Giving people set options to choose from can narrow the realm of
what they consider. Permitting selection of just one worry ("what worries
you *most* . . .") means that the responses only reflected perspectives from
those who were most concerned about a given topic. These are important
qualifications. They mean, for example, that it wouldn't be appropriate
to make claims like "X percent of teens are worried about this topic" nor
would it be right to say that a certain percentage of teens are *not* worried
about a topic just because it wasn't their top concern.

Our subsequent qualitative data collection, particularly teen advisory
council focus groups and interviews (see "Phase 3: Teen Advisory Council

Focus Groups and Interviews") gave us insight into teens' worries (including and well beyond those on our initial list) and other salient topics discussed across the book.

As noted in the Educator Survey (Phase 1a), our youth surveys also included a series of questions to capture participants' attitudes about quandaries or dilemmas that surface routinely in networked life. Participants responded to a series of Likert-type normative statements with a 7-point Likert scale from "Strongly Agree" (7) to "Strongly Disagree" (1) (the scale included "Undecided" as a response option between "Somewhat Agree" and "Somewhat Disagree"). The statements included:

It's reasonable for people to face consequences later in life for social media posts they shared when they were in middle or high school.

It's fair for college admissions to consider applicants' social media posts.

If someone texts you, you should respond as quickly as possible.

Parents should monitor their teens' text messages.

Parents should monitor their teens' social media accounts.

It's okay for people to share violent videos online to call attention to what's going on in the world.

If someone sends a naked picture to someone else, it's their own fault if the picture ends up getting shared with other people.

If someone makes an offensive comment on social media, people have the right to call them out—even if it hurts their reputation.

Being a good friend means being available whenever your friend needs you.

It's okay to take a break from social media for a few days, even though you'll miss some of your friends' posts.

If a friend asks for honest opinions on an anonymous app, you should respond honestly even if it might hurt their feelings.

What people do or say in public is fair for others to record and post on social media.

If you suspect someone of doing something behind your back, it's justified to look through that person's private messages.

Schools should monitor what students are doing on social media.

Participants were also presented with three longer form digital dilemma vignettes on the following topics: the appropriateness of doxing individuals who participate in a hateful protest; the fairness of a college's decision to revoke an offer of admission from students for offensive online speech; and the appropriateness of a parent's actions when discovering evidence of teen sexting. Respondents were offered "Agree" and "Disagree" response options and an opportunity for explanation of their choice in an open-ended format.

These surveys yielded responses from more than 3,600 youths. Because some students left questions blank or did not complete the survey in its entirety, the total number of respondents varies across questions (for example: 3,630 youths responded to the initial worries question and 3,529 provided elaboration; 3,697 provided open-ended responses about the best parts of growing up with today's technologies; Likert responses to the normative statements ranged from 2,909 to 3,453). In instances where we report percentages in relation to certain findings, they are calculated based on the number of responses provided for a given question.

ANALYSIS

We generated descriptive statistics of students' responses to questions about social media app usage, worries about today's technologies, responses to short-form dilemma statements, agree/disagree responses to longer form dilemma vignettes, and reported demographic characteristics.

We conducted in-depth coding and qualitative analysis of students' responses to selected questions. For example, for the "What worries you most about today's digital world? Why is [response] your biggest worry?" questions, our research team analyzed open-ended responses (short, textual data) through a multistep process, looking for themes through inductive and then deductive approaches (including open, axial, and selective coding drawing on Strauss and Corbin[1]). Key to our process was the inclusion of a teen researcher as a full team member. When discrepancies and edge cases arose in our coding, we favored her interpretations. Our coding and analytic process yielded an array of insights about teens' worries about screen time, relational pressures to stay connected, digital drama, sexting, privacy, and digital footprint risks. Quotes illustrating key themes are woven throughout the thematic chapters. In our concluding chapter, we articulate a broader throughline finding—the struggle for digital agency—that emerged as a clear cross-cutting theme across youths' specific concerns. We then completed an additional analytic step after coding, which was key to our analytic process: teen advisory.

PHASE 3: TEEN ADVISORY COUNCIL

From November 2020 to April 2021, we convened a council of twenty-two U.S.-based teens as advisors for our research on teens and digital life. We recruited teen participants through word of mouth, tapping our networks and colleagues at schools and youth-serving organizations to establish a diverse group. Our advisory council sessions unfolded during the COVID-19 pandemic, which meant that they also provided an opportunity to learn about how the lockdown, remote schooling, and social distancing affected teens' digital well-being. This also facilitated inclusion of COVID-19-relevant examples shared in prior chapters. When we began our recruitment process, we wondered how the pandemic circumstances might affect participation. We had our recruitment survey open for approximately two weeks. We received responses from eighty-six interested participants, invited twenty-eight, and ultimately had participation from twenty-two teens.

Our youth advisors were teens between the ages of thirteen and eighteen. The group was roughly two-thirds female; diverse with respect to race, ethnicity, and sexual orientation; living in varied family structures and communities in different regions of the United States; and attending different kinds of schools.

We convened our youth advisors over Zoom, meeting in small groups of approximately three to five members to facilitate rapport and deep discussion. An added benefit of meeting in small groups was that we held multiple discussions on particular topics and then compared similarities and differences across these groups. In total, we held twenty-seven small group discussions with our teen advisory council and conducted twenty-eight individual interviews with council members. Crucially, we (Carrie and Emily) jointly led all youth council sessions with our teen research managers Sol Lange and Chloe Brenner, who codesigned the facilitation guides and asked valuable follow-up questions. Their closer proximity in age to adolescents and their personal experiences prompted them to raise topics such as performative commenting (which we describe in chapter 3) and particular facets of social comparison experiences on social media (like those we describe in chapter 2) that weren't on our adult radar.

Each session was designed around one or two focal topics, but in a semi-structured fashion to allow discussions to follow themes most salient to participants. A key aim of the teen advisory council was to invite teens to be co-interpreters of our survey data. Accordingly, sessions often included sharing thematic quotations from our survey, and our working interpretations of what our coding seemed to reveal about teens' experiences and struggles with digital habits, footprints, civic issues, and more. We worked with our teen advisors to consider alternative interpretations of data, and to explore questions about what might be missing and how experiences with a particular issue vary for different teens.

We audio- and video-recorded all sessions, created verbatim transcriptions, and examined the transcripts for (a) key illustrative cases related to topical themes from our survey data analysis and (b) counter-cases that suggested alternatives or different perspectives. In several cases, we brought key data points from our survey and working arguments about those data to our advisors for their reactions and pushback.

For example, in chapter 5, we present a list of "9 Reasons Why" teens send nudes. We created an initial version of this list based on the insights from our survey data and prior research, and then workshopped the list with our teen advisors. They critiqued, annotated, and revised the "reasons list" through open discussion and Zoom features that provided different feedback and editing modalities (polls, whiteboard, and chat). The final "9 Reasons Why" version we share in chapter 5 reflects their additions, tweaks, and deletions. Among other things, they suggested adding a direct acknowledgment of the idea that sexting could be "pleasurable, exciting, and fun." They also advocated removing the reason "it seems like no big deal because 'everybody does it.'" In this instance, teens clarified that knowing their peers sext is not itself a primary reason to send a nude; rather, peer norms "ease" or normalize sexting decisions made principally for other reasons (e.g., to impress a crush). We followed their guidance and removed the item from the list. Similarly, the opening vignette we share at the beginning of chapter 5 (about a boy showing his friends a nude allegedly from a classmate) is an adapted version of a story shared with us a few years prior. We had our advisory council discuss the vignette in detail so we could understand whether and how it remained relevant, and whether teens felt there were additional aspects of such situations that we should surface for readers. Their reactions helped us understand how sharing of others' nudes without consent plays out in different ways for older versus younger teens.

For each topical chapter, we used similar approaches: vetting our interpretations and arguments with teen advisors and reworking the chapter text to attend to counter-cases or variations.

RELEVANT PRIOR RESEARCH

Between roughly 2008 and 2018, our research team also conducted 378 interviews with young people in the course of various studies we led about social media and digital life. In numerous places in the book, we draw on insights from these interviews and use corresponding footnotes to signal connections to the relevant studies. Details on the methodological approaches relevant to those interviews and their analysis appear in published articles, including:

Emily Weinstein, Evan Kleiman, Peter Franz, Victoria Joyce, Carol Nash, Ralph Buonopane, and Matthew Nock, "Positive and Negative Uses of Social Media among Adolescents Hospitalized for Suicidal Behavior," *Journal of Adolescence* 87 (2021): 63–73.

Carrie James and Megan Cotnam-Kappel, "Doubtful Dialogue: How Youth Navigate the Draw (and Drawbacks) of Online Political Dialogue," *Learning, Media and Technology* 45, no. 2 (2020): 129–150.

Emily Weinstein, "The Social Media See-Saw: Positive and Negative Influences on Adolescents' Affective Well-Being," *New Media & Society* 20, no. 10 (2018): 3597–3623.

Emily Weinstein, "Adolescents' Differential Responses to Social Media Browsing: Exploring Causes and Consequences for Intervention," *Computers in Human Behavior* 76 (2017): 396–405.

Carrie James, Daniel T. Gruner, Ashley Lee, and Margaret Mullen, "Getting into the Fray: Civic Youth, Online Dialogue, and Implications for

Digital Literacy Education," *Journal of Digital and Media Literacy* 4, no. 1 (2016).

Emily Weinstein, Margaret Rundle, and Carrie James, "A Hush Falls Over the Crowd: Diminished Online Civic Expression Among Young Civic Actors," *International Journal of Communication* 9, no. 0 (2015): 84–105.

Emily Weinstein, "The Personal Is Political on Social Media: Online Civic Expression Patterns and Pathways Among Civically Engaged Youth," *International Journal of Communication* 8, no. 0 (2014): 210–233.

Carrie James, *Disconnected: Youth, New Media, and the Ethics Gap* (Cambridge, MA: MIT Press, 2014).

NOTES

INTRODUCTION

1. We credit Elisabeth Soep for this compelling term, which she conceptualized in Elisabeth Soep, "The Digital Afterlife of Youth-Made Media: Implications for Media Literacy Education," *Comunicar* 19, no. 38 (2012): 93–100.

2. Sonia Livingstone and Alicia Blum-Ross, *Parenting for a Digital Future: How Hopes and Fears about Technology Shape Children's Lives* (New York: Oxford University Press, 2020).

3. Participants first selected a response from ten options (randomized order) that were (1) selected based on literature review about salient digital topics and prior fieldwork and (2) pretested with youth. Options included: being asked for inappropriate pictures; comparing to others on social media; connecting with strangers; digital drama and cyberbullying; digital footprints or online posts lasting forever; pressure to always stay connected; risks to private information; seeing inappropriate content; too much screen time; and other (please specify). All participants were prompted for an open-ended explanation (Why is [response] your biggest worry?). This list of options felt relatively robust at the time, though three years later we can certainly identify additional topics we would add if we were redoing our data collection today (e.g., posting about civic issues on social media, echo chambers, and filter bubbles). We are grateful that our subsequent data collection, particularly interviews and teen advisory council discussion, allows us to address a broader range of issues in the chapters of this book.

4. Catherine D'Ignazio and Lauren Klein, *Data Feminism* (Cambridge, MA: MIT Press, 2020), 5.

5. Livingstone and Blum-Ross, *Parenting for a Digital Future*. See also earlier ethnographic work by Lynn Schofield Clark, *The Parent App: Understanding Families in the Digital Age* (Oxford, UK: Oxford University Press, 2012).

6. We credit media researcher Henry Jenkins here, who often uses this phrase when speaking about the optimal roles of adults in young people's digital lives.

7. "I Used to Think . . . Now I Think . . ." Thinking Routine, Project Zero, Harvard Graduate School of Education, accessed April 21, 2021, https://pz.harvard.edu/sites /default/files/I%20Used%20to%20Think%20-%20Now%20I%20Think_1.pdf.

CHAPTER 1

1. Eric J. Vanman, Rosemary Baker, and Stephanie J. Tobin, "The Burden of Online Friends: The Effects of Giving up Facebook on Stress and Well-Being," *Journal of Social Psychology* 158, no. 4 (2018): 496–508.

2. These headline examples were from (1) CNBC, https://www.cnbc.com/2018/05 /25/quitting-facebook-for-5-days-can-lower-your-stress-levels.html#:~:text=In%20 addition%20to%20the%20physiological,worsened%20sense%20of%20well%2 Dbeing; (2) Business Insider, https://www.businessinsider.com/deleting-facebook -could-be-bad-for-you-2018-4; and (3) a YouTube video from Wochit News (link no longer active but previously at https://www.youtube.com/watch/?v=0xk8A-qo79w [screenshot available on request]).

3. Donna Ruch, Arielle Sheftall, Paige Schlagbaum, Joseph Rausch, John Campo, and Jeffrey Bridge, "Trends in Suicide among Youth Aged 10 to 19 Years in the United States, 1975 to 2016," *JAMA Network Open* 2, no. 5 (2019): e193886–e193886; Centers for Disease Control and Prevention (CDC), *Youth Risk Behavior Survey: Data Summary & Trends Report 2009–2019* (2020), https://www.cdc.gov/healthyyouth/data /yrbs/pdf/YRBSDataSummaryTrendsReport2019-508.pdf; Jean Twenge, "Increases in Depression, Self-Harm, and Suicide among US Adolescents After 2012 and Links to Technology Use: Possible Mechanisms," *Psychiatric Research and Clinical Practice* 2, no. 1 (2020): 19–25.

4. Hugues Sampasa-Kanyinga and Rosamund F. Lewis, "Frequent Use of Social Net- working Sites Is Associated with Poor Psychological Functioning among Children and Adolescents," *Cyberpsychology, Behavior, and Social Networking* 18, no. 7 (2015): 380–385; Jean Twenge, "Have Smartphones Destroyed a Generation?" *The Atlantic*, September 2017, https://www.theatlantic.com/magazine/archive/2017/09/has-the -smartphone-destroyed-a-generation/534198/; Kevin Wright, Jenny Rosenberg, Nicole Egbert, Nicole A. Ploeger, Daniel R. Bernard, and Shawn King, "Communica- tion Competence, Social Support, and Depression among College Students: A Model of Facebook and Face-to-Face Support Network Influence," *Journal of Health Commu- nication* 18, no. 1 (2013): 41–57.

5. Sarah M. Coyne, Jeffrey Hurst, William Justin Dyer, and Quintin Hunt, "Suicide Risk in Emerging Adulthood: Associations with Screen Time over 10 Years," *Journal of Youth and Adolescence*, February 2, 2021.

6. Georgia Wells, Jeff Horwitz, and Deepa Seetharaman, "Facebook Knows Instagram Is Toxic for Teen Girls, Company Documents Show," *Wall Street Journal*, September 14, 2021, sec. Tech, https://www.wsj.com/articles/facebook-knows-instagram-is-toxic -for-teen-girls-company-documents-show-11631620739.

7. Susan Harter, *The Construction of Self* (New York: Guilford Press, 1999).

8. Daniel Clay, Vivian Vignoles, and Helga Dittmar, "Body Image and Self-Esteem among Adolescent Girls: Testing the Influence of Sociocultural Factors," *Journal of Research on Adolescence* 15 (2005): 452.

9. A meta-analysis of studies on social media use and body image disturbance found a small, positive effect of social media use on body disturbance overall, which the authors note is significant yet smaller in size than the effect of traditional media on body image. See Alyssa Saiphoo and Zahra Vahedi, "A Meta-Analytic Review of the Relationship between Social Media Use and Body Image Disturbance," *Computers in Human Behavior* 101 (2019): 259–275.

10. Our aim is to use affirming language to represent teens' identities, gender and otherwise. We acknowledge that what counts as affirming language is a moving target over time and may well be different by the time this book is in your hands.

11. See for review: Candice Odgers and Michaeline Jensen, "Annual Research Review—Adolescent Mental Health in the Digital Age: Facts, Fears, and Future Directions," *Journal of Child Psychology and Psychiatry* 61, no. 3 (2020): 336–348.

12. Amy Orben and Andrew Przybylski, "The Association Between Adolescent Well-Being and Digital Technology Use," *Nature Human Behaviour* 3, no. 2 (2019): 173–182.

13. Odgers and Jensen, "Annual Research Review."

14. Michaeline Jensen, Madeleine J. George, Michael R. Russell, and Candice L. Odgers, "Young Adolescents' Digital Technology Use and Mental Health Symptoms: Little Evidence of Longitudinal or Daily Linkages," *Clinical Psychological Science* 7, no. 6 (2019): 1416–1433.

15. Erica Euse, "Maybe Social Media Isn't as Bad for Teens as We Thought," *I-D*, August 26, 2019, https://i-d.vice.com/en_us/article/7x5bpd/maybe-social-media-isnt -as-bad-for-teens-as-we-thought.

16. Three examples: Ine Beyens, J. Loes Pouwels, Irene I. van Driel, Loes Keijsers, and Patti M. Valkenburg, "The Effect of Social Media on Well-Being Differs from Adolescent to Adolescent," *Scientific Reports* 10, no. 1 (2020): 1–11; Jensen et al., "Young Adolescents' Digital Technology Use"; Caroline Pitt, Ari Hock, Leila Zelnick, and Katie Davis, "The Kids Are / Not / Sort of All Right: Technology's Complex Role in Teen Wellbeing during COVID-19," in *Proceedings of the ACM Conference on Human Factors in Computing Systems (CHI '21)* (New York: ACM Press, 2021).

17. "Tech Time Not to Blame for Teens' Mental Health Problems," *UCI News*, August 23, 2019, https://news.uci.edu/2019/08/23/tech-time-not-to-blame-for-teens-mental -health-problems/.

18. Emily Weinstein, Evan Kleiman, Peter Franz, Victoria Joyce, Carol Nash, Ralph Buonopane, and Matthew Nock, "Positive and Negative Uses of Social Media among Adolescents Hospitalized for Suicidal Behavior," *Journal of Adolescence* 87 (2021): 63–73.

19. danah boyd, *It's Complicated: The Social Lives of Networked Teens* (New Haven, CT: Yale University Press, 2014).

20. Philippe Verduyn, Nino Gugushvili, and Ethan Kross, "The Impact of Social Network Sites on Mental Health: Distinguishing Active from Passive Use," *World Psychiatry* 20, no. 1 (2021): 133–134; Ingibjorg Eva Thorisdottir, Rannveig Sigurvinsdottir, Bryndis Bjork Asgeirsdottir, John P. Allegrante, and Inga Dora Sigfusdottir, "Active and Passive Social Media Use and Symptoms of Anxiety and Depressed Mood among Icelandic Adolescents," *Cyberpsychology, Behavior, and Social Networking* 22, no. 8 (2019): 535–542; Philippe Verduyn, Oscar Ybarra, Maxime Résibois, John Jonides, and Ethan Kross, "Do Social Network Sites Enhance or Undermine Subjective Well-Being? A Critical Review," *Social Issues and Policy Review* 11, no.1 (2017): 274–302.

21. Jean Twenge and Gabrielle Martin, "Gender Differences in Associations between Digital Media Use and Psychological Well-Being: Evidence from Three Large Datasets," *Journal of Adolescence* 79 (2020): 91–102.

22. Ine Beyens, Loes Pouwels, Irene I. van Driel, Loes Keijsers, and Patti M. Valkenburg, "Social Media Use and Adolescents' Well-Being: Developing a Typology of Person-specific Effect Patterns," *PsyArXiv*, December 16, 2020.

23. Jessica Piotrowski and Patti Valkenburg, "Finding Orchids in a Field of Dandelions: Understanding Children's Differential Susceptibility to Media Effects," *American Behavioral Scientist* 59, no. 14 (2015): 1776–1789; Anya Kamenetz, *The Art of Screen Time: How Your Family Can Balance Digital Media and Real Life* (New York: PublicAffairs, 2018); Patti Valkenburg and Jochen Peter, "The Differential Susceptibility to Media Effects Model," *Journal of Communication* 63, no. 2 (2013): 221–243.

24. Jacqueline Nesi, Sophia Choukas-Bradley, and Mitchell J. Prinstein, "Transformation of Adolescent Peer Relations in the Social Media Context: Part 1—A Theoretical Framework and Application to Dyadic Peer Relationships," *Clinical Child and Family Psychology Review* 21, no. 3 (2018): 267–294.

25. E.g., Kelly Jakubowski, Tuomas Eerola, Barbara Tillmann, Fabien Perrin, and Lizette Heine, "A Cross-Sectional Study of Reminiscence Bumps for Music-Related Memories in Adulthood," *Music & Science* 3 (2020): 2059204320965058; Alexandra Lamont and Catherine Loveday, "A New Framework for Understanding Memories and Preference for Music," *Music & Science* 3 (2020): 2059204320948315.

26. "Privileged" position in our memories: Jennifer Senior, "Why You Truly Never Leave High School," *New Yorker*, January 18, 2013.

Other references on this phenomenon include Jakubowski et al., "Cross-Sectional Study of Reminiscence Bumps"; Steve Janssen, Antonio Chessa, and Jaap Murre, "Modeling the Reminiscence Bump in Autobiographical Memory with the Memory Chain Model," *Constructive Memory* (2003): 138–147; Steve Janssen, Antonio Chessa, and Jaap Murre, "The Reminiscence Bump in Autobiographical Memory: Effects of Age, Gender, Education, and Culture," *Memory* 13, no. 6 (2005): 658–668.

Note, however, that while a particular peak around the teen years is documented in some studies, others suggest different peaks across a wider period (roughly ages ten to thirty) for various types of memories. Those interested in this research can see for review: Khadeeja Munawar, Sara Kuhn, and Shamsul Haque, "Understanding the Reminiscence Bump: A Systematic Review," *PloS one* 13, no. 12 (2018): e0208595.

27. Katie McLaughlin, Megan Garrad, and Leah Somerville, "What Develops during Emotional Development? A Component Process Approach to Identifying Sources of Psychopathology Risk in Adolescence," *Dialogues in Clinical Neuroscience* 17, no. 4 (2015): 403–410.

28. This developmental reality and its connection to the reminiscence bump is made by Laurence Steinberg in the textbook *Adolescence*, 12th ed. (New York: McGraw-Hill, 2020).

29. Grace Icenogle, Laurence Steinberg, Natasha Duell, Jason Chein, Lei Chang, Nandita Chaudhary, Laura Di Giunta, et al., "Adolescents' Cognitive Capacity Reaches Adult Levels Prior to Their Psychosocial Maturity: Evidence for a 'Maturity Gap' in a Multinational, Cross-Sectional Sample," *Law and Human Behavior* 43, no. 1 (2019): 69–85.

30. Linda Van Leijenhorst, Kiki Zanolie, Catharina S. Van Meel, P. Michiel Westenberg, Serge A. R. B. Rombouts, and Eveline A. Crone, "What Motivates the Adolescent? Brain Regions Mediating Reward Sensitivity across Adolescence," *Cerebral Cortex* 20, no. 1 (2010): 61–69.

31. Betty Jo Casey, Sarah Getz, and Adrianna Galvan, "The Adolescent Brain," *Developmental Review* 28, no 1. (2008): 62–77.

32. Sarah-Jayne Blakemore and Trevor Robbins, "Decision-making in the Adolescent Brain," *Nature Neuroscience* 15, no. 9 (2012): 1184–1191; Laurence Steinberg, "Risk Taking in Adolescence: What Changes, and Why?," *Annals of the New York Academy of Sciences* 1021, no. 1 (2004): 51–58.

33. Dustin Albert, Jason Chein, and Laurence Steinberg, "The Teenage Brain: Peer Influences on Adolescent Decision Making," *Current Directions in Psychological Science* 22, no. 2 (2013): 114–120.

34. Carrie Masten, Naomi Eisenberger, Larissa A. Borofsky, Jennifer Pfeifer, Kristin McNealy, John C. Mazziotta and Mirella Dapretto, "Neural Correlates of Social Exclusion during Adolescence: Understanding the Distress of Peer Rejection," *Social Cognitive and Affective Neuroscience* 4, no. 2 (2009): 143–157; Amanda Guyer, Victoria Choate, Daniel S. Pine, and Eric E. Nelson, "Neural Circuitry Underlying Affective Response to Peer Feedback in Adolescence," *Social Cognitive and Affective Neuroscience* 7, no. 1 (2012): 81–92.

35. Mitch Prinstein and his colleagues' extensive work provides rich empirical and theoretical confirmation of the power of popularity among adolescents. They find that adolescent social status predicts outcomes like future health, professional success, and adult relationships. See, for example, Mitch Prinstein, *Popular: The Power of Likability in a Status-Obsessed World* (New York: Viking, 2018).

36. Deborah Christie and Russell Viner, "Adolescent Development," *BMJ* 330, no. 7486 (2005): 301–304.

37. Erik Erikson, *Identity: Youth and Crisis* (No. 7) (New York: W. W. Norton & Company, 1968).

38. Urie Bronfenbrenner, *The Ecology of Human Development: Experiments in Nature and Design* (Cambridge, MA: Harvard University Press, 1977); Urie Bronfenbrenner and Anne C. Crouter, "Evolution of Environmental Models in Developmental Research," in *The Handbook of Child Psychology*, ed. Paul Mussen (New York: John Wiley & Sons, 1983), 358–414; Urie Bronfenbrenner and Pamela A. Morris, "The Bioecological Model of Human Development," in *The Handbook of Child Psychology: Theoretical Models of Human Development*, ed. William Damon (series ed.) and Richard Lerner (vol. ed.) (New York: John Wiley & Sons, 2006), 793–828.

39. Bronfenbrenner and colleagues' approach has been variously referred to and elaborated on as the bioecological model, the Process-Person-Context-Time (PPCT) model, and ecological systems theory. See Bronfenbrenner and Morris, "Bioecological Model"; Urie Bronfenbrenner, "Developmental Ecology through Space and Time: A Future Perspective," in *Examining Lives in Context: Perspectives on the Ecology of Human Development*, ed. Phyllis Moen, Glenn H. Elder, and Kurt Luscher (Washington, D.C.: American Psychological Association, 1995), 599–618; Urie Bronfenbrenner, *The Ecology of Human Development*.

40. S. Craig Watkins, "Digital Divide: Navigating the Digital Edge," *International Journal of Learning and Media* 3, no. 2 (2012): 1–12.

41. S. Craig Watkins, *The Digital Edge: How Black and Latino Youth Navigate Digital Inequality* (New York: NYU Press, 2018); Henry Jenkins, Sangita Shresthova, Liana Gamber-Thompson, Neta Kligler-Vilenchik, and Arely Zimmerman, *By Any Media Necessary: The New Youth Activism* (New York: NYU Press, 2016).

42. Emily used this metaphor as a description in her 2017 dissertation. Emily Weinstein, "Influences of Social Media Use on Adolescent Psychosocial Well-Being: 'OMG' or 'NBD'?" (EdD diss., Harvard Graduate School of Education, 2017).

43. danah boyd, "Social Network Sites as Networked Publics: Affordances, Dynamics, and Implications," in *Networked Self: Identity, Community, and Culture on Social Network Sites*, ed. Zizi Papacharissi (London: Routledge, 2010), 39–58.

44. danah boyd, "Why Youth ♥ Social Network Sites: The Role of Networked Publics in Teenage Social Life," in *Youth, Identity, and Digital Media*, ed. David Buckingham (Cambridge, MA: MIT Press, 2008), 119–142; danah boyd, "Social Network Sites as Networked Publics"; Alexander Cho, "Default Publicness: Queer Youth of Color, Social Media, and Being Outed by the Machine," *New Media & Society* 20, no. 9 (2018): 3183–3200; Nesi et al., "Transformation of Adolescent Peer Relations in the Social Media Context: Part 1; Nicholas Negroponte, *Being Digital*, 1st ed. (New York: Vintage, 1996).

CHAPTER 2

1. Tristan Harris uses this evocative language to describe persuasive design. See, for example, Tristan Harris, "How Technology Is Hijacking Your Mind—from a Magician

and Google Design Ethicist," *Medium*, May 18, 2016, https://medium.com/thrive
-global/how-technology-hijacks-peoples-minds-from-a-magician-and-google-s-design
-ethicist-56d62ef5edf3.

2. Iver Iversen, "Skinner's Early Research: From Reflexology to Operant Condition-
ing," *American Psychologist* 47, no. 11 (1992): 1318–1327; Burrhus Frederic Skinner,
Science and Human Behavior (New York: Free Press, 1953); Lauren Slater, *Opening Skinner's Box: Great Psychological Experiments of the Twentieth Century* (New York: W. W.
Norton, 2004).

3. Adam Alter and Tristan Harris have both made these clear connections between
variable intermittent rewards and persuasive design features, and described similarities to gambling. E.g., Mattha Busby, "Social Media Copies Gambling Methods to
Create 'Psychological Cravings,'" *Guardian*, May 8, 2018; Shauna Reid, "5 Questions
for Adam Alter," *American Psychological Association* 48, no. 7 (July/August 2017);
Cadence Bambenek, "Ex-Googler Slams Designers for Making Apps Addictive 'Like
Slot Machines,'" *Business Insider*, May 25, 2016.

4. American Gaming Association, *State of the States 2021: The AGA Survey of the Com-
mercial Casino Industry*, May 2021, https://www.americangaming.org/wp-content
/uploads/2021/05/AGA-2021-State-of-the-States_FINALweb-150ppi.pdf.

5. Lucy Foulkes and Sarah-Jayne Blakemore, "Is There Heightened Sensitivity to
Social Reward in Adolescence?," *Current Opinion in Neurobiology* 40 (2016): 81–85.

6. Brian M. Galla, Sophia Choukas-Bradley, Hannah M. Fiore, and Michael Esposito,
"Values-Alignment Messaging Boosts Adolescents' Motivation to Control Social
Media Use," *Child Development* 92, no. 5 (2021): 1717–1734.

7. James Paul Gee, *Good Video Games and Good Learning (New Literacies and Digital
Epistemologies)* (New York: Peter Lang Publishing, Inc, 2007).

8. Mihaly Csikszentmihalyi, *FLOW: The Psychology of Optimal Experience* (New York:
Harper and Row, 1990).

9. Harris, "How Technology Is Hijacking Your Mind."

10. Brandon T. McDaniel and Sarah M. Coyne "'Technoference': The Interference
of Technology in Couple Relationships and Implications for Women's Personal and
Relational Well-Being," *Psychology of Popular Media Culture* 5, no. 1 (2016): 85–98.

11. James A. Roberts and Meredith E. David, "My Life Has Become a Major Distraction from My Cell Phone: Partner Phubbing and Relationship Satisfaction among
Romantic Partners," *Computers in Human Behavior* 54 (2016): 134–141; McDaniel
and Coyne, "'Technoference.'"

12. Genavee Brown, Adriana M. Manago, and Joseph E. Trimble, "Tempted to Text:
College Students' Mobile Phone Use During a Face-to-Face Interaction with a Close
Friend," *Emerging Adulthood* 4, no. 6 (2016): 440–443.

13. Brandon T. McDaniel and Jenny S. Radesky, "Technoference: Parent Distraction
with Technology and Associations with Child Behavior Problems," *Child Development* 89, no. 1 (2018): 100–109.

14. Laura A. Stockdale, Sarah M. Coyne, and Laura M. Padilla-Walker, "Parent and Child Technoference and Socioemotional Behavioral Outcomes: A Nationally Representative Study of 10- to 20-Year-Old Adolescents," *Computers in Human Behavior* 88 (2018): 219–226.

15. Andrew K. Przybylski and Netta Weinstein, "Can You Connect with Me Now? How the Presence of Mobile Communication Technology Influences Face-to-Face Conversation Quality," *Journal of Social and Personal Relationships* 30, no. 3 (2013): 237–246.

16. Eric Suni, "Teens and Sleep," April 17, 2009, Sleep Foundation, https://www .sleepfoundation.org/teens-and-sleep.

17. See for review: Sakari Lemola, Nadine Perkinson-Gloor, Serge Brand, Julia F. Dewald-Kaufmann, and Alexander Grob, "Adolescents' Electronic Media Use at Night, Sleep Disturbance, and Depressive Symptoms in the Smartphone Age," *Journal of Youth and Adolescence* 44, no. 2 (2015): 405–418.

18. Children appear to be especially vulnerable to these impacts. See Anne-Marie Chang, Daniel Aeschbach, Jeanne F. Duffy, and Charles A. Czeisler, "Evening Use of Light-Emitting eReaders Negatively Affects Sleep, Circadian Timing, and Next-Morning Alertness," *Proceedings of the National Academy of Sciences* 112, no. 4 (2014): 1232–1237; Shigekazu Higuchi, Yuki Nagafuchi, Sang-il Lee, and Tetsuo Harada, "Influence of Light at Night on Melatonin Suppression in Children," *Journal of Clinical Endocrinology & Metabolism* 99, no. 9 (2014): 3298–3303.

19. Ben Carter, Philippa Rees, Lauren Hale, Darsharna Bhattacharjee, and Mandar S. Paradkar, "Association Between Portable Screen-Based Media Device Access or Use and Sleep Outcomes: A Systematic Review and Meta-Analysis," *JAMA Pediatrics* 170, no. 12 (2016): 1202–1208; Matthew D. Weaver, Laura K. Barger, Susan Kohl Malone, Lori S. Anderson, and Elizabeth B. Klerman, "Dose-Dependent Associations Between Sleep Duration and Unsafe Behaviors among US High School Students," *JAMA Pediatrics* 172, no. 12 (2018): 1187–1189.

20. Monique K. LeBourgeois, Lauren Hale, Anne-Marie Chang, Lameese D. Akacem, Hawley E. Montgomery-Downs, and Orfeu M. Buxton, "Digital Media and Sleep in Childhood and Adolescence," *Pediatrics* 140, Suppl. 2 (November 1, 2017): S92–S96.

21. Michael B. Robb, *Screens and Sleep. The New Normal: Parents, Teens, Screens, and Sleep in the United States* (San Francisco: Common Sense Media, 2019), accessed April 1, 2021, https://www.commonsensemedia.org/sites/default/files/uploads/research/2019 -new-normal-parents-teens-screens-and-sleep-united-states.pdf.

22. Jason J. Jones, Gregory Kirschen, Sindhuja Kancharla, and Lauren Hale, "Association between Late-Night Tweeting and Next-Day Game Performance among Professional Basketball Players," *Sleep Health* 5, no. 1 (2019): 68–71.

23. American Psychological Association, *Multitasking: Switching Costs* (Washington, DC: American Psychological Association, 2006), accessed March 16, 2019, https:// www.apa.org/research/action/multitask.

24. Kaitlyn E. May and Anastasia D. Elder, "Efficient, Helpful, or Distracting? A Literature Review of Media Multitasking in Relation to Academic Performance," *International Journal of Educational Technology in Higher Education* 15, no. 1 (2018): 13; Larry D. Rosen, L. Mark Carrier, and Nancy A. Cheever. "Facebook and Texting Made Me Do It: Media-Induced Task-Switching While Studying," *Computers in Human Behavior* 29, no. 3 (2013): 948–958; Jessica S. Mendoza, Benjamin C. Pody, Seungyeon Lee, Minsung Kim, and Ian M. McDonough, "The Effect of Cellphones on Attention and Learning: The Influences of Time, Distraction, and Nomophobia," *Computers in Human Behavior* 86 (2018): 52–60. An interesting caveat: Some studies show that action video game playing can reduce task-switching costs, in addition to supporting other skills (such as visual-spatial and perceptual). See, for example, Shawn C. Green, Michael A. Sugarman, Katherine Medford, Elizabeth Klobusicky, and Daphne Bavelier, "The Effect of Action Video Game Experience on Task-Switching," *Computers in Human Behavior* 28, no. 3 (2012): 984–994.

25. Mark L. Carrier, Larry D. Rosen, Nancy A. Cheever, and Alex F. Lim. "Causes, Effects, and Practicalities of Everyday Multitasking," *Developmental Review* 35 (2015): 64–78; May and Elder, "Efficient, Helpful, or Distracting?"

26. Mizuko Itō, Sonja Baumer, Matteo Bittanti, danah boyd, Rachel Cody, Becky Herr-Stephenson, Heather A. Horst, et al., *Hanging Out, Messing Around, and Geeking Out: Kids Living and Learning with New Media* (Cambridge, MA: MIT Press, 2010); Henry Jenkins, *Confronting the Challenges of Participatory Culture: Media Education for the 21st Century* (Cambridge, MA: MIT Press, 2009); Joseph Kahne, Nam-Jin Lee, and Jessica T. Feezell, "The Civic and Political Significance of Online Participatory Cultures among Youth Transitioning to Adulthood," *Journal of Information Technology & Politics* 10, no. 1 (2013): 1–20.

27. Carolyn McNamara Barry and Kathryn R. Wentzel, "Friend Influence on Prosocial Behavior: The Role of Motivational Factors and Friendship Characteristics," *Developmental Psychology* 42, no. 1 (2006): 153–163. For a comprehensive synthesis of research on peer influence, see Matteo Giletta, Sophia Choukas-Bradley, Marlies Maes, Kathryn Linthicum, Noel Card, and Mitchell J. Prinstein, "A Meta-Analysis of Longitudinal Peer Influence Effects in Childhood and Adolescence," *PsyArXiv*, May 19, 2021.

28. Jacqueline Nesi and Mitchell J. Prinstein, "Using Social Media for Social Comparison and Feedback-Seeking: Gender and Popularity Moderate Associations with Depressive Symptoms," *Journal of Abnormal Child Psychology* 43, no. 8 (2015): 1427–1438.

29. Frederick X. Gibbons and Bram P. Buunk, "Individual Differences in Social Comparison: Development of a Scale of Social Comparison Orientation," *Journal of Personality and Social Psychology* 76, no. 1 (1999): 129–142; Nesi and Prinstein, "Using Social Media."

30. This passage describing Essena O'Neill's social media departure appears nearly verbatim on pp. 12–13 of Emily's 2017 dissertation. Emily Weinstein, "Influences of Social Media Use on Adolescent Psychosocial Well-Being: 'OMG' or 'NBD'?" (EdD diss., Harvard Graduate School of Education, 2017).

31. Megan McCluskey, "Teen Instagram Star Speaks Out about the Ugly Truth Behind Social Media Fame," *Time*, November 2, 2015, http://time.com/4096988/teen -instagram-star-essena-oneill-quitting-social-media/.

32. Kristina Rodulfo, "100 Shots, One Day of Not Eating: What Happens When You Say What Really Goes into the Perfect Bikini Selfie?," *Elle*, November 2, 2015, http:// www.elle.com/culture/news/a31635/essena-oneill-instagram-social-media-is-not-real -life/.

33. Hayley C. Cuccinello, "Instagram Star Essena O'Neill Quits Social Media, Exposes the Business Behind Her Pics," *Forbes*, November 3, 2015, http://www.forbes.com /sites/hayleycuccinello/2015/11/03/instagram-star-essena-oneill-quits-social-media -exposes-the-business-behind-her-pics/#571c16901e47.

34. Eline Frison and Steven Eggermont, "Exploring the Relationships Between Different Types of Facebook Use, Perceived Online Social Support, and Adolescents' Depressed Mood," *Social Science Computer Review* 34, no. 2 (2016): 153–171; Erin A. Vogel, Jason P. Rose, Lindsay R. Roberts, and Katheryn Eckles, "Social Comparison, Social Media, and Self-Esteem," *Psychology of Popular Media Culture* 3, no. 4 (2014): 206–222; Nesi and Prinstein, "Using Social Media"; Philippe Verduyn, David Seung-jae Lee, Jiyoung Park, Holly Shablack, Ariana Orvell, Joseph Bayer, Oscar Ybarra, John Jonides, and Ethan Kross, "Passive Facebook Usage Undermines Affective Well-Being: Experimental and Longitudinal Evidence," *Journal of Experimental Psychology: General* 144, no. 2 (2015): 480–488; Emily Weinstein, "Adolescents' Differential Responses to Social Media Browsing: Exploring Causes and Consequences for Intervention," *Computers in Human Behavior* 76 (2017): 396–405.

35. Daniel Kahneman, *Thinking, Fast and Slow* (New York: Macmillan, 2011).

36. Sophia Choukas-Bradley, Savannah R. Robert, Anne J. Maheux, and Jacqueline Nesi, "The Perfect Storm: A Developmental–Sociocultural Framework for the Role of Social Media in Adolescent Girls' Body Image Concerns and Mental Health," *PsyArXiv*, March 18, 2021.

37. Mariska Kleemans, Serena Daalmans, Ilana Carbaat, and Doeschka Anschütz, "Picture Perfect: The Direct Effect of Manipulated Instagram Photos on Body Image in Adolescent Girls," *Media Psychology* 21, no. 1 (2018): 93–110.

38. Allen and colleagues' study focused specifically on differences between cisgender and transgender, nonbinary, and gender nonconforming (TNG) youth, offering important evidence that underscores differences in how TNG youth can use and experience social media. We note that we use the terminology of "heavier internet users" in our text, though the authors measured Problematic Internet Use (PIU). Brittany J. Allen, Zoe E. Stratman, Bradley R. Kerr, Qianqian Zhao, and Megan Moreno, "Associations Between Psychosocial Measures and Digital Media Use Among Transgender Youth: Cross-Sectional Study," *JMIR Pediatrics and Parenting* 4, no. 3 (2021): e25801, 8.

39. Crystal Abidin, "Communicative ♡ Intimacies: Influencers and Perceived Interconnectedness," *Ada: A Journal of Gender, New Media & Technology* 8 (2015): n.p.

40. Harter, *Construction of the Self*; Jerry Suls, René Martin, and Ladd Wheeler, "Social Comparison: Why, With Whom, and With What Effect?," *Current Directions in Psychological Science* 11, no. 5 (2002): 159–163.

41. Daniel T. Gilbert, R. Brian Giesler, and Kathryn A. Morris, "When Comparisons Arise," *Journal of Personality and Social Psychology* 69, no. 2 (1995): 227–236.

42. Robert L. Selman, *The Growth of Interpersonal Understanding: Developmental and Clinical Analyses* (New York: Academic Press, 1980).

43. Laura P. E. Van Der Aar, Sabine Peters, and Eveline A. Crone, "The Development of Self-Views across Adolescence: Investigating Self-Descriptions with and without Social Comparison Using a Novel Experimental Paradigm," *Cognitive Development* 48 (2018): 256–270.

44. Richard W. Robins, Kali H. Trzesniewski, Jessica L. Tracy, Samuel D. Gosling, and Jeff Potter, "Global Self-Esteem across the Life Span," *Psychology and Aging* 17, no. 3 (2002): 423–434.

45. See, for a discussion and review, the section "What Prompts Social Comparison?," in Gibbons and Buunk, "Individual Differences in Social Comparison," 130–131.

46. Ladd Wheeler and Kunitate Miyake, "Social Comparison in Everyday Life," *Journal of Personality and Social Psychology* 62, no. 5 (1992): 760–773.

47. danah boyd, "Social Steganography: Learning to Hide in Plain Sight," *Apophenia*, August 23, 2010, https://www.zephoria.org/thoughts/archives/2010/08/23/social-steganography-learning-to-hide-in-plain-sight.html.

48. Jessica H. Lu and Catherine Knight Steele, "'Joy Is Resistance': Cross-Platform Resilience and (Re)Invention of Black Oral Culture Online," *Information, Communication & Society* 22, no. 6 (May 12, 2019): 823–837.

49. Kishonna L. Gray, *Intersectional Tech: Black Users in Digital Gaming* (Baton Rouge, LA: LSU Press, 2020).

50. Patrick M. Markey and Christopher J. Ferguson, "Internet Gaming Addiction: Disorder or Moral Panic?," *American Journal of Psychiatry* 174, no. 3 (2017): 195–196; Andrew K. Przybylski, Netta Weinstein, and Kou Murayama, "Internet Gaming Disorder: Investigating the Clinical Relevance of a New Phenomenon," *American Journal of Psychiatry* 174, no. 3 (2016): 230–236; Christopher J. Ferguson, Mark Coulson, and Jane Barnett, "A Meta-Analysis of Pathological Gaming Prevalence and Comorbidity with Mental Health, Academic and Social Problems," *Journal of Psychiatric Research* 45, no. 12 (2011): 1573–1578. Note that the above studies are with young adults, not adolescents, although the editorial makes claims about the relevance to kids/young people. To look further at these studies on adolescents, see Jia Yuin Fam, "Prevalence of Internet Gaming Disorder in Adolescents: A Meta-Analysis across Three Decades," *Scandinavian Journal of Psychology* 59, no. 5 (2018): 524–531; Katajun Lindenberg, Sophie Kindt, and Carolin Szász-Janocha, "Characteristics and Conditions Associated with Internet Use Disorders," in *Internet Addiction in Adolescents: The PROTECT Program for Evidence-Based Prevention and Treatment*, ed. Katajun Lindenberg, Sophie

Kind, and Carolin Szász-Janocha (New York: Springer International Publishing), 17–28.

51. James Paul Gee, *What Video Games Have to Teach Us about Learning and Literacy* (London: Palgrave Macmillan, 2003).

52. Mizuko Itō et al., *Hanging Out, Messing Around.*

53. Jordan Shapiro, *The New Childhood: Raising Kids to Thrive in a Digitally Connected World* (London, UK: Hachette, 2019).

54. Adam Gazzaley and Larry D. Rosen, *The Distracted Mind: Ancient Brains in a High-Tech World* (Cambridge, MA: MIT Press, 2016); Adam Gazzaley and Larry D. Rosen, "Remedies for the Distracted Mind," *Behavioral Scientist*, January 1, 2018, https:// behavioralscientist.org/remedies-distracted-mind/.

CHAPTER 3

1. Niobe Way, *Deep Secrets: Boys' Friendships and the Crisis of Connection* (Cambridge, MA: Harvard University Press, 2011).

2. Joanna Yau and Stephanie M. Reich, "Are the Qualities of Adolescents' Offline Friendships Present in Digital Interactions?," *Adolescent Research Review* 3, no. 3 (2018): 339–355.

3. Nesi et al., "Transformation of Adolescent Peer Relations in the Social Media Context: Part 2—Application to Peer Group Processes and Future Directions for Research."

4. Tim is one of the teens who Emily interviewed for her 2017 dissertation, and she shared this quote previously in her dissertation writing(s), including Emily Weinstein, "The Social Media See-Saw: Positive and Negative Influences on Adolescents' Affective Well-being," *New Media & Society* 20, no. 10 (2018): 3597–3623.

5. Weinstein et al., "Positive and Negative Uses of Social Media."

6. Weinstein, "The Social Media See-Saw."

7. David Buckingham, ed., *Youth, Identity, and Digital Media* (Cambridge, MA: MIT Press, 2007); Sherry Turkle, *Life on the Screen: Identity in the Age of the Internet* (New York: Simon & Schuster, 1997).

8. Erving Goffman, *The Presentation of Self in Everyday Life* (London: Harmondsworth, 1978), 56.

9. Alice E. Marwick and danah boyd, "I Tweet Honestly, I Tweet Passionately: Twitter Users, Context Collapse, and the Imagined Audience," *New Media & Society* 13, no. 1 (2011): 115.

10. Robin I. M. Dunbar, "The Social Brain: Psychological Underpinnings and Implications for the Structure of Organizations," *Current Directions in Psychological Science* 23, no. 2 (2014): 109–114.

11. Robin I. M. Dunbar, "The Social Brain Hypothesis," *Evolutionary Anthropology: Issues, News, and Reviews* 6, no. 5 (1998): 178–190.

12. Robin I. M. Dunbar, "Do Online Social Media Cut through the Constraints That Limit the Size of Offline Social Networks?," *Royal Society Open Science* 3, no. 1 (2016): 150292.

13. Mark S. Granovetter, "The Strength of Weak Ties," *American Journal of Sociology* 78, no. 6 (1973): 1360–1380.

14. Marwick and boyd, "I Tweet Honestly . . ."

15. Marwick and boyd, "I Tweet Honestly . . ."

16. In their book *Instagram: Visual Social Media Cultures (Digital Media and Society)* (Cambridge, UK: Polity Press, 2020), Tama Leaver, Tim Highfield, and Crystal Abidin trace the history of Snapchat Stories and intentionally ephemeral sharing opportunities. The feature began as a distinct aspect of Snapchat and was adopted by Instagram. As Leaver and colleagues describe, the inclusion of Stories reflected a successful effort to enable more relaxed sharing on the Snapchat platform.

17. Jean M. Twenge, A. Bell Cooper, Thomas E. Joiner, Mary E. Duffy, and Sarah G. Binau, "Age, Period, and Cohort Trends in Mood Disorder Indicators and Suicide-Related Outcomes in a Nationally Representative Dataset, 2005–2017," *Journal of Abnormal Psychology* 128, no. 3 (2019): 185–199; CDC, *Youth Risk Behavior Survey*.

CHAPTER 4

1. This story is based on an actual tea account, and the examples are verbatim except for names—but Mill High School is a pseudonym.

2. This apt comparison was also made about YikYak in a February 4, 2015 article by John Patrick Pullen for *TIME* Magazine, https://time.com/3694578/you-asked-what-is-yik-yak/.

3. Weinstein et al., "Positive and Negative Uses of Social Media."

4. Nesi et al., "Transformation of Adolescent Peer Relations in the Social Media Context: Part 2."

5. "How Are Photos and Videos Chosen for Search & Explore?," Instagram, accessed February 1, 2021, https://help.instagram.com/487224561296752.

6. Alice Marwick and danah boyd, "'It's Just Drama': Teen Perspectives on Conflict and Aggression in a Networked Era," *Journal of Youth Studies* 17, no. 9 (2014): 1187–1204.

7. Sarah Jackson, Moya Bailey, and Brooke Foucault Welles, *#HashtagActivism: Networks of Race and Gender Justice* (Cambridge, MA: MIT Press, 2020).

8. Bari Weiss covered some of the controversy unfolding at other NYC private schools in April 2021. Relevant posts include Bari Weiss, "The Goal of This Newsletter," *Common Sense with Bari Weiss*, April 19, 2021, https://bariweiss.substack.com/p/the-goal-of-this-newsletter; and Bari Weiss, "You Have to Read This Letter," *Common Sense with Bari Weiss*, April 17, 2021, https://bariweiss.substack.com/p/you-have-to-read-this-letter.

9. John Suler, "The Online Disinhibition Effect," *CyberPsychology & Behavior* 7, no. 3 (2004): 321–326.

10. E.g., Michal Dolev-Cohen and Azy Barak, "Adolescents' Use of Instant Messaging as a Means of Emotional Relief," *Computers in Human Behavior* 29, no. 1 (2013): 58–63.

11. Suler, "Online Disinhibition Effect"; Noam Lapidot-Lefler and Azy Barak, "Effects of Anonymity, Invisibility, and Lack of Eye-Contact on Toxic Online Disinhibition," *Computers in Human Behavior* 28, no. 2 (2012): 434–443.

12. Suler, "Online Disinhibition Effect."

13. As described in Elizabeth Englander, *25 Myths about Bullying and Cyberbullying* (Hoboken, NJ: Wiley Blackwell, 2020), 84.

14. E.g., Noam Lapidot-Lefler and Michal Dolev-Cohen, "Comparing Cyberbullying and School Bullying among School Students: Prevalence, Gender, and Grade Level Differences," *Social Psychology of Education: An International Journal* 18, no. 1 (2015): 1–16.

15. For a classic paper on this topic, see David Elkind, "Egocentrism in Adolescence," *Child Development* 38 (1967): 1025–1034. Also, though Elkind postulated a decline in egocentrism around ages fifteen to sixteen, subsequent research indicates that it remains relevant to adolescents' thinking into later adolescent years (e.g., ages eighteen to twenty-one; see Paul D. Schwartz, Amanda M. Maynard, and Sarah M. Uzelac, "Adolescent Egocentrism: A Contemporary View," *Adolescence* 43, no. 171 [2009]: 441–448).

16. Robert L. Selman, *Promotion of Social Awareness: Powerful Lessons for the Partnership of Developmental Theory and Classroom Practice* (New York: Russell Sage Foundation, 2003); Silvia Diazgranados, Robert L. Selman, and Michelle Dionne, "Acts of Social Perspective Taking: A Functional Construct and the Validation of a Performance Measure for Early Adolescents," *Social Development* 25, no. 3 (2018): 572–601.

17. Christian K. Tamnes, Knut Overbye, Lia Ferschmann, Anders M. Fjell, Kristine B. Walhovd, Sarah-Jayne Blakemore, and Iroise Dumontheil, "Social Perspective Taking Is Associated with Self-Reported Prosocial Behavior and Regional Cortical Thickness across Adolescence," *Developmental Psychology* 54, no. 9 (2018): 1745–1757.

18. Dan Olweus, *Bullying at School: What We Know and What We Can Do* (Oxford, UK: Wiley-Blackwell, 1993).

19. Englander, *25 Myths about Bullying and Cyberbullying*; Sameer Hinduja and Justin Patchin, *Bullying Beyond the Schoolyard: Preventing and Responding to Cyberbullying* (Thousand Oaks, CA: Sage, 2015).

20. For a synthesis and overview of multiple studies carried out by the authors, including their 2019 survey findings, see Sameer Hinduja and Justin W. Patchin, "Cyberbullying: Identification, Prevention, and Response" (Cyberbullying Research Center, 2020), accessed March 12, 2021, https://cyberbullying.org/Cyberbullying-Identification-Prevention-Response-2020.pdf.

21. Englander, *25 Myths about Bullying and Cyberbullying*.

22. Englander, 90.

23. Sameer Hinduja and Justin W. Patchin, "Connecting Adolescent Suicide to the Severity of Bullying and Cyberbullying," *Journal of School Violence* 18, no. 3 (2019): 333–346.

24. Megan A. Moreno, Aubrey D. Gower, Heather Brittain, and Tracy Vaillancourt, "Applying Natural Language Processing to Evaluate News Media Coverage of Bullying and Cyberbullying," *Prevention Science: The Official Journal of the Society for Prevention Research* 20, no. 8 (2019): 1274–1283.

25. Nesi et al., "Transformation of Adolescent Peer Relations in the Social Media Context: Part 2."

26. Kishonna Gray's ethnographic work reveals layered dynamics through which racism, sexism, heterosexism, and other "intersecting oppressions" permeate online games and gaming cultures. Gray also identifies the ways in which Black men and Black women find "solace" (p. 104), empowerment, and strategies of resistance in these contexts. Gray, *Intersectional Tech.*

27. boyd, "Social Steganography."

28. Catherine Sebastian, Essi Viding, Kipling D. Williams, and Sarah-Jayne Blakemore, "Social Brain Development and the Affective Consequences of Ostracism in Adolescence," *Brain and Cognition, Adolescent Brain Development: Current Themes and Future Directions* 72, no. 1 (2010): 134–145.

29. Caitlin Elsaesser, Desmond Upton Patton, Emily Weinstein, Jacquelyn Santiago, Ayesha Clarke, and Rob Eschmann, "Small Becomes Big, Fast: Adolescent Perceptions of How Social Media Features Escalate Online Conflict to Offline Violence," *Children and Youth Services Review* no. 122 (2021): 105898.

30. Desmond U. Patton, David Pyrooz, Scott Decker, William R. Frey, and Patrick Leonard, "When Twitter Fingers Turn to Trigger Fingers: A Qualitative Study of Social Media-Related Gang Violence," *International Journal of Bullying Prevention* 1, no. 3 (2019): 1–13.

31. Jeffrey Lane, *The Digital Street.* (Oxford, UK: Oxford University Press, 2018).

32. Desmond U. Patton, Jeffrey Lane, Patrick Leonard, Jamie Macbeth, and Jocelyn R Smith Lee, "Gang Violence on the Digital Street: Case Study of a South Side Chicago Gang Member's Twitter Communication," *New Media & Society* 19, no. 7 (2016): 1000–1018.

33. Cho, "Default Publicness."

CHAPTER 5

1. Pamela K. Kohler, Lisa E. Manhart, and William E. Lafferty, "Abstinence-Only and Comprehensive Sex Education and the Initiation of Sexual Activity and Teen Pregnancy," *Journal of Adolescent Health* 42, no. 4 (2008): 344–351; Kathrin F. Stanger-Hall and David W. Hall, "Abstinence-Only Education and Teen Pregnancy Rates: Why We Need Comprehensive Sex Education in the U.S," *PLOS ONE* 6, no. 10 (October 14, 2011): e24658.

2. Katrien Symons, Koen Ponnet, Michel Walrave, and Wannes Heirman, "Sexting Scripts in Adolescent Relationships: Is Sexting Becoming the Norm?," *New Media & Society* 20, no. 10 (2018): 3836–3857.

3. Two recent (as of this writing) meta-analyses of sexting: Sheri Madigan, Anh Ly, Christina L. Rash, Joris Van Ouytsel, and Jeff R. Temple, "Prevalence of Multiple Forms of Sexting Behavior among Youth: A Systematic Review and Meta-Analysis," *JAMA Pediatrics* 172, no. 4 (2018): 327–335. In this analysis, reported means for prevalence are as follows: sending sexts (0.15, 95% CI, 0.13, 0.17), receiving (0.27, 95% CI, 0.23, 0.32), forwarding (0.12, 95% CI, .08, 0.16), having a sext forwarded without consent (0.08, 95% CI, 0.05, 0.12); Cristian Molla-Esparza, Josep-Maria Losilla, and Emelina López-González, "Prevalence of Sending, Receiving and Forwarding Sexts among Youths: A Three-Level Meta-Analysis," *PLOS ONE* 15, no. 12 (December 7, 2020): e0243653. In this analysis, reported means for prevalence are as follows: sending sexts (0.14, 95% CI 0.12, 0.17), receiving (0.31, 95% CI 0.26, 0.36), forwarding (0.07, 95% CI 0.05, 0.09). The authors also note that all sexting experiences increased with age and became more prevalent in recent years.

4. See, for example, Elizabeth Englander and Meghan McCoy, "Sexting-Prevalence, Age, Sex, and Outcomes," *JAMA Pediatrics* 172, no. 4 (2018): 317–318; Madigan et al., "Prevalence of Multiple Forms of Sexting Behavior"; Elizabeth Reed, Marissa Salazar, Alma I. Behar, Niloufar Agah, Jay G. Silverman, Alexandra M. Minnis, Melanie L. A. Rusch, and Anita Raj, "Cyber Sexual Harassment: Prevalence and Association with Substance Use, Poor Mental Health, and STI History among Sexually Active Adolescent Girls," *Journal of Adolescence* 75 (2019): 53–62.

5. Justin W. Patchin and Sameer Hinduja, "The Nature and Extent of Sexting among a National Sample of Middle and High School Students in the U.S," *Archives of Sexual Behavior* 48, no. 8 (2019): 2333–2343.

6. Relevant research includes: Eric Rice, Harmony Rhoades, Hailey Winetrobe, Monica Sanchez, Jorge Montoya, Aaron Plant, and Timothy Kordic, "Sexually Explicit Cell Phone Messaging Associated with Sexual Risk among Adolescents," *Pediatrics* 130, no. 4 (2012): 667–673; Michele L. Ybarra, and Kimberly J. Mitchell, "'Sexting' and Its Relation to Sexual Activity and Sexual Risk Behavior in a National Survey of Adolescents," *Journal of Adolescent Health* 55, no. 6 (2014): 757–764; Patchin and Hinduja, "Nature and Extent of Sexting"; Joris Van Ouytsel, Michel Walrave, and Koen Ponnet, "An Exploratory Study of Sexting Behaviors among Heterosexual and Sexual Minority Early Adolescents," *Journal of Adolescent Health: Official Publication of the Society for Adolescent Medicine* 65, no. 5 (2019): 621–626.

7. E.g., Elizabeth Englander, "Sexting in LGBT Youth" (presentation, Virtual Annual Conference of the American Academy of Child and Adolescent Psychiatry, October 12–24, 2020); Ybarra and Mitchell, "'Sexting' and Its Relation to Sexual Activity."

8. Van Ouytsel, Walrave, and Ponnet, "An Exploratory Study of Sexting Behaviors"; Englander, "Sexting in LGBT Youth."

9. Cho, "Default Publicness."

10. Laurence Steinberg, "Cognitive and Affective Development in Adolescence," *Trends in Cognitive Sciences* 9, no. 2 (February 2005): 72; emphasis added.

11. Camille Mori, Jessica E. Cooke, Jeff R. Temple, Anh Ly, Yu Lu, Nina Anderson, Christina Rash, and Sheri Madigan, "The Prevalence of Sexting Behaviors Among Emerging Adults: A Meta-Analysis," *Archives of Sexual Behavior* 49, no. 4 (2020): 1103–1119; Madigan et al., "Prevalence of Multiple Forms of Sexting Behavior."

12. Justin Lehmiller, Justin R. Garcia, Amanda N. Gesselman, and Kristen P. Mark, "Less Sex, but More Sexual Diversity: Changes in Sexual Behavior during the COVID-19 Coronavirus Pandemic," *Leisure Sciences* 43, no. 1–2 (2020): 295–304.

13. Joris Van Ouytsel, Ellen Van Gool, Michel Walrave, Koen Ponnet, and Emilie Peeters, "Sexting: Adolescents' Perceptions of the Applications Used for, Motives for, and Consequences of Sexting," *Journal of Youth Studies* 20, no. 4 (2017): 446–470; Elizabeth Englander, "Coerced Sexting and Revenge Porn Among Teens," *Bullying, Teen Aggression & Social Media* 1, no. 2 (2015): 19–21; HyeJeong Choi, Joris Van Ouytsel, and Jeff R. Temple, "Association between Sexting and Sexual Coercion among Female Adolescents," *Journal of Adolescence* 53 (2016): 164–168.

14. Anne J. Maheux, Reina Evans, Laura Widman, Jacqueline Nesi, Mitchell J. Prinstein, and Sophia Choukas-Bradley, "Popular Peer Norms and Adolescent Sexting Behavior," *Journal of Adolescence* 78 (2020): 62–66, 62.

15. Elkind, "Egocentrism in Adolescence."

16. Amy Alberts, David Elkind, and Stephen Ginsberg, "The Personal Fable and Risk-Taking in Early Adolescence," *Journal of Youth and Adolescence* 36, no. 1 (2007): 71–76.

17. Planned Parenthood, "All about Consent" (2019), accessed June 6, 2020, https://www.plannedparenthood.org/learn/teens/sex/all-about-consent.

18. Michelle Drouin and Elizabeth Tobin, "Unwanted but Consensual Sexting among Young Adults: Relations with Attachment and Sexual Motivations," *Computers in Human Behavior* 31 (2014): 412–418.

19. Elizabeth Englander, "Low Risk Associated with Most Teenage Sexting: A Study of 617 18-Year-Olds," (Bridgewater, MA: MARC, 2012), https://vc.bridgew.edu/marc_reports/6.

20. Michelle Drouin, Manda Coupe, and Jeffrey Temple, "Is Sexting Good for Your Relationship? It Depends . . . ," *Computers in Human Behavior*, no. 75 (2017): 749–756.

21. Cho, "Default Publicness."

22. Elizabeth Englander, "What Do We Know About Sexting, and When Did We Know It?," *Journal of Adolescent Health* 65, no. 5 (2019): 577–578; emphasis added.

23. Jeremy Adam Smith, "Can Sexting Increase Relationship Satisfaction?," *Greater Good*, September 2016, https://greatergood.berkeley.edu/article/item/can_sexting_increase_relationship_satisfaction.

24. Anna Ševčíková, "Girls' and Boys' Experience with Teen Sexting in Early and Late Adolescence," *Journal of Adolescence* 51 (2016): 156–162.

25. Poco D. Kernsmith, Bryan G. Victor, and Joanne P. Smith-Darden, "Online, Offline, and Over the Line: Coercive Sexting among Adolescent Dating Partners," *Youth & Society* 50, no. 7 (2018): 891–904.

26. Elizabeth Reed, Marissa Salazar, and Anita Raj, "Nonconsensual Sexting and the Role of Sex Differences," *JAMA Pediatrics* 172, no. 9 (2018): 890.; Reed et al., "Cyber Sexual Harassment."

27. Jennifer Wolak and David Finkelhor, "Sextortion: Key Findings from a Survey of 1,631 Victims," Crimes Against Research Center / THORN, June 2016, http://unh .edu/ccrc/pdf/Key%20Findings%20from%20a%20Survey%20of%20Sextortion%20 Victims%20revised%208-9-2016.pdf.

28. Bianca Klettke, David J. Hallford, Elizabeth Clancy, David J. Mellor, and John Toumbourou, "Sexting and Psychological Distress: The Role of Unwanted and Coerced Sexts," *Cyberpsychology, Behavior and Social Networking* 22, no. 4 (2019): 237–242.

29. Sameer Hinduja and Justin W. Patchin, "Digital Dating Abuse among a National Sample of U.S. Youth," *Journal of Interpersonal Violence*, January 8, 2020, 0886260519897344; Lauren A. Reed, Richard M. Tolman, and L. Monique Ward, "Snooping and Sexting: Digital Media as a Context for Dating Aggression and Abuse Among College Students," *Violence Against Women* 22, no. 13 (2016): 1556–1576; Lauren A. Reed, Jenny McCullough Cosgrove, Jill D. Sharkey, and Erika Felix, "Exploring Latinx Youth Experiences of Digital Dating Abuse," *Social Work Research* 44, no. 3 (2020): 157–168.

30. Julia Lippman and Scott W. Campbell, "Damned If You Do, Damned If You Don't . . . If You're a Girl: Relational and Normative Contexts of Adolescent Sexting in the United States," *Journal of Children and Media* 8, no. 4 (2014): 371–386.

31. Molla-Esparza et al., "Prevalence of Sending"; Madigan et al., "Prevalence of Multiple Forms of Sexting Behavior."

32. M. Johnson, F. Mishna, M. Okumu, and J. Daciuk, *Non-consensual Sharing of Sexts: Behaviours and Attitudes of Canadian Youth* (Ottawa: MediaSmarts, 2018), accessed February 12, 2021, https://mediasmarts.ca/sites/default/files/publication -report/full/sharing-of-sexts.pdf.

33. Van Ouytsel et al., "Sexting: Adolescents' Perceptions."

34. Van Ouytsel et al., "Sexting: Adolescents' Perceptions."

35. Johnson et al., *Non-consensual Sharing of Sexts.*

36. M. Dolores Gil-Llario, Vicente Morell-Mengual, Martha Cecilia Jiménez-Martínez, Paula Iglesias-Campos, Beatriz Gil-Julia, and Rafael Ballester-Arnal, "Culture as an Influence on Sexting Attitudes and Behaviors: A Differential Analysis Comparing Adolescents from Spain and Colombia," *International Journal of Intercultural Relations* 79 (2020): 145–154.

37. Johnson et al., *Non-consensual Sharing of Sexts*.

38. Research points to the power of norms in shaping sexual behaviors, even at the macro level. An interesting example: One large study that examined beliefs and behaviors across seventeen European countries revealed a relationship between cultural beliefs about the appropriate age for first sexual encounters and the actual ages at which people in those contexts become sexually active. See Aubrey Spriggs Madkour, Margaretha de Looze, Ping Ma, Carolyn Tucker Halpern, Tilda Farhat, Tom F. M. Ter Bogt, Virginie Ehlinger, Saoirse Nic Gabhainn, Candace Currie, and Emmanuelle Godeau, "Macro-Level Age Norms for the Timing of Sexual Initiation and Adolescents' Early Sexual Initiation in 17 European Countries," *Journal of Adolescent Health* 55, no. 1 (2014): 114–121; Gil-Llario et al., "Culture as an Influence on Sexting Attitudes and Behaviors."

39. Patchin and Hinduja, "Nature and Extent of Sexting"; Jeff R. Temple, Jonathan A. Paul, Patricia van den Berg, Vi Donna Le, Amy McElhany, and Brian W. Temple, "Teen Sexting and Its Association with Sexual Behaviors," *Archives of Pediatrics & Adolescent Medicine* 166, no. 9 (2012): 828–833.

40. Molla-Esparza et al., "Prevalence of Sending"; Madigan et al., "Prevalence of Multiple Forms of Sexting Behavior."

41. Madigan et al., "Prevalence of Multiple Forms of Sexting Behavior."

42. Peggy Orenstein, *Girls & Sex: Navigating the Complicated New Landscape* (New York: HarperCollins, 2016).

43. Lippman and Campbell, "Damned If You Do, Damned If You Don't," 381.

44. Lauren A. Reed, Margaret P. Boyer, Haley Meskunas, Richard M. Tolman, and L. Monique Ward, "How Do Adolescents Experience Sexting in Dating Relationships? Motivations to Sext and Responses to Sexting Requests from Dating Partners," *Children and Youth Services Review* 109 (2020): 104696.

45. Gender differences in sexting behaviors is an ongoing area of research. Understanding sexting decision-making in light of gender and intersections with other identities is also important. Notably, a small study focused on digital dating abuse among Latinx youth found that girls were more likely to say that they experienced pressure to sext, to have sent an unrequested nude, *and* to have perpetrated pressure on their partner to sext (the latter was statistically significant). Reed et al., "Exploring Latinx Youth Experiences."

46. Cyberbullying Research Center, "Sexting Laws Across America," accessed August 9, 2019, https://cyberbullying.org/sexting-laws.

47. Katie Lannan, "Alternatives to felony pitched for teens who share sexual images," *Daily Hampshire Gazette*, December 3, 2019, https://www.gazettenet.com/Alternatives-to-pitched-for-teens-who-share-sexual-images-31007643.

48. "Nonconsensual Pornography (Revenge Porn) Laws in the United States," Ballotpedia, accessed April 17, 2021, https://ballotpedia.org/Nonconsensual_pornography_(revenge_porn)_laws_in_the_United_States.

49. Lannan, "Franklin Lawmaker"; Shira Schoenberg, "Gov. Charlie Baker Refiles Bill to Address 'Sexting' and 'Revenge Porn,'" MassLive, February 6, 2019, sec. News, https://www.masslive.com/news/2019/02/gov-charlie-baker-refiles-bill-to-address -sexting-and-revenge-porn.html; Cyberbullying Research Center, "Sexting Laws in Massachusetts," accessed April 17, 2021, https://cyberbullying.org/sexting-laws /massachusetts.

50. Justin W. Patchin and Sameer Hinduja, "It Is Time to Teach Safe Sexting," *Journal of Adolescent Health* 66, no. 2 (2020): 140–143.

51. Lippman and Campbell, "Damned If You Do, Damned If You Don't"; Amy Adele Hasinoff, *Sexting Panic: Rethinking Criminalization, Privacy, and Consent* (Champaign: University of Illinois Press, 2015).

52. Johnson et al., *Non-consensual Sharing of Sexts*.

53. Jennifer S. Hirsch and Shamus Khan, *Sexual Citizens: A Landmark Study of Sex, Power, and Assault on Campus* (New York: W. W. Norton & Company, 2020).

54. Hirsch and Kahn, *Sexual Citizens*, xv.

55. Hirsch and Kahn, 144.

56. Patchin and Hinduja, "It Is Time to Teach Safe Sexting."

57. Gail Dines, "Pornography" presentation, Digital Media and Mental Health Research Retreat, Children and Screens, virtual, May 24–25, 2021.

58. Culture Reframed, "Solving the Public Health Crisis of the Digital Age," accessed September 3, 2021, https://www.culturereframed.org.

59. Culture Reframed, "Solving the Public Health Crisis of the Digital Age."

60. Ana J. Bridges, Robert Wosnitzer, Erica Scharrer, Chyng Sun, and Rachael Liberman, "Aggression and Sexual Behavior in Best-Selling Pornography Videos: A Content Analysis Update," *Violence Against Women* 16, no. 10 (2010): 1065–1085. Note: The Bridges et al. (2010) content analysis is a widely cited study of 304 scenes from popular pornographic videos and found that 88.2 percent contained physical aggression. Fritz et al.'s (2020) descriptive analysis of free pornographic content from Pornhub and Xvideos found lower prevalence of physically aggressive acts (45 percent of Pornhub scenes and 35 percent of Xvideo scenes; across these scenes, 97 percent had women as the targets and women's reactions to the aggression was "rarely negative"). Niki Fritz, Vinny Malic, Bryant Paul, and Yanyan Zhou, "A Descriptive Analysis of the Types, Targets, and Relative Frequency of Aggression in Mainstream Pornography," *Archives of Sexual Behavior* 49, no. 8 (2020): 3041–3053.

61. Fritz et al., "A Descriptive Analysis."

62. Fritz et al., "A Descriptive Analysis."

63. Malachi Willis, Sasha N. Canan, Kristen N. Jozkowski, and Ana J. Bridges, "Sexual Consent Communication in Best-Selling Pornography Films: A Content Analysis," *Journal of Sex Research* 57, no. 1 (2020): 52–63.

64. Eric W. Owens, Richard J. Behun, Jill C. Manning, and Rory C. Reid, "The Impact of Internet Pornography on Adolescents: A Review of the Research," *Sexual Addiction & Compulsivity* 19, no. 1–2 (2012): 99–122.

65. Elisha Fieldstadt, "Billie Eilish Reveals She Watched Porn at Young Age, Calls It 'a Disgrace,'" *NBC News*, December 15, 2021, https://www.nbcnews.com/news/us -news/billie-eilish-reveals-watched-porn-young-age-calls-disgrace-rcna8863.

CHAPTER 6

1. Taylor Lorenz, Kellen Browning, and Sheera Frenkel, "TikTok Teens and K-Pop Stans Say They Sank Trump Rally," *New York Times*, June 21, 2020, https://www .nytimes.com/2020/06/21/style/tiktok-trump-rally-tulsa.html.

2. Jenkins et al., *By Any Media Necessary*.

3. Constance A. Flanagan and Nakesha Faison, "Youth Civic Development: Implications of Research for Social Policy and Programs," *Social Policy Report* 15, no. 1 (2001): 3–14.

4. boyd, "Why Youth ♥ Social Network Sites"; Henry Jenkins, Sam Ford, and Joshua Green, *Spreadable Media: Creating Value and Meaning in a Networked Culture* (New York: NYU Press, 2013).,

5. Notably, in 2020–2021, when we asked teens and young adults about the term, "slacktivism," the reaction was either a blank stare or "Is that like using Slack (the digital communications platform) for activism?" This was suggestive of both the growing popularity of the tool, Slack, and perhaps of a fading hold of the discourse that equates online actions with laziness.

6. Evgeny Morozov, "The Brave New World of Slacktivism," *Foreign Policy*, May 19, 2009, https://foreignpolicy.com/2009/05/19/the-brave-new-world-of-slacktivism/.

7. Malcolm Gladwell, "Small Change: Why the Revolution Will Not Be Tweeted," *New Yorker*, September 27, 2010, https://www.newyorker.com/magazine/2010/10 /04/small-change-malcolm-gladwell.

8. Zeynep Tufekci, *Twitter and Tear Gas: The Power and Fragility of Networked Protest* (New Haven, CT: Yale University Press, 2017), xxvi.

9. Ethan Zuckerman, "New Media, New Civics?," *Policy & Internet* 6, no. 2 (2014): 151–168.

10. Jennifer Earl and Katrina Kimport, *Digitally Enabled Social Change: Activism in the Internet Age* (Cambridge, MA: MIT Press, 2013).

11. Evgeny Morozov, "From Slacktivism to Activism," *Foreign Policy*, September 5, 2009, https://foreignpolicy.com/2009/09/05/from-slacktivism-to-activism/.

12. Danielle Allen and Jennifer S. Light, eds., *From Voice to Influence: Understanding Citizenship in a Digital Age* (Chicago: University of Chicago Press, 2015).

13. Jackson, Bailey, and Welles, *#HashtagActivism*. See also Catherine Knight Steele, "Black Bloggers and Their Varied Publics: The Everyday Politics of Black Discourse

Online," *Television & New Media* 19, no. 2 (2018): 112–127; Zizi Papacharissi, *Affective Publics: Sentiment, Technology, and Politics* (Oxford, UK: Oxford University Press, 2014).

14. Jackson, Bailey, and Welles, *#HashtagActivism*; Ian P. Philbrick and Sanam Yar, "What Has Changed Since George Floyd," *New York Times*, August 3, 2020, https://www.nytimes.com/2020/08/03/briefing/coronavirus-vaccine-tropical-storm-isaias-tiktok-your-monday-briefing.html.

15. Breanna Draxler, "Harnessing People Power to Protect Alaska's Last Remaining Wilderness," *YES! Magazine*, January 27, 2021, https://www.yesmagazine.org/environment/2021/01/27/alaska-arctic-national-wildlife-refuge-tiktok.

16. Joseph Kahne, Ellen Middaugh, and Danielle Allen, "Youth, New Media and the Rise of Participatory Politics," in Allen and Light, *From Voice to Influence*, 41.

17. Though we focus here on informal avenues for participation, social media also enable direct engagement with politicians and social media-fueled windows into the nuts and bolts of policymaking. Leaver and colleagues' description of Alexandria Ocasio-Cortez's Instagram use offers an illustrative example. Leaver, Highfield, and Abidin, *Instagram*, 155.

18. Kahne et al., "Youth, New Media."

19. Similarly, sociologist Lynn Schofield Clark discusses "online artifacts of political engagement," which she defines as "photos, memes, quoted sayings, and original or curated commentary that evince young people's emotional investment and participation in unfolding events" (236). As these media are shared on different social media platforms by peers, they can draw "newcomers" into political activities such as walkouts. Lynn Schofield Clark, "Participants on the Margins: Examining the Role That Shared Artifacts of Engagement in the Ferguson Protests Played Among Minoritized Political Newcomers on Snapchat, Facebook, and Twitter," *International Journal of Communication* 10 (2016): 235–253. In their more recent ethnographic research with high school students, Regina Marchi and Schofield Clark observed the ways in which liking and sharing news about current events—what they refer to as "connective journalism"—can be a "first step" in a "continuum of communicative action" that includes adding one's feelings about such issues and then involvement in political organizing and action. Regina Marchi and Lynn Schofield Clark, "Social Media and Connective Journalism: The Formation of Counterpublics and Youth Civic Participation," *Journalism* 22, no. 2 (February 1, 2021): 285–302. Online information practices are increasingly recognized by researchers as sites of political agency, especially for historically marginalized youth. Based on their qualitative research, Amana Kaskazi and Vanessa Kitzie assert that "information practices function as a form of political participation; practices such as seeking, sharing, and assessing constitute keyways for participants to engage with locally and culturally meaningful political information and challenge the status quo." Amana Kaskazi and Vanessa Kitzie, "Engagement at the Margins: Investigating How Marginalized Teens Use Digital Media for Political Participation," *New Media & Society*, April 15, 2021, https://doi.org/10.1177/14614448211009460.

20. See Emily Weinstein, "The Personal Is Political on Social Media: Online Civic Expression Patterns and Pathways Among Civically Engaged Youth," *International Journal of Communication* 8 (2014): 210–233.

21. Emily Weinstein, Margaret Rundle, and Carrie James, "A Hush Falls Over the Crowd? Diminished Online Civic Expression Among Young Civic Actors," *International Journal of Communication* 9 (2015): 83–105.

22. See Ellen Middaugh, Benjamin Bowyer, and Joseph Kahne, "U Suk! Participatory Media and Youth Experiences with Political Discourse," *Youth & Society* 49, no. 7 (2017): 902–922; Kjerstin Thorson, "Facing an Uncertain Reception: Young Citizens and Political Interaction on Facebook," *Information, Communication & Society* 17, no. 2 (2014): 203–216; Kjerstin Thorson, Emily K. Vraga, and Neta Kligler-Vilenchik, "Don't Push Your Opinions on Me: Young Citizens and Political Etiquette on Facebook," in *Presidential Campaigning and Social Media: An Analysis of the 2012 Campaign*, ed. John Allen Hendricks and Dan Schill (Oxford, UK: Oxford University Press, 2017), 74–93; Ariadne Vromen, Brian D. Loader, Michael A. Xenos, and Francesco Bailo, "Everyday Making through Facebook Engagement: Young Citizens' Political Interactions in Australia, the United Kingdom and the United States," *Political Studies* 64, no. 3 (2016): 513–533.

23. Soep, "Digital Afterlife of Youth-Made Media."

24. Desmond Upton Patton, Douglas-Wade Brunton, Andrea Dixon, Reuben Jonathan Miller, Patrick Leonard, and Rose Hackman, "Stop and Frisk Online: Theorizing Everyday Racism in Digital Policing in the Use of Social Media for Identification of Criminal Conduct and Associations," *Social Media + Society* 3, no. 3 (2017): 2056305117733344.

25. Nina Eliasoph, *Avoiding Politics: How Americans Produce Apathy in Everyday Life* (Cambridge, UK: Cambridge University Press, 1998); Thorson, "Facing an Uncertain Reception."

26. Neta Kligler-Vilenchik, "Friendship and Politics Don't Mix? The Role of Sociability for Online Political Talk," *Information, Communication & Society* 24, no. 1 (2021): 118–133.

27. Howard Gardner and Katie Davis, *The App Generation: How Today's Youth Navigate Identity, Intimacy, and Imagination in a Digital World* (New Haven, CT: Yale University Press, 2013).

28. Kaskazi and Kitzie, "Engagement at the Margins."

29. Erikson, *Identity: Youth and Crisis.*

30. Michael J. Nakkula and Eric Toshalis, *Understanding Youth: Adolescent Development for Educators* (Cambridge, MA: Harvard Education Press, 2006), 33.

31. Flanagan and Faison, "Youth Civic Development"; James Youniss, Jeffrey A. McLellan, and Miranda Yates, "What We Know about Engendering Civic Identity," *American Behavioral Scientist* 40, no. 5 (1997): 620–631.

32. Jennifer Graham, "Cancel Culture Is Entering a Dangerous New Phase," *Deseret News*, August 22, 2020, https://www.deseret.com/indepth/2020/8/22/21362516

/cancel-culture-forgiveness-j-k-rowling-carson-king-apology-moral; Adam B. Vary, "J. K. Rowling's Book Sales Lagging Despite Industry Boom in June," *Variety*, July 16, 2020, https://variety.com/2020/film/news/jk-rowling-book-sales-harry-potter-12347 08777/.

33. Jonah Engel Bromwich, "Everyone Is Canceled," *New York Times*, June 28, 2018, https://www.nytimes.com/2018/06/28/style/is-it-canceled.html.

34. Zeynep Tufekci, "The Social-Media Mob Was Good," *The Atlantic*, May 28, 2020, https://www.theatlantic.com/technology/archive/2020/05/case-social-media-mobs /612202/.

35. Valeriya Safronova, "James Charles, From 'CoverBoy' to Canceled," *New York Times*, May 14, 2019, https://www.nytimes.com/2019/05/14/style/james-charles -makeup-artist-youtube.html.

36. Sanah Yar and Jonah E. Bromwich, "Tales from the Teenage Cancel Culture," *New York Times*, October 31, 2019, https://www.nytimes.com/2019/10/31/style /cancel-culture.html.

37. Diana C. Mutz, *Hearing the Other Side: Deliberative Versus Participatory Democracy* (Cambridge, UK: Cambridge University Press, 2006).

38. Flanagan and Faison, "Youth Civic Development"; James Youniss and Miranda Yates, *Community Service and Social Responsibility in Youth* (Chicago: University of Chicago Press, 1997).

39. Eli Pariser, *The Filter Bubble: How the New Personalized Web Is Changing What We Read and How We Think* (New York: Penguin Press, 2012); Cass R. Sunstein, *#Republic: Divided Democracy in the Age of Social Media* (Princeton, NJ: Princeton University Press, 2017).

CHAPTER 7

1. Kate Robertson, "Alexi McCammond, Teen Vogue Editor Resigns after Fury over Past Racist Tweets," *New York Times*, March 18, 2021, https://www.nytimes.com/2021 /03/18/business/media/teen-vogue-editor-alexi-mccammond.html.

2. Hannah Natanson, "Harvard Rescinds Acceptances for at Least Ten Students for Obscene Memes," *Harvard Crimson*, June 5, 2017, https://www.thecrimson.com /article/2017/6/5/2021-offers-rescinded-memes/.

3. Bill Murphy Jr., "Meet the 10 Harvard Students Who Just Ruined Their Lives," *Inc.*, June 6, 2017, https://www.inc.com/bill-murphy-jr/harvard-facebook-group -admitted-students-offer-rescinded.html.

4. Soep, "Digital Afterlife of Youth-Made Media."

5. Brady Robards and Siân Lincoln, *Growing Up on Facebook* (New York: Peter Lang, 2020); "scroll-back method," 51; "panic," "urgency," 63; "anxiety," 62, 63; "therapeutic," 73, 181; "memory 'sparks,'" 96.

6. Robards and Lincoln, *Growing Up on Facebook*, 96.

7. Adriana Manago's detailed discussion of digital media and identity processes outlines a suite of relevant opportunities and challenges relevant to adolescent development. Adriana M. Manago, "Identity Development in the Digital Age: The Case of Social Networking Sites," in *The Oxford Handbook of Identity Development*, ed. Kate C. Mclean and Moin Syed (New York: Oxford Press, 2014), 508–524.

8. Erikson, *Identity: Youth and Crisis.*

9. Turkle, *Life on the Screen.*

10. Erikson, *Identity: Youth and Crisis.*

11. Katie Davis and Emily Weinstein, "Identity Development in the Digital Age: An Eriksonian Perspective," in *Identity, Sexuality, and Relationships among Emerging Adults in the Digital Age*, ed. M. F. Wright (Hershey, PA: IGI Global, 2017), 1–17.

12. Shanyang Zhao, Sherri Grasmuck, and Jason Martin, "Identity Construction on Facebook: Digital Empowerment in Anchored Relationships," *Computers in Human Behavior* 24, no. 5 (2008): 1816–1836.

13. Robards and Lincoln, *Growing Up on Facebook*, 4.

14. Patton et al., "Stop and Frisk Online," 2056305117733344.

15. boyd, "Social Steganography."

16. boyd, "Social Steganography." See also James C. Scott, *Domination and the Arts of Resistance: Hidden Transcripts* (New Haven, CT: Yale University Press, 1992); Lane, *Digital Street.*

17. Margo Gardner and Laurence Steinberg, "Peer Influence on Risk Taking, Risk Preference, and Risky Decision Making in Adolescence and Adulthood: An Experimental Study," *Developmental Psychology* 41, no. 4 (2005): 625–635.

18. Lauren E. Sherman, Ashley A. Patyon, Leanna M. Hernandez, Patricia M. Greenfield, and Mirella Dapretto, "The Power of the Like in Adolescence: Effects of Peer Influence on Neural and Behavioral Responses to Social Media," *Psychological Science* 27, no. 7 (July 1, 2016): 1027–1035.

19. Laurence Steinberg, "A Social Neuroscience Perspective on Adolescent Risk-Taking," *Developmental Review* 28, no. 1 (2008): 78–106.

20. Leaver, Highfield, and Abidin, *Instagram.*

21. Tama Leaver and Tim Highfield, "Visualising the Ends of Identity: Pre-Birth and Post-Death on Instagram," *Information, Communication & Society* 21, no. 1 (2018): 30–45.

22. Leaver and Highfield, "Visualising the Ends"; Leaver, Highfield, and Abidin, *Instagram.*

23. Dan Levin, "A Racial Slur, a Viral Video, and a Reckoning," *New York Times*, December 26, 2020, sec. U.S., https://www.nytimes.com/2020/12/26/us/mimi-groves-jimmy-galligan-racial-slurs.html.

24. On the statement "It's fair for college admissions to consider applicants' social media posts," 33 percent (1,147) of youth disagreed, 31 percent (956) were

undecided, and 39 percent (1,322) agreed. On the statement "It's reasonable for people to face consequences later in life for posts shared in middle or high school," 40 percent (1,382) of youth disagreed, 25 percent (849) were undecided, and 35 percent (1,214) agreed. On the statement "If someone makes an offensive comment on social media, people have the right to call them out—even if it hurts their reputation," 17 percent (599) disagreed, 20 percent (688) were undecided, and 63 percent (2,159) agreed.

25. Merrill Perlman, "The Rise of 'Deplatform,'" *Columbia Journalism Review*, February 4, 2021, https://www.cjr.org/language_corner/deplatform.php.

26. Brooke Erin Duffy and Ngai Keung Chan, "'You Never Really Know Who's Looking': Imagined Surveillance across Social Media Platforms," *New Media & Society* 21, no. 1 (January 1, 2019): 119–138.

27. Rachel Buchanan, Erica Southgate, and Shamus P Smith, "'The Whole World's Watching Really': Parental and Educator Perspectives on Managing Children's Digital Lives," *Global Studies of Childhood* 9, no. 2 (June 1, 2019): 167–180.

28. Ben Wolford, "Everything You Need to Know about the 'Right to Be Forgotten,'" *GDPR.EU*, n.d., https://gdpr.eu/right-to-be-forgotten.

29. Kate Eichhorn, *The End of Forgetting: Growing Up with Social Media* (Cambridge, MA: Harvard University Press, 2019). For a discussion of the Star Wars Kid, see pp. 121–122.

30. Leo Kelion, "Google Wins Landmark Right to Be Forgotten Case," *BBC*, September 24, 2019, https://www.bbc.com/news/technology-49808208.

31. Aaron Krolik and Kashmir Hill, "The Slander Industry," *New York Times*, April 24, 2021, sec. Technology, https://www.nytimes.com/interactive/2021/04/24/technology/online-slander-websites.html.

32. Graeme Wood, "America Has Forgotten How to Forgive," *The Atlantic*, March 19, 2021, https://www.theatlantic.com/ideas/archive/2021/03/america-has-lost-ability-forgive/618336/.

33. Carol S. Dweck, *Mindset: The New Psychology of Success* (New York: Ballantine, 2007).

34. Carol Tavris and Elliot Aronson, *Mistakes Were Made (But Not by Me): Why We Justify Foolish Beliefs, Bad Decisions, and Hurtful Acts* (New York: Harcourt, 2007).

35. Loretta Ross, "I'm a Black Feminist. I Think Call-Out Culture Is Toxic," *New York Times*, August 17, 2019, sec. Opinion, https://www.nytimes.com/2019/08/17/opinion/sunday/cancel-culture-call-out.html; Jessica Bennett, "What If Instead of Calling People Out, We Called Them In?," *New York Times*, November 19, 2020, sec. Style, https://www.nytimes.com/2020/11/19/style/loretta-ross-smith-college-cancel-culture.html.

36. As we describe in the appendix, we collected survey responses from students in fifteen middle and high schools. In the survey questionnaire we used at the first two participating schools in our study, this option was phrased as "threats to private information." We modified the language to "risks to private information" after data

collection at the first two sites. Why? In short, we were sufficiently surprised that privacy issues topped the concerns list that we conducted additional pretesting of our item to further check its interpretation. While this didn't alert us to any obvious misunderstandings, it raised a question for us about whether it was possible that some students interpret the word "threats" as inherently acute because of the term's frequent use in relation to physical fights and bullying. We therefore decided to shift to "risks." This did not change the popularity of the response item, though, which was the top response overall and either the most prevalent or second most prevalent worry selected by students at fourteen of our fifteen school sites.

37. Based on their focus group study with young adults, Hargittai and Marwick (2016) describe a "privacy paradox: namely, concern over privacy, but little presence of privacy-protective behavior" (3738). Eszter Hargittai and Alice Marwick, "'What Can I Really Do?' Explaining the Privacy Paradox with Online Apathy," *International Journal of Communication* 10 (2016): 3737–3757. Davis and James (2013) similarly show that tweens have clear conceptions of privacy. Katie Davis and Carrie James, "Tweens' Conceptions of Privacy Online: Implications for Educators," *Learning, Media and Technology* 38, no. 1 (2013): 4–25.

38. Ralf De Wolf, "Contextualizing How Teens Manage Personal and Interpersonal Privacy on Social Media," *New Media & Society 22*, no. 6 (2020): 1060.

CONCLUSION

1. Carrie James, Emily Weinstein, and Kelly Mendoza, "Teaching Digital Citizens in Today's World: Research and Insights Behind the Common Sense K–12 Digital Citizenship Curriculum" (San Francisco: Common Sense Media, 2019), https://www.commonsense.org/education/sites/default/files/tlr_component/common_sense_education_digital_citizenship_research_backgrounder.pdf.

2. As Livingstone and Blum-Ross put it aptly, "anxious parents read the runes to figure out which of their child's behaviors may yield future benefits or harms, which newly sparked interests could chart a profitable path to adulthood, which missed opportunities will later be regretted, and which easily overlooked problems signal trouble to come." Livingstone and Blum-Ross, *Parenting for a Digital Future*, 9.

3. Albert Bandura, "Social Cognitive Theory: An Agentic Perspective," *Annual Review of Psychology* 52, no. 1 (2001): 1–26.

4. Seligman's research on learned helplessness serves as a compelling example of the ways inhibited control and agency can lead to depression. See, for example, Christopher Peterson, Steven F. Maier, and Martin E. P. Seligman, *Learned Helplessness: A Theory for the Age of Personal Control* (New York: Oxford University Press, 1995).

5. Albert Bandura, "Adolescent Development from an Agentic Perspective," in *Self-Efficacy Beliefs of Adolescents*, ed. Frank Pajares and Timothy Urdan (Greenwich, CT: Information Age, 2006), 5.

6. Tom Harrison, *Thrive: How to Cultivate Character So Your Children Can Flourish Online* (London, UK: Robinson, 2021), 83.

7. Overall, some parents are permissive in allowing tech access (*"enablers"*), while others aim to restrict screen time (*"limiters"*). But there is a third path: "Digital *mentors"* whose tech parenting is focused on actively talking to kids about online skills and experiences and working to understand and positively shape kids' tech use. Digital mentoring may have benefits: survey data (though correlational in nature) indicates that children who have been digitally mentored appear least likely to engage in problematic behavior online. Alexandra Samuel, "Parents: Reject Technology Shame," *The Atlantic*, November 4, 2015.

Importantly, adopting a successful mentoring approach to digital parenting isn't simply a matter of choosing to model/guide versus limit. As Livingstone and Blum-Ross's work illustrates powerfully, parenting strategies play out in the context of socioeconomic realities, inequities, and parents' work schedules. From a resources and time perspective, families are differently positioned to mentor and support their children's' digital activities and opportunities toward digital agency. Livingstone and Blum-Ross, *Parenting for a Digital Future*.

8. Katie Davis, *Technology's Child: Digital Media's Role in the Ages and Stages of Growing Up* (Cambridge, MA: MIT Press, 2023).

9. Davis, *Technology's Child*.

10. Kathryn C. Montgomery, Jeff Chester, and Tijana Milosevic, "Children's Privacy in the Big Data Era: Research Opportunities," *Pediatrics* 140, Suppl. 2 (November 1, 2017): S117–S121; Jenny Radesky, Yolanda Linda Reid Chassiakos, Nusheen Ameenuddin, Dipesh Navsaria, and the Council on Communication and Media, "Digital Advertising to Children," *Pediatrics* 146, no. 1 (July 1, 2020): e20201681.

11. "I Used to Think . . . Now I Think . . ."

APPENDIX

1. Anselm L. Strauss and Juliet Corbin, *Basics of Qualitative Research: Techniques and Procedures for Developing Grounded Theory* (Thousand Oaks, CA: Sage, 1998).

INDEX